★★★

A Dying Breed

The True Story of a World War II Air Combat Crew's Courage, Camaraderie, Faith, and Spirit

x—x—x—x—x—x—x—x—x—x—x—x—x—x—x

Neal B. Dillon

Hellgate Press
Grants Pass, Oregon

A Dying Breed

Published by Hellgate Press
© 2000 by Neal B. Dillon

Interior design by Eliot House Productions
Cover art by Alfred G. Vetromile/U.S. Airforce Art Collection Series 10–3*126.86
Cover design by J. C. Young

Please direct any comments, questions, or suggestions regarding this book to:

Hellgate Press
Editorial Department
P.O. Box 3727
Central Point, Oregon 97502-0032

(541) 245-6502
(541) 245-6505 fax
info@psi-research.com email

Dillon, Neal B., 1939-
    A dying breed : the true story of a World War II air combat crew's amazing courage,
    touching comaraderie, uplifting faith, and indomitable spirit / Neal B. Dillon.
        p. cm.
    Includes bibliographical references.
    ISBN 1-55571-529-X (paper)
  1. World War, 1939-1945—Aerial operations, American. 2. United States. Army Air
Forces. Bombardment Group, 384th. 3. World War, 1939-1945—Regimental
histories—United States. 4. Bomber pilots—United States—Biography. 5. Bombing,
Aerial—Germany. 6. Prisoners of war—Germany—Biography. 7. World War,
1939-1945—Prisoners and prisons, German. I. Title.

D790 .D53 2000
940.54'4973—dc21

00-044985

Printed and bound in the United States of America
First Edition 10 9 8 7 6 5 4 3 2 1

♲ Printed on recycled paper when available.

Contents

Book III: Grounded Eagles

Foreword

When Captain Robert Dillon approached me about writing a foreword for his father's book, I was immediately taken with the title. Was there a double meaning? Was this a challenge for the reader? Was it more than a story about men fighting and dying? Why *A Dying Breed*?

I discovered a touching story about ordinary American kids overcoming extraordinary obstacles, about authentic American heroes. Soon I was with them on their first combat mission. I marveled at the author's ability to capture the crew's great faith, incredible courage, and determination. I, too, embrace the author's conviction that this story must not be permitted to die when the last World War II Eighth Air Force crew member is gone.

This story of courage under fire, of good cheer in the face of adversity, of common sense solutions to brand new problems of aerial warfare had to be preserved and passed on. It took an admiring brother-in-law, an Air Force veteran, to capture the story. So, I applaud *A Dying Breed* for preserving the lore. What had to be told has now been told.

I, like the author, was a beneficiary of the legacy of the Eighth Air Force crews and was also honored to be a crew member. I knew then, we were standing on the shoulders of giants. I now realize my check rides and unit evaluations were being judged by the standards set by previous crews of the Eighth Air Force. Later, I was a bomb squadron commander and wing commander in the Eighth and held up this heritage to inspire my crews. (It always worked!)

In 1993, I was selected for the best job in the United States Air Force — commander of the Mighty Eighth! I got to meet and talk intimately with many of these wonderful veterans firsthand as a guest at their annual reunions. I delighted in their stories, marveled at their courage and humility, and treasured their friendship. I remember wishing that someone would capture their experiences in print as oral histories, to preserve the heritage.

You can imagine my delight when I received the manuscript for *A Dying Breed*, and read the author's moving story about his boyhood hero, Technical Sergeant John S. Honeycutt. The book is about one crew's amazing courage, touching camaraderie, uplifting faith, and indomitable spirit. But, it is more, much more. It is a tale about the giants of the Mighty Eighth who created a tradition. That tradition, the humor, the perseverance in adversity, the lessons learned, were already a legacy for me and for others of our era. These men, and men like them, were already our heroes. Now, thanks to Neal Dillon, they can be your heroes too.

—Stephen B. Croker, Lt. Gen, USAF (RET.)
Former Commander of the Eighth Air Force

★ ★ ★

Preface

Our country was in harm's way at the outbreak of World War II. In patriotic response, a generation of young Americans, the likes of which we are not likely to see again, raised their right hands in thousands of recruiting stations all across this great country and swore to protect and defend it. In order to challenge this threat to our way of life, America began to assemble a mighty air armada in 1942–43. Its purpose was to destroy the German war machine and the industries that fed it. The body of this armada was the Eighth Air Force. Its heart was the bomber group and the lifeblood was the air combat crew.

The primary instrument of destruction selected to defeat the German war machine was the B-17, *Flying Fortress*. To the American public in 1943, the B-17 bomber was a massive, sophisticated, and powerful flying machine. It was a mighty symbol of America's burgeoning military strength. The human element, the bomber crew, was rarely considered, as the great bomber seemed to overshadow them. Yet, in control of this huge flying machine of powerful engines, servo-mechanisms and a formidable array of machine guns, were young men — just recently high school and college boys.

This book honors one such B-17 bomber crew:

1st Lt. William (Bill) Kaczaraba
    Pilot
    Bold Leader

2nd Lt. Myron (Mike) Clinton Morgan, Sr.
    Copilot
    Brave As They Come

viii ★★★ *A DYING BREED*

2nd Lt. Theodore (Ted) Matthew Wirth
    Bombardier
    Quiet Warrior

2nd Lt. Marvin Lewis Horsky
    Navigator
    The Joker

T/Sgt. John Samuel (Sam) Honeycutt
    Engineer/ Top Turret Gunner
    Led by Example

T/Sgt. Wilber Allen Peifer
    Radio Operator
    German by Birth, American by Choice

S/Sgt. Solomon (Shorty) Craden
    Ball Turret Gunner
    Gallant Fighter

S/Sgt. Harry Alexander (Gilly) Gilrane
    Right Waist Gunner
    Fightin' Irishman

S/Sgt. Peter (Pete) Franklin Parker
    Left Waist Gunner
    Old War Horse

S/Sgt. George Gibson (Gibby) Polley, Jr.
    Tail Gunner
    A Crack Shot

This is the story of ten young Americans who answered their country's call to arms; how they adjusted to service life, how they trained, how they fought, and how they coped as prisoners of war.

★ ★ ★

Acknowledgments

Many kind people took time out of their hectic lives to assist me in the preparation of this book. Special thanks to my wife, Lucy Ann, for her assistance in preparing the draft and for supporting me in writing this book. Also, for tolerating my impatience, seclusion, and social restrictions over seven years.

I would like to convey my sincere appreciation to the many people and organizations listed below who all had a hand in preparing this book.

The 384th Bombardment Group (H) Historian, Mr. Clint Orean, for permission to use information contained in his *Facts and Happenings, Station 106, Grafton Underwood, England* document.

The Mighty Eighth Air Force Heritage Museum Archivist, Mr. John B. Edwards, for providing assistance in locating records, pictures, and various information on the 384th Bomb Group (BG)and the 547th Squadron (SQ).

Mr. George G. Polley, III (son of S/Sgt. George G. Polley, Jr.) for permission to use information contained in his father's memoirs.

Mrs. Madelyn Morgan (wife of 2nd Lt. Myron (Mike) C. Morgan, Sr.) for permission to use information contained in her husband's memoirs, *Fly for Your Life.*

My deepest appreciation for the response from those living crew members, who flew with my brother-in-law during World War II and who gave this story wings. Thanks for the interviews, the questionnaires you completed, the copies of logs, articles, documents, photographs, comments and tapes you provided, and the many phone calls you received and made. You are:

Mr. Theodore M. Wirth, Mr. Harry A. Gilrane, and Mr. Solomon Craden.

I am indebted to my sister, Pauline (Polly) Honeycutt, who saved all of Sam's pictures, letters, awards, documents, and other data during the war years and thereafter until I resurrected them from her scrapbooks.

Special thanks to my brother, John, for his many hours of proofreading and critical corrections he inserted into the manuscript. His dedication to the completion of this book is also an expression of his love for our brother-in-law.

Thanks to all of these kind people and organizations for supporting what I hope is a story that will remind all that freedom is the sole possession only of those who have the courage to defend it.

★★★

From the Author

During my youth I lived for extended periods of time with my sister, Pauline, and her husband, Sam Honeycutt. As a teenager, in the '50s, World War II seemed like ancient history to me, so naturally, I had little interest in the subject. From time to time I would notice an odd looking book in their bookcase dated 1946 and entitled, *As Briefed, A Family History of The 384th Bomb Group.* During my sophomore year of high school, I read this book several times in an attempt to grasp its meaning.

On occasions, but only at my persistent questioning, Sam would call forth his memories of the air battles over Germany and Nazi occupied Europe during the war. I remember, on one occasion, how he expressed his experiences to me:

> *"I recall such things as the smell of smoke and sweat in the aircraft oxygen system. Such things as the sucking grip of the oxygen mask on my cold, tired face for eight or nine hours; of flak clouds bursting around us while over targets such as Bremen, Kiel, Emden, and many others; of the shock of losing three of four engines to flak and fighters; and the gut-wrenching fear of a wheels-up crash landing. But worst of all seeing your friends go down in B-17s around you and then seeing their empty beds that had been full the night before. These are my memories and I share them with you, although, I know you cannot possibly understand them."*

In 1991, Sam prevailed upon me to write a book about his crew so that others may learn from the sacrifices and hardships they suffered. This book is the culmination of that promise to him eight years ago.

Dedication

This book was written as a labor of love and is dedicated
to my brother-in-law, John Samuel (Sam) Honeycutt,
B-17 crewmates, and to all members of the
384th Bomb Group who served during WWII.

★★★
Book I

A Gathering of Eagles

★ ★ ★

CHAPTER

1

Eaglets

World War II Army Air Corps flyers were an elite group, all young volunteers, specially recruited and trained to perform highly skilled combat jobs. The degree of competence required for pilots, copilots, navigators, bombardiers, engineers, radio operators, and gunners, was so high that all crewmen, once qualified, received immediate rank as either Commissioned Officers or Non-Commissioned Officers[1] (NCOs).

Flying attracted young, free-spirited, fun loving individuals. They were well-educated non-conformists. At the same time, they possessed a great sense of patriotism and loyalty to their country and were more than eager to do their part in the war.

These young American flyers fought a type of war in the air that the world had never experienced and would likely never see again. All fought bravely with great pride — these heroes of the air war. Most survived, many died, and many languished as prisoners of war.

Who were these young eaglets soon to become war eagles? What towns, cities, or rural areas of the country could produce such future air warriors at this critical hour? No one could predict from where they would come, but

Image 1.1: Bill Kaczaraba, age 18, a few months after high school graduation.

come they did with backgrounds as varied as their names. Our future war eagles typified that diversity.

William (Bill) Kaczaraba (Image 1.1), son of Stefan and Mary Kaczaraba, was born in New York City, New York on August 14, 1919. His parents were from the Ukrainian area of Russia; thus, he was a first generation Russian-American. During his early years he lived in New York City with his parents, and two sisters, Anne and Francis.

Bill's family moved to Somerville, New Jersey when he was in grade school. In 1937, Bill graduated from Somerville High School after taking college preparatory courses. He was employed in several manual occupations in the Somerville area until 1941. Bill's last civilian job was as a Jr. Science Aide with the U.S. Navy at Norfolk, Virginia where he worked on operations and maintenance of anti-magnetic mine equipment from September 1941 until January 1942.

Eager to get a crack at the German war machine when war broke out in December 1941, Bill enlisted as an aviation cadet in the Army Air Corps on March 16, 1942 in Richmond, Virginia.

Myron (Mike) Clinton Morgan, Sr. (Image 1.2), son of Marshall Blain and Anna Alice Morgan, was born in Morgantown, West Virginia on May 12, 1918. During his early years he lived in Morgantown with his parents, two sisters, Geraldine (Jerry) Bossart and Ernestine Hines (Tinnie); and his three brothers, James (Jim), John, and Geneve (Nevy).

Mike was in grade school when he first became interested in flying. His first close up

Image 1.2: Mike Morgan, high school summer vacation in 1936, 18 years of age.

look at an airplane was at the local airport. It was an open cockpit bi-plane, a WACO. His dad took him to the Chicago World Fair in 1933 where Mike was treated to his first airplane ride. From that day on he was in love with flight.

He attended and graduated from Morgantown High School where he excelled in academics. In sports he participated in basketball and football. If study and sports did not occupy all of his time, he also played the trombone. In his free time he worked at an ice cream store (Higgins Dairy) and also had a paper route.

Following high school graduation, he attended and graduated from West Virginia University with a Bachelor of Science Degree in Forestry. During college he spent his summers in Colorado employed as a forest ranger.

Mike did not believe in all work and no play, and during his sophomore year in college he met and started dating the beautiful Miss Madelyn Ellen Robinson.

He always thought about flying and when he was a Junior at West Virginia University, a flying school was started and he was one of the first to sign up. He earned a private pilot's license when he graduated in June 1941.

When the Japanese bombed Pearl Harbor in 1941, Mike was working in North Carolina. He left his job in March 1942, and enlisted in the Army Air Corps as an aviation cadet in Pittsburgh, Pennsylvania.[2]

Theodore (Ted) Wirth (Image 1.3), was born in Nebraska City, Nebraska on March 13, 1916. He graduated from St. Bernards Academy and attended the University of Nebraska, College of Agriculture for a year, then went to work on the family farm.

Ted entered the U.S. Army as a private in 1941. Later that year, he married the lovely Miss Charlotte McGowen. After successfully passing the aviation cadet exams in 1942, he was accepted into the Army Air Corps and was selected to attend bombardier school in Big Springs, Texas.[3]

Marvin Lewis Horsky was born in Omaha, Nebraska in 1920, and lived there during his childhood. He was attending the

Image 1.3: Ted Wirth, shortly after attending the University of Nebraska, 19 years of age.

University of Nebraska majoring in accounting when the war erupted. In May, 1942 he left the university and entered the Army Air Corps Aviation Cadet program to serve his country.

Image 1.4: John Samuel (Sam) Honeycutt, high school graduation day in 1942, 19 years of age.

John Samuel (Sam) Honeycutt (Image 1.4), son of David Brown and Bessie Morgan Honeycutt, was born in Rowan County, North Carolina on September 22, 1921. During his early years he lived near Salisbury, North Carolina with his parents, two sisters: Pauline and Janie Belle, and four brothers: Ray, David, Edgar, and Kenneth. His father was a farmer and sawmill operator causing the family to move several times during Sam's early years.

The family moved to Virgilina, Virginia where his father started a sawmill operation during Sam's first year of high school. During his sophomore year, Sam fell in love with a local girl, Pauline Francis Dillon. Sam's family left the area that same year but Sam decided not to leave so he could complete his last two years of high school. Of course, he had no desire to leave his only true love, Pauline as well. During these last two years of high school Sam made a living by working various jobs and by driving a school bus. He lived in an unheated room with no electricity over an abandoned grocery store during his high school years. He graduated from Bethel Hill High School in May 1942 and married Pauline the same month. Sam answered his country's call to arms and enlisted in the U.S. Army on August 15, 1942 at Camp Lee, Virginia.

Solomon (Shorty) Craden, son of Samuel and Rachel Craden, was born in Milwaukee, Wisconsin on May 31, 1921. His parents were from Russia, thus, he was a first generation Russian-American.

During his early years he lived in Milwaukee with his large family. He had six sisters: Lillian, Sara, Fanny, Esther, Mary, and Jeanette; and four brothers: Nathan, Mac, Sam, Jack, with Sol as the youngest.

After graduating from Milwaukee's North Division High School in May, 1942, he attended a vocational school and was then employed by International Harvester Company as a sheet metal worker. Driven by his sense of patriotism, he enlisted in the U.S. Army on August 18, 1942 at Ft. Sheridan, Illinois.[4]

Harry Alexander (Gilly) Gilrane (Image 1.5), was born in Norfolk, Virginia on January 25, 1922. His parents were from Ireland, making Gilly a first generation Irish-American. During his childhood, Harry and his family made several trips to visit their relatives in Ireland. On a few occasions he witnessed pitched battles in the streets of Belfast between the Black and Tans and the IRA.

Harry's family moved to Brooklyn, New York when he was four years old and continued to live there during his school years. As a boy he became inter-

Image 1.5: Harry Alexander (Gilly) Gilrane with future wife, Dotty, age 18.

ested in aviation and joined the Eagle Club. The Eagle Club promoted the science of flight by encouraging young men to build and fly experimental, remote-controlled airplanes. He enjoyed these flying activities and his love for flight never abated.

During high school he played football and also played a mean trumpet. After many arguments with his parents, Harry received permission to enlist in the Army Air Corps. In 1942, at 19, Harry combined his patriotism and his love of flight by enlisting in the service of his country.[5]

Wilber A. Peifer was born in Germany in 1920. He immigrated to the United States with his parents when he was twelve-years-old. He lived his early years in Pontiac, Michigan. Wilber joined the regular Army in 1938 to serve his adopted country.

Peter (Pete) Franklin Parker was born in Westlake, Ohio in 1921. As a teenager he worked for Western Auto in Westlake before the war and when not working loved to hunt small game in the woods of Ohio. He enlisted to serve his country shortly after war was declared on Germany.

George Gibson (Gibby) Polley, Jr. was born in Marblehead, Massachusetts on February 25, 1922. The house on Circle Street where he was born was known as the Flood Ireson House. (Flood was the sea captain made famous in the Whittier poem *Flood Ireson's Ride*.) His mother was the former Helen Stillman; known on the Vaudeville circuit as Dixie, the psychic and singer. His father was George Gibson Polley; a rather famous daredevil, Polley, The Human Fly, and was also Helen's partner in the mind-reading act. Named after his father, George Gibson Polley, Jr., he soon became known as "Gibby." At first his life was rather aristocratic with servants and chauffeured Essex automobiles. This ended with the sudden death of his father and the stock market crash in 1929. After that his mother moved back to her hometown of Marblehead, and made the best of it with her three sons: Herbert, Gibby, and Stillman. She eventually married Horace Snow and had two more sons, Robert and Donald, and then two daughters, Helen and Patricia.

During the Depression, life was difficult, especially for a family of nine. Gibby would go to the corner market each morning to get a cardboard box. He would then cut it to fit the inside soles of his worn-out shoes. The cardboard would last most of the day. He was fortunate to be the second oldest. That meant he was only the second in line to wear the clothes that were handed down until they were outgrown.

When the United States was drawn into the war, Gibby's older brother Herbert, known as Bud, entered the service first and ended up in the Army's 3rd Armored Division. Bud was killed in action in May 1943 during the North Africa invasion. Gibby entered the Army Air Corps in August 1942 and his younger brother, Stilly, entered soon after and eventually served in Europe in the Signal Corps.[6]

★★★★★

These sons of America, unskilled in the art of war, were quickly trained by accelerated Army methods to master air combat duties. They were ten youths hastily thrown together and trained in ground and airborne duties in less than eight months, and soon would be pitted against what was then the world's mightiest air force: the German Luftwaffe. The balance of power looked quite lopsided at the time.

★★★

2

Crew Duties and Training

The term *Flying Fortress* as a description of the Boeing B-17 was coined by a journalist during the presentation of the prototype bomber in Seattle, Washington, 1935. The Boeing Aircraft Company, which manufactures the B-17, was quick to adopt the name and proudly embellished the center motif on the control columns of its production aircraft with the name. It became famous with the public some years before it actually participated in air combat.

In truth the *Flying Fortress* was not a fortress at all, but an aluminum shell that offered little protection against flak[1], cannon fire, or bullets. Nevertheless, due to its sound design, rugged construction, and redundant systems, it proved to be extremely durable and reliable against the enemy's efforts to shoot it down.

The B-17 had a ten-man crew and with the exception of the pilot, copilot, and bombardier, everyone else was a gunner. The crew would fly the B-17F and B-17G, both models having nine .50 caliber machine guns.

The pilot, 1st Lt. William (Bill) Kaczaraba, is a cocky, determined, 24-year-old sometimes prone to foul language. The copilot, 2nd Lt. Myron (Mike) Morgan, Jr. is a 24 year old happy-go-lucky, Clark Gable look-alike with nerves of steel. Both sat up front on the flight deck or cockpit. As you look forward the pilot occupies the left seat while the copilot is on the right. The cockpit contains all the necessary flight instrumentation and controls to fly the B-17 (Image 2.1).

The pilot is the airplane's commander. He is responsible for the safety and efficiency of the crew at all times — not just when flying and fighting, but for the full 24 hours of every day. His crew is made up of specialists. How well each crew member performs and how well each contributes as a member of the combat team, will in large part depend on how well Lt. Kaczaraba performs his role as the airplane commander. During training he must observe and understand each of the crew as individuals. He must learn their personal idiosyncrasies, capabilities, and also their shortcomings. He must gain the crew's respect, confidence, and trust, which will form the glue of discipline that will bond them together in combat. He must master his job and prove that he knows how to fly in a tight formation. He must be fair and impartial in his decisions and when circumstance permits, allow the crew to discuss a course of action when their lives are at stake.

The crew's respect for Lt. Kaczaraba will grow out of respect for him as an individual — not simply for the position he holds. The discipline that he must develop within the crew will breed comradeship and high morale as natural by-products. Lt. Kaczaraba must be prepared to brief the crew before each mission regarding the purpose of the mission, conditions that may be encountered, and the role that each member must play for mission success. In short, he will become their coach in a life and death game with little room for error.

The copilot is the pilot's executive officer, chief understudy, and strong right hand (both figuratively and literally). He must become familiar with all of the pilot's responsibilities and duties and be fully qualified to fly the B-17 when necessary. He must understand engine controls to ensure smooth performance while cruising, maintaining, or changing formation position, climbing and descending. During missions he is the engineering officer and is required to maintain a complete log of performance data.

Lt. Morgan must become a qualified B-17 instrument pilot and be able to fly tight formations in any assigned position, day or night, and be proficient at navigation, day or night, by pilotage, dead reckoning, or by radio aids (primarily the radio in the cockpit).

In front and below the cockpit is the bombardier's, (2nd Lt. Ted Wirth) and the navigator's (2nd Lt. Marvin Lewis Horsky) positions. Lt. Wirth is the "old man" of the crew at 27. He qualified for air cadet training from the regular Army and has a lovely wife, Charlotte, waiting for him. Lt. Horsky,

Image 2.1: B-17 main instrument panel cluster contains instrumen s for flying in England's normal murk. At right are the engine performance gages normally monitored by Lt. Morgan. At left is the pilot directional indicator (PDI), whose needle is to be kept centered during the bomb run and is normally monitored by Lt. Kaczaraba.

navigator, age 21, is a recent college student before the Army turned him into a navigator.

Access to the bombardier and navigator's area is via a removable folding, two-piece, plywood door located between the pilot and copilot's seats. This is the most forward station of the B-17. Once inside this area you can stand up and observe the navigator's seat and small table on the left.

The bombardier's position is in the forward nose of the ship (Images 2.2, 2.3, and 2.4). Lt. Wirth has his instruments on a panel to his left (Image 2.5). During the bomb run he will sit in a small chair directly over and behind the Norden bombsight (Image 2.6).

Lt. Horsky doubles as a gunner. He has a single .50 caliber machine gun to defend the front of the aircraft. In the B-17, model G, there is a nose hatch located in this section on the left side of the fuselage to provide for emergency exits.

Lts. Wirth and Horsky will be extremely critical to the ultimate success of the crew's future bombing missions. They must function as a team to get to the target area, deliver the bomb load, and return to base.

Lt. Horsky, as the navigator, will have the responsibility to lay out the mission course to and from the target, record estimated times of arrival (ETA) at key points along the course, determine key course alterations points, and the initial point (IP)for the bomb run.

The IP is the last navigation check before the bomb run at which time Lt. Wirth will actually fly the aircraft to the target and release the bomb load using the highly accurate Norden Bombsight (Image 2.7).

Accurate and effective bombing will be the job of the bombardier, Lt. Ted Wirth, and the ultimate purpose of the B-17 and its crew. Every other function is preparatory to hitting and destroying a target. Getting Lt. Wirth over the target will be the primary purpose of each mission. His job, putting bombs on the target, will require close cooperation with Lt. Kaczaraba and a mutual understanding of duties. During the brief interval on the bomb run, usually less than three minutes, Lt. Wirth will be in absolute command. He will tell Lt. Kaczaraba what is needed and until the bombs leave the racks his word is law. Lt. Wirth will control the aircraft on the bomb run, either through the auto-pilot or Pilot Directional Indicator (PDI). The auto-pilot connects directly to the bombsight; the PDI transmits desired course changes to Lt. Kaczaraba via a needle instrument on the cockpit panel.[2]

During the bomb run, Lt. Wirth must ignore flak and fighter opposition. German fighter pilots will not always leave the bombers to avoid anti-aircraft (AA) ground fire over the target and there will be times when they will press home their attacks through their own flak. Lt. Wirth must

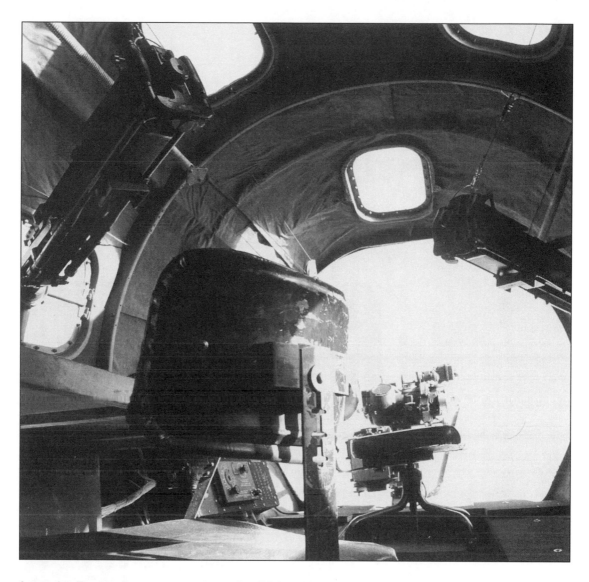

Image 2.2: To enter the nose compartment, Lts. Wirth and Horsky must crawl through the passage under the cockpit floor, past an escape hatch and through a small opening in the bulkhead. This is the view forward as they crawl into the nose. Left is Lt. Horsky's table and chair. Lt. Horsky's cheek gun is in a ball mount, suspended by a combination of springs and cables to make it easier to move while tracking enemy fighters.

Image 2.3: Navigator at his small table in the forward nose of ship plotting a course for Germany.

Image 2.4: Lt. Horsky's tools spread across his table in the nose compartment. His job is to keep the pilot informed of aircraft position, and upcoming course corrections and to plot the course back to base from any point during the mission. Though a combination of pilotage and dead reckoning (visual landmarks and time-distance), with these tools he keeps track of progress.

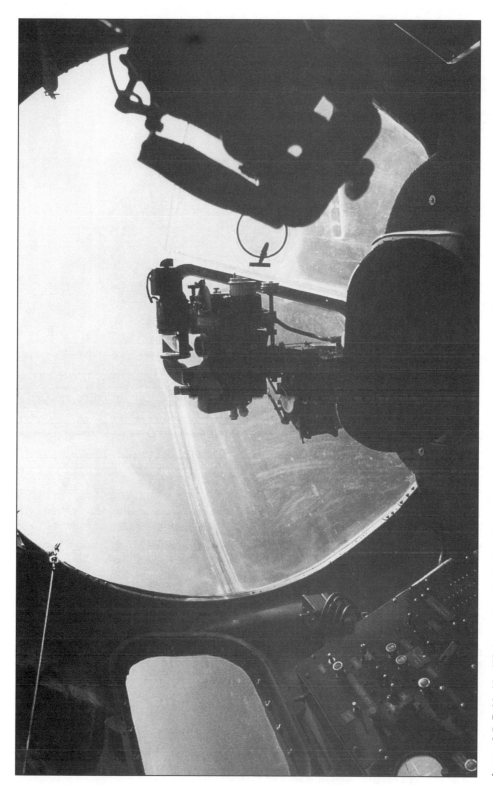

Image 2.5: Behind Lt. Wirth's seat, to the left, is the control panel that provides him the necessary information to program the bombsight. The switches control the bomb bay doors and arm the bombs. Lights give the status of the bomb load. The intervalometer is at bottom left. This controls the timing bomb release — either a salvo (all bombs at once) or at intervals to "walk" the bombs across the target. In the center is the Norden bombsight. This bombsight, a closely guarded secret during WWII, computes aircraft flight variables and bomb ballistics to arrive at a solution — a point in space from which the bombs are released to strike the target.

Image 2.6: The crew fly and fight to put Lt. Wirth in a position to destroy the target.

Image 2.7: The Norden Bombsight.

ignore multiple head-on attacks by German Bf109 and Fw190 fighters, no matter how ferocious. The wall of angry flak must also be ignored.

The navigator, Lt. Horsky, will be tasked with getting the B-17 to and from the objective, furnishing Lt. Kaczaraba with flight directions, keeping the flight log book, and manning a nose gun in the event of fighter attacks. He must be well versed on weather, flak concentrations, and the type of formation being flown.

Navigation is a combination of dead reckoning, (using speed and elapsed time between checkpoints to compute position), pilotage (watching the ground for visible landmarks), radio use, and celestial navigation. Lt. Horsky has his own Plexiglas bubble just forward of the cockpit through which he can shoot his celestial navigational fixes. In combat, all bombing targets will be approached by pilotage. The aircraft's positional accuracy is expected to stay within one-quarter mile at all times during the mission.

Instrument calibration will also be an important duty of Lt. Horsky since all navigation and bombing depends directly on the accuracy of his instruments. Instruments to be calibrated include the altimeter, compasses, airspeed indicator, astro-compass, astro-graph, drift meter, and sextant.

Before each mission Lt. Kaczaraba and Lt. Horsky will study the route to be flown and select alternate airfields. Lt. Kaczaraba will advise Lt. Horsky on the expected weather, and the airspeed and altitude the mission will be flown. Checkpoints are discussed. Once in the air, Lt. Kaczaraba needs to fly consistent airspeed and course-and notify Lt. Horsky of any changes. Lt. Horsky is expected to give Lt. Kaczaraba position reports at regular intervals.

Additional duties of Lt. Horsky will include familiarity with the oxygen system, gun turrets, fuel transfer system, and radios. He must know the location of all fuses and lights affecting navigation. He must be well versed in emergency procedures such as crash landings, bailing out, ditching, and manual operation of the landing gear, bomb doors, and flaps.

The top turret is located just behind and above the two pilot's seats (Image 2.8). This "top gun" position is home for the engineer and top turret gunner, T/Sgt. John Samuel (Sam) Honeycutt (Images 2.9 and 2.10). He is a 21-year-old possessing good engineering aptitude, which was rigorously tested by the Army Air Corps engineer's course. Sam is the only married NCO having a wife (Pauline) waiting back home. He stands on a steel platform inside his electrically powered turret, which houses twin .50 caliber machine guns. The turret and its weapons are able to rotate 360 degrees horizontally and up to 85 degrees vertically. When not occupying the turret Sam will stand or sometimes sit in a small jump seat between and slightly behind the two pilots. In this position, he will monitor certain gauges on the cockpit instrument panel and will call out take-off and landing speeds.

Image 2.8: T/Sgt. John Honeycutt, senior enlisted crew member, is the flight engineer and top turret gunner. During takeoff, he assists the pilots in monitoring the engines and systems. As the bomber approaches hostile airspace, he climbs into the top turret.

Image 2.9: From this position atop the bomber, the top turret gunners responsibility is to cover the sky above and call out the positions of attacking fighters for the other gunners.

Image 2.10: The top turret gunner's view to the six o'clock position. This early turret was an enclosure of steel and Plexiglas that provided a surprisingly restricted view. Later turrets were completely enclosed in Plexiglas, affording far better visibility.

In addition, Sam is responsible for the bomb bay area located just behind the top turret and separated from it by a plywood door. This door is normally closed to keep out cold air. Inside the bomb bay an eight-and-a-half-inch wide catwalk supported by offset steel beams extend rearward six-and-one-half feet to a similar plywood door. This narrow walkway allows about 15 inches of chest space to walk back and forth, with vertical clearance just over five feet. These dimensions necessitate a crouched, sideways movement back and forth through this low, narrow passage. There are waist-high rope lines that run fore and aft on both sides of this cramped passage, which provide some support. The bombs hang from shackles located on either side of the catwalk. Should the bombs fail to release, Sam must leave his top turret, enter the extremely cold, wind-blown area, negotiate the wide-open bomb bay area, and physically kick the bombs loose while hanging on for dear life (Images 2.11 and 2.12).

Sam must know more about the B-17 than any member of the crew, including the aircraft commander. He is the senior NCO aboard, is a qualified combat flight engineer, and must know his airplane, engines, and armament thoroughly. The lives of the entire crew, the safety of the equipment, and the success of a mission will rest squarely on his shoulders. In emergencies, it is Sam to whom Lt. Kaczaraba will turn.

During training Lt. Kaczaraba will teach Sam as much about flying as possible. His reasoning being that the more completely Sam understands the function of the equipment, the more valuable he will be if and when something goes wrong. He must be well versed in all emergency procedures and able to assist in flying the aircraft when necessary.

Working closely with the copilot, Lt. Mike Morgan, he will check engine operation, fuel consumption, and the operation of all equipment. He will also work with the bombardier, Lt. Ted Wirth, to cock, lock, and load the bomb racks. He must be thoroughly familiar with the armament, and know how to strip, clean, and reassemble the weapons almost without thought.

The top turret is the most comfortable battle station where Sam can see 360 degrees horizontally and can alert the other gunners of any enemy plane positioning for an attack.

At the aft end of the bomb bay is the radio compartment. Entry and exit from the bomb bay to the radio compartment is via another small plywood door that is also normally closed to keep out the cold air. This small room contains the B-17's communications equipment, which includes receivers, transmitter, external signal earphones, and other communication devices. It also contains a small table and swivel chair for the radio operator (Image 2.13).

The radio operator, T/Sgt. Wilber Allen Peifer, is 24-years-old and an excellent operator but will have the least glamorous job in the crew. He has a compartment in the center of the fuselage. He must sit for hours on end, static crackling in his ears, giving position reports every 30 minutes, assisting the navigator in taking fixes, and informing headquarters of targets attacked and the results. Sending distress signals is also Wilber's responsibility. He must keep his equipment in good working order, maintain a log, preflight test his radio equipment, and frequently act as the crew photographer. Finally, he is responsible for the first-aid equipment, which the crew fervently hopes will remain unused.

A plywood door provides exit from the radio compartment aft into the aircraft waist section. The ball turret is located about four feet past this door

Image 2.11: Looking aft through the bomb bay from the top turret gun mount position. This narrow catwalk is the only route fore and aft. This pathway must be traversed while wearing a high altitude flight suit and lugging a portable oxygen bottle. Through the bulkhead door aft is the support structure for the ball turret — its yellow oxygen bottle attached.

Image 2.12: Looking from inside the bomb bay toward the cockpit. Numbered bomb shackles correspond to lights on Lt. Wirth's control panel. At lower left is a bright green walk-around oxygen bottle. These portable bottles can be refilled by the main oxygen system at an outlet at every crew battle station.

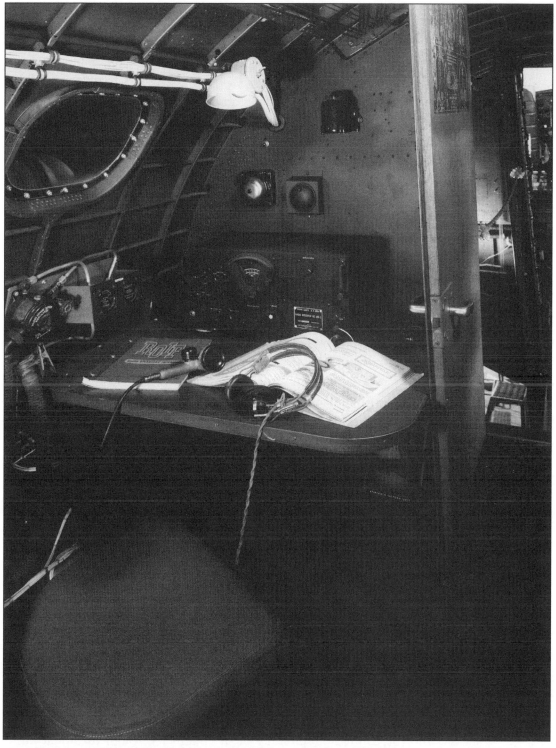

Image 2.13: T/Sgt. Wilber Peifer, the radio operator, is positioned in the center of the B-17 just aft of the bomb bay.

and is mounted half in and half out of the lower fuselage of the aircraft (Image 2.14). This is the battle station of the ball turret gunner. The ball turret will be ably manned by S/Sgt. Solomon (Shorty) Craden, age 21. Shorty is a big-hearted, cocky kid who has more tall stories than Paul Bunyan. For entry, this turret is hand cranked into a position where the electrically powered twin "50s" are pointed straight downward. Once in this position, a hinged panel, 21 inches wide by 21 inches long, is exposed allowing Shorty to pass through this tiny portal and into his battle station (Image 2.15). Once inside the turret, he assumes a crossed-leg sitting position, and when strapped into place can traverse his weapon 360 degrees and almost 90 degrees vertically. He will be responsible for defending the total underside of the aircraft for his are the only weapons available for this purpose (Image 2.16).

Small men are generally selected as ball turret gunners and Shorty is no exception at 5'1" and 105 pounds. Even at his height and weight there is no room for a chest parachute in these cramped quarters. He wears only a seat pack parachute in case of an emergency. Shorty will keep his Sperry-built power turret in constant rotation on lookout and to aim. He will not climb into his battle station until well after takeoff, and climb out again before landing. Though definitely not for the claustrophobic, the ball turret is statistically the safest position on the airplane, from the standpoint of numbers and types of battle wounds. It is, however, never occupied during take-offs and landings for obvious reasons.

About eight feet aft of the ball turret are the two waist gunner's positions, one on the right and one on the left. The right waist gunner position will be the battle station of S/Sgt. Harry Alexander (Gilly) Gilrane who also doubles as the assistant radio operator (Image 2.17). Gilly is a good-looking, big, dark-haired 21-year-old. Having received extensive training in radio principles, his skills are on a par with the primary radio operator, T/Sgt. Wilber Peifer. The left waist gunner position will be the battle station of S/Sgt. Peter (Pete) Franklin Parker. Pete, age 23, got his natural shooting eye from hunting squirrels in the wooded hills of Ohio. Each gunner has a single, post-mounted, manually aimed .50 caliber machine gun for defense. When the B-17 is at high altitude and the sub-freezing temperatures are as low as 60 degrees below zero, the waist gunners have the coldest battle stations in the B-17. The waist gunners are responsible for defending the flanks of the aircraft (Image 2.18).

All gunners have been well trained in aircraft identification, possess a good sense of timing, and know where to place their shots for maximum effect. With the enemy fighter's high rates of closure, the B-17's evasive action, and the rolling and pitching of the bomber through turbulent air, it will be difficult, if not impossible, to get a clean shot.

Image 2.14: The Sperry ball turret battle station of the ball turret gunner, S/Sgt. Sol Craden.

Image 2.15: This is S/Sgt. Craden's view as he enters his battle station. The ball turret, to be entered, must be positioned with the guns pointed straight down. This exposes the hatch to the inside of the B-17. Sol steps into the heel plates and curls himself into the ball. Once inside and the hatch closed behind, Sol is alone in his sphere, communicating with other crew members only through the interphone. Below are the charging handles for arming the machine guns.

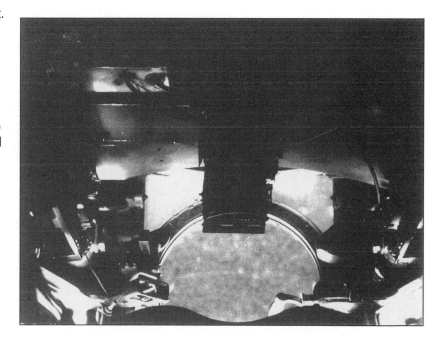

Image 2.16: Looking toward the six o'clock position from inside the ball turret. Enclosed in his sphere of glass and steel, suspended below the fuselage, Sol guards the B-17's belly. At left is the barrel of one of his two .50 caliber machine guns.

Image 2.17: Looking forward from the main entry door through the waist area up to the ball turret support structure. The large plywood box at right contains ammunition for the right waist gun. The flexible track keeps the belts of the .50 caliber ammunition feeding smoothly to the gun.

Image 2.18: Waist gunners, S/Sgt. Gilrane and Parker, must fight the 150 MPH slipstream to maneuver their 65 pound machine guns throughout their range of travel while tracking incoming fighters. They must also remember not to shoot parts of the B-17.

The waist gunners will have the distinction of manning the positions suffering the highest casualty rates. It is the least well protected, and the windiest; frostbite is a common concern. They must wrestle 65-pound Browning .50 caliber machine guns against the B-17's slipstream of 150+ MPH while taking care not to entangle themselves in oxygen, inter-phone, and electric connections, or slip on brass shell casings piling up around their feet.

Continuing aft, on the left, about six feet beyond the waist gunners battle stations is the waist door.[3] This hatch serves as the normal main entry to the aircraft and also serves as an emergency escape hatch for the radio operator, ball turret gunner and both waist gunners.

Lastly, in the extreme rear of the aircraft is the home of the tail gunner, S/Sgt. Gibson (Gibby) Polley, Jr. This battle station will be ably defended by this tall, slim, easy-going, 20-year-old New Englander who looks so young that he could pass for a junior in high school. In order to gain access to his battle station, Gibby must crawl around the tail wheel housing and assume a cramped and uncomfortable position. He must sit on a large, hard, canvas-covered bicycle-like seat having no backrest or arms (Image 2.19). His tail weapons consist of twin mounted, manually aimed, .50 caliber machine guns (Image 2.20). He is provided with a small escape hatch slightly behind him and to his left for use in an emergency. Gibby will be responsible for defending the rear of the B-17 from the bulk of enemy fighters, this being the usual attack approach taken by the German pilots (Image 2.21). In addition, he will be indispensable during aircraft take-off and landings. Located in his area is an electric torch, coined an Aladdin lamp. During inclement weather, Gibby's job will be to keep this light flashing to guide the aircraft following behind.

During takeoff or landing, Shorty and Gibby will occupy positions in the radio compartment. Shorty is out from underneath the aircraft for obvious reasons of safety. Gibby, with his allotment of ammunition, is there to reduce the inherent tail-heaviness of the B-17.

The B-17's oxygen system will sustain the crew when the aircraft climbs above 10,000 feet into the high, thin air. Once the crew dons oxygen masks and hooks into the main breathing system at each battle station, they can execute their tasks just as at lower altitudes. There are also 13 portable "walk-around" bottles with at least one at each battle station. These containers allow each crew member to move freely about the aircraft above 10,000 feet, are good for a 6–12 minute supply (depending on individual exertion), and are rechargeable by a valve located near the top turret position. As a precaution, each crew member will be trained to observe each other when above 10,000 feet for signs of oxygen deprivation. If a crew

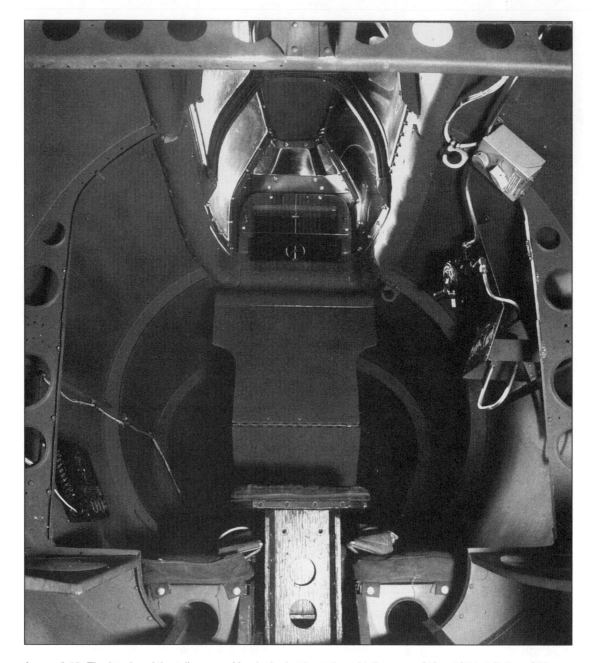

Image 2.19: The interior of the tail gun position is the battle station of tail gunner, S/Sgt. "Gibby" Polley. Gibby must sit or kneel for hours on a bicycle-type seat, reaching around the armor plate to fire his twin .50 caliber machine guns.

Image 2.20: "Gibby" is responsible for protecting the rear area. The battle station, located directly below the tails large rudder affords him a panoramic view of an air battle. His guns have the ring and bead gun sight that rises and falls with the movement of the guns. The entire aiming assembly is connected to the guns by cables.

Image 2.21: Gibby's view looking from inside his battle station from the six o'clock position.

member shows signs of being oxygen deprived, an unaffected member will provide a fresh oxygen bottle.

Following completion of their individual job specialties training at various Army Air Corps Bases, the crew came together at Moses Lake, Washington for second phase crew training in May, 1943. Crew 31-M, as they are impersonally listed on Special Order No. 127, will be heavily engaged for the next three months in practice missions, hoping one day to have a chance to learn formation flying when enough B-17s are available to make up a formation.

Lts. Kaczaraba and Morgan soon demonstrate to the rest of the crew what the B-17 can do in their expert hands and they quickly fall in love with their flying fort. Each crew member practices his own specialty. Lt. Ted Wirth proves how much of his training with the Norden bombsight he has absorbed by demonstrating some good, high-level bombing on the practice range near Walla Walla, Washington.[4] The waist gunners, Gilly and Pete, practice deflection shooting at tow-target sleeves over the desert in

Washington state. They will soon find out that this will be a far different proposition than firing at German Fw190s and Me109s.

During their second phase of crew training at Moses Lake, Gilly receives two visitors on the same day. Soon after arriving at the Moses Lake Base, Gilly is scheduled to fly a practice mission with another crew that includes his close friend, S/Sgt. John Babb of Boston, Massachusetts. While waiting to board the B-17, a jeep roars up and Gilly is informed that he has a visitor. The visitor is Major "Wild Bill" Donavan, a friend of Gilly's father. (Major Donavan will become a well-known general later in the war.) Gilly is excused from the practice mission and told to get into the jeep to be driven to his meeting with Major Donavan. That afternoon, they enjoy many pleasant exchanges of information regarding their heritage and family ties in Ireland.

The second visitor was also to become well-known later in the war, not only to Gilly, but to other Eighth Air Force airmen as well. This visitor is none other than the Grim Reaper. Later that day Gilly is informed that S/Sgt. John Babb, along with the rest of the crew, were all killed when their B-17 exploded on a practice bombing run over the desert. The Grim Reaper had missed his opportunity to gather Gilly into his fold only by the grace of God and the luck of the Irish.

This experience firmed up Gilly's personal faith in his Lord. He did not publicly express his faith or attend church on a regular basis; nevertheless, from that day on he possessed a strong belief in God. Each night Gilly prayed to his Lord to protect and watch over him. He thought of the Lord as a little guy on his shoulder watching over him in times of danger. During Gilly's combat missions the Grim Reaper will pay him more visits. These visits will be deadly contests between the Grim Reaper and the little guy on his shoulder for possession of Gilly's life and soul.

Flying both day and night exercises during the second phase crew training period, with a few 48-hour passes thrown in, the two months at Moses Lake pass quickly. The feeling of being transformed from ten individuals into a combat-ready team begins to settle in. The rest of the crew respects each man's judgment regarding his specialty. As the training nears completion the crew feels a growing confidence in having Lts. Kaczaraba and Morgan up front at the controls. Although still untested rookies, they believe strongly they have learned enough and deserve a chance to prove themselves in battle. Being young, eager and perhaps a bit cocky, little thought is given at this point to the perils of aerial combat soon to come.

At Topeka Army Air Base, Kansas, the crew receives their final processing orders on August 5, 1943 for departing the continental United States.

They are finally on their way to combat duty. This is the real thing, and each man has doubts as to how he will react to actual combat. Each believes, however, that he can put to good use the accumulated skills he has acquired through months of hard training while living in tar-paper huts and tents.

The crew will be transported to England by ship. It is just after noon on August 27th, when the *General William E. Black* ship eases out from the pier at the Norfolk, Virginia Naval Shipyard and into the Atlantic Ocean. Its decks are temporarily cleared of all passengers and the ship heads for the open sea.

Passengers are divided into two sleeping shifts, the "Up" and "Down." The Up shift passengers remain on deck and attempt to sleep with no facilities at all, while the Down shift goes to the cabins and attempts to sleep with very few facilities. However, fatigue wins out, and soon any corner where there is room turns into a bed. So it continues until the end of the voyage.

Each morning the crew, along with all the other passengers, form long lines for morning chow, which is eaten standing up at high tables. After eating, most of the crew goes back to bed for the rest of the morning.

Then at noon, everyone musters on the deck with life jackets on. The order is given for "attention" and all is silent. For a while the crew stands at attention. Then whispers increase to a higher volume until it is difficult for a man to hear his neighbor. Suddenly a stern voice yells, "At Ease," and the noise falls away again.

Sam stands by the rails for long periods of time watching the water slide by and aches for his new bride, Pauline. On the way over, a severe storm is experienced and sea sickness is the worst part of the trip. The good part about this storm is that it may keep submarines from attacking.[5]

Finally, in the early morning hours of September 2nd, the *General William E. Black* slips into the Firth of Clyde, Scotland. Gilly wakes and viewing land for the first time in six days, wakes the rest of the crew. The *General William E. Black* cast anchor off Glenrock, Scotland waiting permission to proceed into the shipyard and dock.

All day long the ship lies off the coast of Scotland. In the distance the Scottish Mountains appear in the mist and today the crew got their first introduction to the long days in the British Isles. It is still light outside at 2330 hours.

During the night the ship docks and the next morning the crew disembarks. The Scottish people seem to be pleased to see the American airmen. While boarding a train and passing through several towns, everyone waves their hands in delighted welcome. The train heads south through the moorlands into England. Prior to reporting to their assigned base, the crew receives a week of intensive ground-school on combat tactics in the European Theater of Operations (ETO)[6] at the Combat Crew Replacement Center in Stowe, England.

Finally, at about 2030 hours on Sunday, September 12, 1943, their train grinds to a halt at Cranford, just outside Kettering, Northamptonshire. It is dusk when the crew, dragging their duffel bags, file from the train and assemble in the railroad siding. Trucks wait to carry them through the quaint villages of Cranford and Grafton Underwood that will soon become familiar to them. They travel on to the airfield that is to become their home. For the first time in their twelve-month Army careers, they are finally "permanent party" upon reporting to their assigned air base in central England.

★★★

Book II

War Eagles

3

Life at Grafton-Underwood

Grafton-Underwood Air Base, England (Image 3.1), which had been a typical Royal Air Force (RAF) Base, was turned over to the United States Army Air Force in June, 1943.

Situated in the heart of the English Midlands, Grafton-Underwood (Station 106) is about 90 miles north of London in the county of Northamptonshire, on land owned by one of the largest land owners in England, his grace the Duke of Buccleuch and Queensbury. The nearest town is Kettering, four miles to the southwest, on the main railway line from London to Scotland. Originally the airfield, at the north end of the village of Grafton-Underwood, was built for the RAF. The airfield is typical of those constructed then, covering approximately 500 acres. The flying field consists of three intersecting runways (6,000 feet, 5,200 feet, and 4,200 feet) having a perimeter track with 50 dispersal's surrounding them. The technical site of the airfield consists of a control tower, two aircraft hangars, workshops, briefing and debriefing huts, offices, maintenance sheds, fuel stores, gunnery and skeet shoot ranges, bomb dumps and ammunition stores. The domestic site includes barracks, mess halls, shower houses, a base hospital, a base chapel, clubs, and a cinema — enough to cater to 3,000 personnel.

There is some green grass, but mostly mud, mud, and more mud. In the fall and winter months, the base receives heavy rain and during this time is known as "Grafton-Undermud."

The crew reports for duty at Grafton-Underwood on Monday, September 13, 1943 and is assigned to the 384th Bomb Group, 547th Bomb Squadron.[1] Lt. Giles F. Kauffman's crew reports the same day and is also assigned to the 547th.[2] Lt. Kaczaraba's crew had trained with this crew back at Moses Lake, Washington and all were close friends.

The squadron clerk provides directions to their living quarters. They are assigned a barrack, which is a major improvement over the tarpaper huts and tents that had been their home for the last year. The barrack is located fairly close to the mess hall, which always seems to be warm. (Later on, the crew will stash their shaving kits and do personal cleanups there, removing the black soot of spent cordite gun powder after combat missions.) Once in the 547th Squadron area, new hut-mates inform the crew that their assigned beds were provided courtesy of the boys shot-down on the recent Nantes (France) and Emden (Germany) raids. These new friends are also more than eager to relate horror stories about air combat and what will happen to rookie crews flying the "tail-end Charlie"[3] position.

One such horror story involved Technical Sergeant Irwin J. (Sam) Pire, Jr. His crew was forced to bail out of their disabled B-17 on a mission to Frankfurt and as Sergeant Pire floated down, he watched in horror as his bombardier, 2nd Lt. Hart, fell to his death because his chute failed to open.

Each crew member is assigned an iron bed and the hut has a table and a cast iron coal stove. From time to time there will be a shortage of coke and coal and this will necessitate "midnight requisitions" to other areas of the base. It all balances out, however, as today's prey is the predator of tomorrow.

The mess hall food is not the worst in the world, but it is a close second. Pancakes served are about the size of small tires and nearly as tough. Dried eggs are always served, except before combat missions. They stink to high heaven, and even after the cook's doctored them with onions and other unknown ingredients, they still reek.

Gambling is allowed in the Officers' Club (Image 3.2) and the Non-commissioned Officers' Club, the Zebra Club (Image 3.3). When off duty, most of the crew plays cards, shoots pool or just drinks warm English beer known as bitters. Except, of course, Sam — his free time is spent writing letters to Pauline. If there is anyone on earth close to a saint, it is Sam.

Off base, each of the crew must learn to deal with a new country, its customs, and its people. The local press has written much about what the Americans and British think of each other. It is true that English and

Image 3.1: Grafton-Underwood.

Image 3.2: Officers' Club.

Image 3.3: For enlisted men there are the Aero Club, the Zebra Club, and the "Privates and Corporals Bar."

American customs and viewpoints differ greatly, secretly however, the English are admired for standing up to the "Hun" under very trying conditions.

During their spare time, Gilly, Pete, Sam, Shorty, Wilber, and Gibby hop aboard large Army trucks for Liberty Runs into the local town of Kettering. These wild and hair-raising runs are at breakneck speeds without lights due to the mandatory blackouts. Once in town each settles down to the normal GI custom of dancing, drinking, and socializing with the English women— all except Sam. He is usually at the Salvation Army or St. Vincent DePaul Canteen writing letters to his true love. The unmarried crew members want women. In turn, the English women want food, cigarettes, gum, and men, not necessarily in that order.

Since all airmen are checked for venereal disease after each trip to town, the NCOs develop a novel method for Sam to avoid these unnecessary treatments. The NCOs would get the military police's attention at the entrance to Grafton-Underwood while Sam entered at another location. It worked without exception.

A trip to London is the primary objective of the crew when the first leave is granted. Their London trip is classically English. The crew proceeds from Grafton-Underwood to Kettering. They stand on a small platform and wait impatiently while the stationmaster sells tickets, moves baggage, and signals the train in and out. The compartment-type coaches, with an aisle running down one side only, are cozy and even private, if passengers are few. They are lightweight in construction, make quick starts and stops, and thrill each passenger with rough rides.

In London, the crew checks in at Red Cross Clubs such as the Jules Club or Van Dyke Club. Later, they ride the Underground all around the city visiting historical sites including Westminster Abbey, Big Ben, Piccadilly Circus, Hyde Park, Trafalgar Square, Leichester Square with its many theaters, Buckingham Palace, and the Mall. The crew will make two trips to London prior to their first combat mission on October 2, 1943.

Back at Grafton-Underwood, a B-17, A/C #41-24525, had been transferred from the 96th Bomb Group on September 13, 1943 for assignment to the crew. It is a common practice of air crews to name their B-17s and Lt. Kaczaraba's crew chose *What's Cookin', Doc?*. A saying popularized by cartoon character Bugs Bunny; in today's vernacular, a rough translation might be "What's Happening, Man?" The crew (Image 3.4), however, usually refers to their B-17 simply as *Doc* (Image 3.5).

The crew will confer upon their B-17 a personality akin to that of a living entity. These feelings toward a machine, based on past association, sentiments, or pride give it a special status, setting it apart from others of the same production line.

Image 3.4: The *What's Cookin', Doc?* crew at Grafton-Underwood, England. Back Row, left to right: 2nd Lt. Theodore Wirth, bombardier; 1st Lt. William Kaczaraba, pilot; 2nd Lt. Marvin Horsky, navigator; 2nd Lt. Myron Morgan, copilot. Front row, left to right: T/Sgt. Wilber Peifer, radio operator; (unknown Polish trainee) S/Sgt. George Polley, Jr., tail gunner; S/Sgt. Harry Gilrane, right waist gunner; S/Sgt. Peter Parker, left waist gunner; S/Sgt. Solomon Craden, ball turret gunner and T/Sgt. John Honeycutt, engineer/top turret gunner.

Image 3.5: B-17, *What's Cookin', Doc?* (USAAF S/N 41-24525). Image taken at Grafton-Underwood, England. Note the grapefruit-size flak hole in fuselage and the collapsed landing gear.

During the training period from September 23rd, until the crew's first combat mission, the following events take place at Grafton-Underwood.

On Thursday, September 23, the 384th bombers made a return trip to Nantes, France, an important shipping center inland on the Loire River, below the bulge in the Peninsula of Brittany. The target was a vessel in excess of 8,000 tons, which is used as a submarine repair shop. Observations as to whether the ship was struck could not be readily obtained due to widespread smoke and flames obscuring the area. One large ship was observed to have received a direct hit, but whether it was the floating submarine repair plant remained undetermined. Returning crewmen reported the target area was heavily hit.

On Sunday, September 26, Nantes-bound for the third time, the 384th BG formation was recalled due to bad weather when it reached the English Channel. The target was the same submarine repair vessel, which evidently had escaped the previous bombing.

Also on this date, information is received that T/Sgt. George Bossinger, a top turret gunner, missing since the Villa-Coublay mission on June 26, 1943, is enroute to England after making good his escape from enemy-occupied France. Sgt. Bossinger was a member of the crew of the plane piloted by Lt. Deltan G. Wheat. Lt. Wheat and seven other members of the group are known to be prisoners of war. The only man unaccounted for is Lt. David G. McMullen, the copilot.

On Monday, September 27th, a protective covering of clouds hid the important port city of Emden, Germany from the group's bombers, so the city of Aurich, to the northeast, took the full brunt of a penetration into Nazi land. The planes carried 1,000 pounders[4] under each wing on external bomb racks in addition to the loads in their bomb bays. The wing was led by the group's commanding officer, Colonel Julius Lacey. Colonel Lacey's formation found a huge opening in the overcast, which enabled the bombardiers to get in an effective bomb run.

On Tuesday, September 28th, several high decorations were awarded combat crewmen. The Silver Star, the third highest award for gallantry in action, was presented to T/Sgt. Raymond P. Gregori, a tail gunner, for his meritorious conduct during the mission on Gelgenkirchen, Germany, August 12th.

Approximately 15 minutes before his B-17 reached the target, Sgt. Gregori received a severe shoulder wound during an attack by enemy fighters, which virtually riddled his compartment and damaged his guns. It was a full 25 minutes after the target had been bombed that his crewmates discovered that Gregori had been wounded. All this time, though weak from loss of blood and in shock, he remained by his guns. The entire tail section was so full of bullet holes that it looked like a sieve. Every window, with the exception of the bulletproof one, had been shot out and the wind through the tail was terrific. Sgt. Gregori was blue from the cold. The heating unit of his electrically heated suit had been damaged. The temperature at that time, with the plane flying at 28,000 feet, was 40 degrees centigrade below zero.

Brigadier General Robert Travis, 41st Combat Wing Commander, awarded three Distinguished Flying Crosses (DFC) on this date.

Lt. Edgar E. Ulrey, copilot, was awarded the DFC for his action on a mission to Gelsenkirchen, Germany. During the Gelsenkirchen mission, August 12th, Lt. Ulrey's plane was subjected to heavy anti-aircraft fire and determined enemy fighter attacks. Over the target, the pilot, 1st Lt. Charles W. Bishop, was wounded and Lt. Ulrey assumed command. Damage to the oxygen system necessitated leaving the formation and it was only through violent evasive action and skillful use of cloud cover that Lt. Ulrey was able to save his crew and ship from destruction and make a safe return to base.

Cpt. Robert R. Fryer was awarded the DFC for his completion of 25 operational missions as a pilot. He was assigned as the 384th assistant group operations officer.

S/Sgt. James W. McKenn, a ball turret gunner, and the most decorated man in the entire group, received the DFC in recognition of his completion of 15 operational missions and for the destruction of two enemy fighter planes. He already held the Air Medal, with three Oak Leaf Clusters, and the Purple Heart.

Prior to the crew's first combat mission, duty time is spent on air training to become familiar with flight inbound/outbound routes, control tower communications, and taxiing. During this time many practice missions are carried out as well as the individual crew members learning their specific duties. Standard operating procedures (SOP) are regulations that are to be ingrained in the minds of the crew. One such SOP involves communications for the take-off. Once at their B-17 and ready for a mission, pilots are under strict instructions not to call over the radio telephone (R/T) for instructions. Instead, either flares or biscuit gun (aldis lamp) signals, are used. The sequences for flares are:

A. Start engines = yellow-yellow flare

B. Taxi = yellow-green flare

C. Take-off = green-green flare

D. Stop taxiing, hold position or do not take-off until further instructed = three red-red flares.

If biscuit guns signals are used, they are:

A. Green light = cleared to taxi, take-off or land

B. Red light = do not take-off, do not land, or stop taxiing

C. White light = return to dispersal's.

From September 19 to October 1, 1943, the crew logs 19 hours and five minutes of local flying time. This is in addition to the 96 hours and 30 minutes logged stateside. As of October 1, 1943, the crew has logged a total of 115 hours and 35 minutes of flying time.[5]

Additional ground training is also received when other crews with combat experience tell what they know and what to expect. In a few weeks *Doc's* crew will be giving the same advice to new replacements after the extremely high losses of aircraft and crews during October. It will be a short period of time between being rookies to seasoned veterans.

Combat tours consist of 25 missions against the Germans. The Army Air Corps has decided that a ten percent loss rate on each mission is acceptable. Since the average loss rate is usually higher than ten percent, each crew member is well aware that the odds of surviving 25 combat missions will be almost nil. Each feels that he is well trained, but still has doubts as to how well he will perform in combat. The only way each man can go on, is to believe that it can't happen to him.

Pitiful Pioneers

T he crew of the *What's Cookin', Doc?* are now well aware, based on the horror stories from their 384th Bomb Group hut mates, that on every mission they will be exposed to the wrath of German fighters and flak. Each knows that his chances of surviving would be much improved if he stayed in the barracks, yet all are eager to get on with the job they have been trained to do. Each approaches his future with an optimistic attitude.

The massive number of aircraft in a bombing formation is, in itself, extremely dangerous. During the summer and fall of 1943 as many as 1,300 bombers take off from England to bomb enemy targets in Germany or occupied Europe. Assembling such a large number of heavy bombers from fields all over central and eastern England, and flying in close formation, is a hazardous task. It's the equivalent of 1,300 civilian aircraft forming up in bad weather, with no radar guidance, in an area about ten square miles. To do so is a great feat even in good weather. The poor visibility arising out of the ever-present fog and overcast causes many airborne collisions. (There were approximately 100 air crashes in the Eighth Air Force while forming up over England during World War II.)

Aerial warfare in World War II is a new and different type of combat. No soldier has ever experienced this type of warfare. The battlefields for airmen are high in the sky and deep in enemy territory. They are far above the wet, muddy, frozen battlefields of the ground forces, and after a battle, they are able to return to the warmth and security of their barracks. Yet, the airman's battle is no less deadly and than the soldier's on the ground. An airman's chances of being killed, wounded, or becoming a prisoner of war are, in fact, much greater.

Fighter pilots receive most of the glory and promotions but the bomber crews are exposed to greater risks and must have more courage in combat. In the summer and fall of 1943, as Eighth Air Force bombers venture deep into enemy territory, they are escorted by fighters only to the extent of the fighter plane's range, usually at the German border. The German pilots stay outside the range of the American fighters and wait for the them to turn back. The enemy fighters then pounce on the unescorted bombers to prevent them from destroying the German war machine. German fighter planes relentlessly attack the bombers in relays from Luftwaffe Air Bases strung all along the routes to and from the targets and when the German fighters let up near the bomb area, the American airmen are challenged with a sky filled with flak. The probability of survival is not promising.

The number of B-17 bombers missing in action in the Eighth Air Force is greater than that of fighter aircraft. During 1943, up until October, there had been 900 Eighth Air Force B-17s that failed to return from their missions. As a result, 9,000 B-17 airmen were killed or taken prisoner. The fighter losses amounted to 160 fighters shot down, resulting in 160 airmen killed or taken prisoner.

The B-17, with its supercharger, is designed to fly at high altitudes close to the stratosphere where the air is so thin that a crew member cannot breathe without supplemental oxygen. Combat crews must wear oxygen masks at altitudes above 10,000 feet. The oxygen masks are plugged into the bomber's oxygen system to furnish the essential breath of life. When an airman's oxygen supply is cut off due to battle damage, he develops anoxia and has symptoms similar to alcoholic intoxication that becomes progressively worse until he lapses into unconsciousness. If oxygen is not restarted within a short time, he dies.

Casualties are great for those unlucky airmen caught in a burning bomber. Only about half of the airmen are able to exit before the aircraft explodes, and half of those are injured. If the aircraft is in a spin or dive, it is more difficult, if not impossible, to get out. If the bail-out is successful, the ordeal still may not be over, since the landing itself may prove to be hazardous. Combat B-17 bomber flying is a very precarious job.

For the first six months of its existence, from June 22, until December 20, 1943, the 384th Bomb Group's bombing offensive was carried out by a small group of pitiful pioneers. The 384th Bomb Group Squadron had an average of 48 available aircraft. This figure is misleading, due to normal maintenance and battle damage repairs. The 384th could, on the average, dispatch 20 B-17s on each mission. So much has been written about the 1,000+ aircraft raids of 1944–45, and so little about the unprotected bomber crews that waged the savage air war during the summer and fall of 1943. During this period the 384th Bomb Group suffered grievous combat losses. Ill fortune on these missions was all too frequent.

The following provides information on the sacrifices during the June through December period of 1943 and the January 1944 through April 1945 period of the group's air combat operations.[1]

	6/22/43 to 12/20/43	12/22/43 to 4/25/45
Missions:	44	272
*A/C MIA:	59	100
A/C MIA per mission:	1.34	.37
A/C MIA per month:	9.8	6.25
Total sorties:	**880	***8,468
A/C MIA by percent of total sorties:	6.8%	1.17%
Percent of total A/C MIA:	37%	63%

*A/C MIA = Aircraft Missing In Action
**Average 20 A/C dispatched per mission times 44 missions = 880
***Average 32.5 A/C dispatched per mission times 272 missions = 8,468

On its first mission on a June 22, 1943 raid to Antwerp, Belgium, the 384th put up 20 B-17s, consisting of the original crews. Of these, 75 percent were shot down over Europe during the next three-and-a-half months of combat operations. The casualties of the 150 crewmen on these aircraft tell a grim story, 32 percent dead, 54 percent prisoners of war, 5.3 percent returned, and 8.7 percent evaded or escaped.

In less than four months of combat operations, the 384th had suffered a 75 percent loss of the original aircraft and crews. These losses well illustrate the 384th Bomb Group's Pitiful Pioneer's determination and the Germans' air and ground forces determination to stop them.

The German Luftwaffe and anti-aircraft ground crews were both effective foes who gave as well as they got. This is evidenced by the 384th Bomb Group's Enemy Aircraft Claims (EAC) of 165 enemy fighters and its own losses of 159 B-17s missing in action.

Welcome to Air Combat

It is late Friday evening, October 1, 1943 as the mist begins to lift from the far ends of the runways. At 2050 hours the base communications tele-printer clatters out the message, "Stand By For B/Cast — Urgent Secret." This is the signal for Major William Dolan, (Image 5.1) the Intelligence (S-2) Officer, and Major Thomas Bechett, the Operations (S-3) Officer, to alert the men of their sections. The day for which the Doc crew had trained individually for more than a year, and as a crew for the past six months, has finally arrived.

A blackjack game between Shorty and Gilly is in progress when a private from operations, who has a southern drawl, comes into the hut and says, "Standby alert, you guys." The crew went out to stand in the mud that three days of rain left. They look up to where a few stars are showing through patches of clouds. "It'll clear," Pete predicts. They argue awhile about clouds banked against the southeastern night horizon because Germany lies in that direction.

Back in the hut Shorty and Gilly restart their blackjack game. Pete and Wilber are lying on the bed and Sam is, again, writing a letter home. Gibby is sitting on his bunk discussing the gear to be worn during the upcoming combat raid with a tail gunner from another squadron. They talk about the new type of microphones that fit in a flier's oxygen mask. It is Gibby's way of mentally checking out his equipment.

Back at the blackjack game, Shorty throws down, in disgust, four cards that total 22. "Sweatin's the hardest part of it," he shouts. No one had been talking about sweatin', but everyone knew what he meant.

Pete blurts out, "You get past the sweatin' and the rest is easy." He sits on the edge of his bunk and while he argues he sews a new pair of earphones into the fuzzy inside of his flying helmet. The blackjack game continues.

At 2300 hours, the printer order comes in and is translated into duty assignments. Lt. Lowell Hassen, the assistant communications officer, carries the long mes-

Image 5.1: It was "Pop" Dolan, the only staff officer to serve the group through the entire war period, who was the embodiment of the spirit of the 384th Bombardment Group.

sage to the Intelligence (S-2) and Operations (S-3) room, where the high-geared human machinery begins to carry out the much-exercised procedures. Officers who are to participate in the briefing are working on their maps and notes while the jeeps from squadron operations begin making their rounds of the barracks, awakening the men who are assigned to fly.

About 2330 hours the same private from operations comes into the hut again and this time it's, "The alert's on, y'all. Kaczaraba's, Kauffman's, and Price's crew in here. Chow at 0430[1] hours, briefing at 0530." Shorty hurls a few good-natured epithets as the private exits the hut. Pete joins Shorty and Gilly and the blackjack game continues.

Sam rolls over beneath his pile of gray and brown blankets and tells everybody to shut up, but the nervous chatter continues. Suddenly, those not playing cards go outside to recheck the sky. The southeast sky is now clear. The crew's worst fears are confirmed—tomorrow they will fly their first combat mission. Eager to relieve some of their fears, they all go to bed. Thus, the blackjack game finally ends.

Sam relates his first mission breakfast and the briefing for the NCOs:

"It is early Saturday morning, October 2, and I am dreaming of the big Post Exchange (PX) across the pond, the U.S. of A. Suddenly, a

loud voice cuts through the silence. Half-awake, I hope that the voice is just part of my dream, but it isn't. The hand of a private from operations jerks at the covers of each crew member and shouts, 'Get up, y'all are flyin' today.'

"I lay for a few more minutes, hoping he will leave in disgust and take his southern drawl with him but he doesn't. Using the light from the window I see that it is only 0400 hours.

"Shorty declares, 'Hey, let's give the army a break and heed the invitation of Major Al Nut (Major Alfred Nuttall) and go flying today.' It's too early for laughs, even from Shorty.

"I stumble out of my rack to get the other NCOs up while Lt. Kaczaraba is probably doing the same with the officers. Playing nursemaid to a bomber crew is causing both of us to lose lots of shuteye. With everyone now up and dressed, we all make our way to, hopefully, the first of many pre-mission breakfasts.

"It's hard to describe our first pre-mission breakfast. It is pretty good, real fried eggs with pancakes and coffee as black as soot. On non-mission days, it's scrambled artificial dried eggs with pancakes and the same old black-as-soot coffee. This time Shorty doesn't even insult the cooks as we leave the mess hall.

"Next, we proceed to the briefing room. There, using blackboards and movie screens, the brass will tell us what kind of a job we'll do this day. Entering the briefing room, Gilly notices the long stretch of string marking the map route for today's raid. 'They must've run out of string,' he mutters.

"The NCOs and officers are briefed separately, and then there are special briefings for the radio operator, navigator, and bombardier. The briefing is similar to a coach talking to you before you go out for the first half, except that you probably won't think of that simile until a long time after you're home from the raid.

"'Gentlemen, the target today presents possibly the most interesting task yet,' begins the briefing officer, Mr. S-2 himself, Major 'Pop' Dolan. He goes on to talk for five or six minutes before we hear the words Emden, Germany. He speaks of flak intensity and fighter strength and what the target means in the scheme of things to the air war. He says who's going and how many. It's a small force and we relax until his talk gets into flak. Then we tighten up. The old crew members swear to each other that they'll take fighters all day long but that damn flak gets to them. Major Dolan talks about other things that are secret and pretty soon he finishes his briefing. You expect to hear someone say, 'Let's go get 'em, men!' or something like that. No one does and *the crews get up and start hauling their flight kits and flight clothing to their assigned B-17s."*

The crew, minus the officers, arrives at the circle of concrete, known as the hardstand, where *Doc* is waiting. The zippered bags full of heated suits, shoes and paraphernalia are left at the hardstand and the crew heads for the armament shop.

In the oily atmosphere of the armament shop each NCO takes his .50 caliber machine gun out of its cover, breaks it down, cleans it, adjusts headspace and oil buffers, and puts it back together. The armament men did this same job on the same guns a few hours before, now they stand around watching. They don't resent that their hard work is being repeated. There is nothing to resent for everyone realizes that the crew's very lives depend on these guns. Sam gets his two top turret guns and Shorty gets the two for his ball turret. The waist gunners, Gilly and Pete, get their single guns and the one that fits in the nose, since Lt. Horsky, who will man the nose gun, is still being briefed. Gibby gets his two tail guns.

Back at the *Doc* each crew member positions his gun(s) and checks out his gear. About this time the sun is coming up, bright and hazy yellow, just like an Indian summer back home. Gilly hands out the emergency kits and Pete checks out his gear once more, just for the hell of it. Pete is talking to one of the ground crew about soy beans and they both seem to know a lot about soy beans. They talk a long time about them because it is the kind of day they would be harvesting soy beans if they were back home. But they aren't back home, they are waiting to go to a very interesting target, Major Dolan had said.

Lt. Morgan recalls the officer's first briefing and the crew's nervous condition prior to combat:

"We anticipate a rough mission despite rumors circulating that it will be an easy one. After breakfast, we trudge to the briefing room through the usual mire of 'Grafton-Undermud.'

"We are assembled in the briefing room and Major Dolan starts the meeting by raising the curtain covering the map on the wall. 'Our target for today is Emden, Germany. A port city just inside the border of Germany and across the bay from northwest Holland. Emden, we are told, has tripled its shipping capacity since heavy destruction wrecked Hamburg and other points. Although a city no larger than Reno, Nevada, war goods that would fill 1,000 American freight cars leave the port every day. Much of the iron ore from Sweden and Norway is

unloaded here. Today we will pound the harbor installations, marshaling yards, and canals, which carry raw materials to the industrial Ruhr Valley. Brigadier General Travis, Commander of the 103rd Combat Wing,[2] will lead today's raid. Major Alfred Nuttall will lead the 384th.'

"It is great to have seasoned combat veterans leading us on our first mission as we have a bad case of nerves. We board our transport truck to take us to the hardstand where Doc is parked and undergoing its early morning preflight. Gilly is checking the oxygen stations, Sam is checking the bomb racks, Lt. Kaczaraba and myself are checking out the controls/instruments but secretly we all try to check out our nerves. Everyone is somewhat on edge and butterflies are fluttering inside us. I make frequent piss calls behind the plane. Others put on their oxygen masks and try to clear their brains. Those that smoke cannot get cigarettes to their mouths because their hands are shaking so badly."

Later on, after a few missions, the crew will learn that overcoming fear is one of the things each man must do. They will take action to stay alive. Sam recalls the long wait before the first mission's takeoff:

"In spite of the early morning wake-up at 0400 hours and briefing at 0530 hours for this, our first mission, we do not start engines until 0830 hours. It is 0840 hours before we assume our takeoff positions inside the aircraft. The crew waits while Lts. Kaczaraba, Morgan, and I run the engines through for the last time prior to takeoff. It is time and we are all in our individual aircraft positions to take Doc down the runway to join the rest of our group's B-17s.

"It is 0845 hours before Doc rolls out to the perimeter track. We follow the aircraft in front of us to the takeoff runway. For the next five minutes I observe aircraft rumbling down the runway, one every 45 seconds. It is 0850 hours, we roll onto the runway, apply full brakes, rev up our 1200 HP Wright Cyclone engines and … wait. Soon the green 'Go' light is flashed and we are ready for takeoff.

"With the brakes still set power is increased to full throttle raising the engines' roar to a deafening level and causing the entire plane to shudder. Now the brakes are released and I feel a surge as Doc accelerates down the runway. After 14 months of training and preparing for this moment … We are on our way!

"Any B-17 crew member will tell you that the takeoff is what he sweats the most, except for actual combat. We are rolling down the runway, however, 5,000 feet later we still have not broken the earth's *grip. The end of the runway is coming up, Lt. Kaczaraba pulls back fully on the yoke and our aircraft wheels finally clear terra firma.*

"We have on board, ten 500 pound bombs and a heavy gun load. What some of us didn't know is that the gunners in the rear of Doc *felt that they would need all the ammunition they could get, so they added eight more cases of .50 caliber ammunition. Our crew may go down fighting but it won't run out of ammo. We're off on mission number one; only 24 more to go, I hope."*

"Pilot to navigator. Pilot to navigator." "Go ahead, pilot." "You all squared away?" "Roger." Strung out across the English sky 4,000 to 5,000 gunners, pilots, bombardiers and navigators are covering the same checklists.

Doc continues to climb. Kauffman's guys are just below to the left in *Tough Shit*. Kelly's ship, *Little America* leads, up above and in front.

"Top turret to pilot. Top turret to pilot." "Pilot to top turret. Go ahead, Sam." "Shall we try out our guns when we clear the coast?" "As soon as we clear the coast, Roger."

The fields down below grow small as *Doc* gains altitude. "Co-pilot to crew. We're getting up there now. Better go on oxygen. Check in, will you?" The responses start with a New England accent from the tail and move up through the ship.

Up ahead the 384th Bomb Group's lead navigator checks his course as the formation turns away from England and starts over the English Channel. "Copilot to gunners. Try 'em out now if you want to."

The inside of *Doc* is filled with the sound of pounding as the twin top turret and ball turret guns open up. The tail guns are in the rear of the B-17 and are not audible and the waist guns are single machine guns and don't pound. All gunners check in and for a long time the interphone is quiet.

Lt. Morgan continues to narrate the mission on his first approach to the enemy coast:

"I am surprised at the length of time required for the forming up of our bomb group with the other groups, wings, then divisions. We consume almost two hours forming up and now we are 30 minutes late departing the English coast. In a few minutes we are up to 15,000 feet above the North Sea with a course set for Emden, Germany. I settle in for an easy mission.

"About 60 miles from the enemy coast, Major Nuttall, the 384th leader, is signaled on the Very High Frequency (VHF) radio band by the 1st Air Division Leader, General Travis to take the lead. The 384th now assumes the lead.

"The sky above 15,000 feet is clear even though a continuous under-cast blocks visual contact with the ground. The early morning sun paints patterns on the clouds, providing many colorful scenes for us to enjoy. We're all scanning the sky trying to peer beyond the flimsy clouds that edge the horizon. The interphone sounds again. 'Gettin in there now, you guys. Better be on watch.' That's Lt. Kaczaraba.

"Above in his top turret position, Sam informs us of about 25 P-47 escorts approaching the formation. Our "little friends" as we call them. They continue on toward the front of our bomber formation. Later, I observe more of their kind.

"We are crossing the enemy coast into Holland and we receive a shower of flak as black puffs explode slightly below and in front of Doc.

"Up ahead billowing cumulus clouds are forcing our formation to climb higher to maintain visual contact with each other. We climb up to 25,000 feet and visibility is good. The temperature outside is −35 degrees centigrade. My feet and hands are starting to get cold.

"Again, up ahead, the clouds look like mountains and are even higher than our present altitude of 25,000 feet. We climb to 27,000 feet. The temperature is −45 degrees centigrade. My feet and hands are numb."

"Well, there's the black shit exploding ahead of us." That's Lt. Kaczaraba. Everyone can't see what he's talking about, but Shorty clears it up. "That stuff's thick enough to fly through on instruments. Hope to see us on the other side."

Doc goes into the flak that comes up all around. Some watch the flak, some don't, because this day Emden earns the title of flak champion. It isn't easy to look at it and not want to run away.

"Anybody want to get out and walk?" That's Shorty, and this time the entire crew laughs like hell because they are right in the middle of it. *Doc* is not taking hits and that's a good feeling. But for some of the other bomb groups this is not so. Way back in the tail Gibby is calling out, in a flat tone, B-17s that have been hit and going down.

Off to the ten o'clock position a burst of flak lingers and Lt. Morgan is on the interphone again. "The fighters will be in now." They are. The orange and black Ju88 German fighters come up and take a swipe, and the Me110 fighters cut in with their tail twin fins high. The Me210 fighters slash at another squadron while other 110s and 210s lay back on the edge of the sky and lob rockets in orange arcs at our B-17s.

Lt. Wirth relates his experience of the first bomb run:

"We are making our approach to the Initial Point (IP), which is the position from where we start our bomb run. Near the target the German

88mm flak guns concentrate on our formation and it is necessary to cut the IP short. This causes the bomb run to be only 15 miles. We bomb through a nine-tenths overcast by the Path Finder Fix (PFF)[3] method. Today, the PFF equipment is aboard the aircraft of Major Nuttall, our group operations officer. Bombs away. I observe many more joining ours on the descent to the Emden harbor installations, marshaling yards, and canals."

Shorty shares the crew's first enemy fighter attacks:

"As I inform the crew that all bombs are away, an Me109 comes up from under Doc *for a belly attack. The German fighter makes an unsuccessful pass and zooms upward and over our tail. It happened so fast that we never fired a round. The fighter's speed and turns were much faster than we had trained for. It was as if the entire attack was in slow motion on our part, yet the pass only took about five seconds. We are stunned, shocked, and disappointed with our reaction … we were spellbound!*

"At last we are on our way home. I sight down my twin .50 caliber machine guns at a Ju88 fighter passing under us. The corner of my eye catches the patterns of fields far below. I think, how strange, they're just like the fields back home.

"The enemy fighters had gone but now they return. A pack of 110s gang up on a Fort that's limping home on three engines. Flames are sifting out of the last operating engine. The Fort starts to slide off to the south. Out of the ship comes little black dots. The dots are men who ate breakfast with us in England a million years ago this morning. Three parachutes blossom and drift down, while the Fort, bulky and big, heads off to the south. It lumbers along, losing altitude, still smoking. The last I see, it is a lumbering giant shuffling down a long hill into a mist. It isn't easy to watch."

The crew reports flak coming up but it is mostly on the division in front of the 384th formation. The exploding flak forms a large black cloud, which makes forward visibility very difficult. Each time Lt. Kaczaraba reaches for the cockpit controls a black puff billows outside and causes him to crouch in his seat to avoid the danger. This continues for a few minutes and it plays havoc with his nerves.

The formation makes a sharp turn and high tails it for home. The flak continues to follow, even in sharp banks and turns. It finally falls behind as the formation departs the Emden defense zone.

The formation flies back to and is now over the North Sea, as briefed. Once again, the air division commander assumes the lead. Now within 60 miles of the English coast, the 384th Bomb Group is again called by the air division commander to take over the lead. The formation is approximately 30 miles off course as the 384th takes over the lead and sets a course correction. Soon the formation passes over the designated point of return on the English coast. The 384th flies to Grafton-Underwood without any further incident. Mission number one down, only 24 more to go.

The *Doc's* crew is not quite finished with their first mission; debriefing is next. Debriefing plays a very important part of each mission because it is the only way that high command can determine the effectiveness of the raid, and of course, how many planes may have been lost and how many men escaped from the missing aircraft. During debriefing each crew member is offered refreshments while he tries to unwind and collect his thoughts.

Prior to the debriefing, the Air Division Commander, General Travis, who had led the raid, has high praise for our bomber crews:

> *"It went off like a military drill. It's not often you come back from a mission in which everything went so well. Usually you have a bad taste in your mouth about something, but this one went off without a hitch. The flak was intense in front of us but it was inaccurate. When we reached the Fresian Islands (these are several small islands west of the Denmark coast) we could barely make them out. The weather became increasingly bad as we went in, but our bombs went down together over the target and I have every reason to believe they did the job. The discipline of our men, the general lack of unnecessary talking, and the eagerness with which they obeyed orders particularly impressed me. It was a good show and I was very much pleased with it."*

Next the debriefing officer discusses the mission with each member of the crew.

"I liked the flak the Germans threw up at us very much. It looked very pretty mushrooming out of the clouds below our ship. They were slightly off the beam on their marksmanship," said Lt. Morgan.

"The result of our bombing could not be observed because of thick layers of clouds that blanketed the target. We dropped our 500 pounders right where the target was supposed to be, but you'll have to ask the Heinies about the amount of damage we inflicted," added Lt. Wirth.

"It was practically a milk run," said Shorty, "not much excitement and not much to see. We went over and returned without any trouble."

Shorty's statement pretty much summed up the crew's opinion. This, their first mission, would later prove to be their only milk run as the rest would all prove to be much more terrifying and traumatic. But this one had served to build up their confidence. They may not be so lucky the next time.

Each crew member talked to the intelligence officer who recorded what had happened and sent it up to command. Command recorded what the intelligence officer sent and forwarded it up to headquarters. After that, the official communiqués are written in the stiff phrases that high command uses.

But the communiqués can't tell about the crew members who go to Emden, Bremen, or Kiel, and they can't tell about sweatin' out the long hours before the mission. Most of all, the communiqués can't tell about Pete and Shorty's fear of fighters, Lt. Kaczaraba and Gilly's hate of flak, Sam's need for prayer, Lt. Morgan's frequent piss calls behind the plane, Lts. Horsky and Wirth's frostbitten toes and fingers, or Gibby's half-eaten sandwich when *Doc* lands back on the friendly fields of England.

★ ★ ★

CHAPTER

6

Heroes Reprimand

It is pitch dark at 0400 hours when the operations clerk with a southern drawl comes into the barrack on this Friday, October 8, 1943 to get the crew out of bed for another crack at Germany.

Shorty wisecracks to the clerk, "You must be confused. The British bomb by night. We bomb by day. Wake us up at noon!" This remark didn't strike the clerk as funny but it got a big laugh from the other NCOs. Shorty is always good for keeping the crew in good spirits.

In spite of the last mission to Emden, Germany where they experienced only flak that was mostly inaccurate and low over the target area, the crew is still eager to get at Adolf. Somehow, each senses that this mission will be much worse.

A hasty breakfast is consumed. Mission briefing is next at 0630 hours. The briefing officer begins by informing the crews of the target for today:

"Today's target will be Bremen, Germany, the originating point of Germany's U-boat campaign. We will attack the dock area to the center of the city. Major William Gilmore will lead the 384th. We will put up 18 aircraft over the target."

Following additional briefings, the crew boards transport trucks to take them out to *Doc*. An eerie calm prevails as the crew travels to *Doc's* parking ramp. Each man sifts through his innermost thoughts. Will I let my crew down? How will I react to fighters and flak searching for me? Will I do my duty? These and a thousand other thoughts haunt their minds. The crew would soon realize that whether it's your second or 22nd mission, the butterflies run rampant in their stomachs.

The crew waits outside *Doc* for the mission briefing from their coach and aircraft commander, Lt. Kaczaraba. Now they huddle, somewhat like a football team around their coach on the sidelines. After Lt. Kaczaraba completes the mission briefing each crew member is confident that he will atone for the lack of defensive action on his last raid to Emden.

The first raid has instilled the crew with confidence. They are no longer individual players, but a highly trained, highly organized, and skilled team. Today they are a team of ten, all with a job to do — Pilot, Co-pilot, Navigator, Bombardier, Engineer, Radio Operator, Ball Turret Gunner, Right and Left Waist Gunners, and Tail Gunner.

Doc is fueled, loaded with bombs and waiting to be coaxed into the air. Each man becomes part of *Doc* and knows it like his own body. Every aspect and detail of their B-17 is deeply ingrained within each of them.

Communications on and checked, synchronize watches, it's time. Now a sputter, followed by the explosion of each 1200 horsepower Wright Cyclone engine. *Doc* is revved up and ready to go, green takeoff flares are sighted, throttles are pushed forward, and one of the most formidable fighting machines built by man is on its way as this 30 ton instrument of destruction hurdles down the runway, engines roaring. It is an overwhelming experience.

The lead aircraft in the group, once airborne, proceeds for 90 seconds, then banks sharply to indicate its turning point as it starts a long left turn. Each trailing aircraft turns as soon as the aircraft in front turns. The first of the group's B-17s levels off at an altitude of 1,000 feet, waiting for the remainder to get airborne. Takeoffs are completed and group assembly is in progress. Other formations, bombers and fighters, from airfields all over England are on their routes to join the 384th. The group's wing and division rendezvous point is not far away.

It is an amazing sight to witness such a large force of bombers assembling for a mission. The time and maneuvering necessary to accomplish this feat is truly mind-boggling. This is the largest strike force ever assembled to date.

The next two hours are required to form, first, the 384th Bomb Group, next, the 41st Combat Wing and then, the 1st Bomber Division. Now assembled, this mighty air armada stretches for almost 20 miles and consists of more than 500 B-17 and B-24 heavies. The armada flies in a combat box formation, which provides a clear field of fire for the bomber's defensive guns (Image 6.1).

Gibby has the best view of this truly striking picture and attempts to describe this amazing scene:

> *"Scattered over this small area of East Anglia are the 1st, 2nd, and 3rd Bomb Divisions flying at altitudes from 5,000 to 10,000 feet. I almost expect to see mid-air crashes at any time as one group slides*

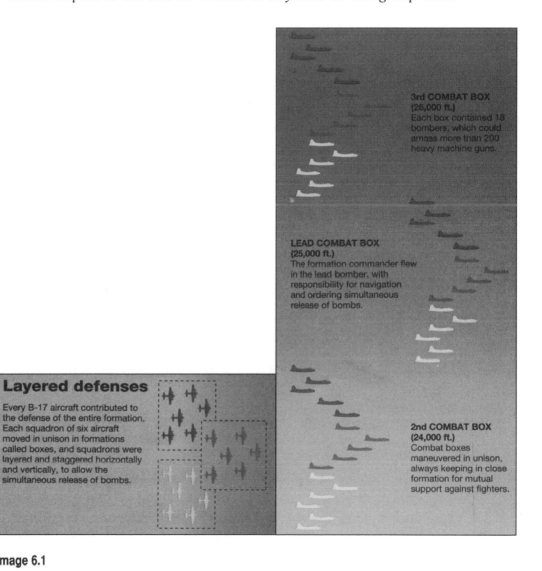

**3rd COMBAT BOX
(26,000 ft.)**
Each box contained 18 bombers, which could amass more than 200 heavy machine guns.

**LEAD COMBAT BOX
(25,000 ft.)**
The formation commander flew in the lead bomber, with responsibility for navigation and ordering simultaneous release of bombs.

Layered defenses

Every B-17 aircraft contributed to the defense of the entire formation. Each squadron of six aircraft moved in unison in formations called boxes, and squadrons were layered and staggered horizontally and vertically, to allow the simultaneous release of bombs.

**2nd COMBAT BOX
(24,000 ft.)**
Combat boxes maneuvered in unison, always keeping in close formation for mutual support against fighters.

Image 6.1

under another or groups appear to be on a head-on collision course, but do not actually collide. I try, in my mind, to describe this thrilling picture but just cannot do it justice."

At 1030 hours the groups, wings, and divisions have assembled, as briefed. The armada is heading for the Cromer navigational fix and are to depart from there in correct combat positions at 10,000 feet. Cloud cover is ahead, communications must now be clear and concise. A midair collision is a very real threat in the English pea soup.

The armada is flying a course straight across the channel, over the Dutch coast to the city of Alkmaar, Germany. Sam reports two 384th Bomb Group B-17s turning back. He does not know why. The formation is at 25,000 feet and the outside air temperature is −45°C. The formation crosses the Dutch coast and all of northern Holland is clearly visible. Flak greets the intruders with minor burst but it is inaccurate and below the formation.

German air space is entered, altitude is 26,000 feet. The outside air temperature is −50°C. At this altitude oxygen masks are collecting moisture and freezing quickly. Masks and hoses must be broken up every few minutes to keep the passages free. Hands and feet are so cold that they are numb. Hands can be warmed occasionally, but feet remain almost frozen and lifeless with no feeling at all. This is in spite of thermal clothing consisting of long johns, a sweater, flying coveralls, gloves, an electric blue suit, and wool-lined boots.

The coldest battle stations on the *Doc* are those of the waist gunners for both waist battle stations are large open spaces. The severe cold freezes oxygen masks to faces and frequent adjustments are necessary to break up the ice in order to keep the oxygen flowing. It will take hours for the waist gunners to get their body temperatures back to normal after landing if they are lucky enough to get back to the friendly fields of England.

Over German territory now and no enemy fighters or any serious flak yet, but they are out there … waiting.

Gibby recalls the crews encounter with enemy fighters and flak prior to reaching the target:

"Our P-47 Thunderbolt fighter escorts now peel off, leaving the formation and heading back to England. Unescorted and on our own, the formation heads deeper into Nazi Germany. We are alert for an attack … here they come. German Me109s and Fw190 fighters come at us four abreast with their 13mm cannons flashing as if searching for each of us. B-17s are going down all around, out of control. Sam reports a B-17 in another formation going down. There are ten fine young men in it.

I see no parachutes. Seeing a B-17 go down is a sight you never forget, especially when your friends are in it.

"Doc is now being attacked, mainly from my position in the rear as we are flying the rookie "tail-end Charlie" position. After a battle of almost an hour the Germans are turned back. They have had enough and high tail it for home to lick their wounds. I know, however, that it will be just as bad on our return home.

"We are 15 miles from the target, Bremen. The initial point (IP) is reached and the approach is started for the bomb run. Flak is coming up, heavy, accurate, and at proper altitude. It fills the sky with jagged metal. You just have to take it. You can't fight back. You can't do anything except fly through it. The bomb run is coming up. This is the most dangerous part of the mission for our B-17 must fly straight and level for 15 miles to allow Lt. Wirth to zero in on the target. In fear I brace and lock my legs in place as we start our bomb run."

Lt. Morgan's view is from the cockpit and he tells how it is up front during the bomb run:[1]

"We are making our turn toward the target. A solid black cloud of flak is at our exact altitude. I can barely make out the formation ahead of us plowing into the flak clouds. Soon we will be following the same path!

"Approaching the target, the turbulence of the exploding German 88mm ground anti-aircraft guns trembles within my body. The 384th is the last group over the target and the German 88s have our range and altitude right on the nose. Flying straight and level through the target area means we are sitting ducks. We are over the target only five or six minutes but it seems like an eternity. The constant droning of the motors, and the excited chatter between crew members describing the ever changing battle scenes are the only sounds present inside the cockpit.

"Outside of the cockpit, the unreal, ever changing scenes are almost indescribable. There are continuous and mountainous clouds of black smoke from exploding 88mm anti-aircraft shells. One to the left, one to the right, then another under us that lifts Doc upwards, along with the familiar sounds of metal fragments pelting the stomach of Doc.

"This spellbinding scene changes from one frightening nightmare to another. Our left wingman's B-17 is on fire from a direct flak hit. The bomber is struggling to stay airborne, now an erratic turn to the left and it noses down into a deadly spiral. Watching in horror, I strain to see how many chutes blossom and float down. Three chutes bloom to

life. Three friends will live. Seven others go down with their B-17. Seven friends will die.

"Now my right wingman's B-17 takes a direct hit and explodes into a giant ball of fire and smoke. Ten young lives are snuffed out inside this ball of fire. This heartbreaking scene is repeated over and over until we reach the target and we prepare to release our bomb load."

Now it's Lt. Wirth's turn to put the bombs on the target. He takes us into the final minutes of the bomb run:

"I am in total concentration on the task at hand. Flak is extremely heavy. Doc is taking flak hits but I cannot be deterred from my work. I open the bomb bay doors, bombs are released and shipyards and docks below feel the force of five tons of destruction from Doc, *joined by many others in their descent to Bremen."*

Shorty recalls, from his ball turret position, the target area's destruction:

"As our bombs are released, I feel Doc *lift a few hundred feet in altitude, as anticipated. This upward thrust serves to place* Doc *slightly above the flak. Lt. Kaczaraba is turning to a heading of 360 degrees north, toward the sea. Flak is still following us but we are slowly ... it seems to take an eternity ... slowly leaving the flak area. We are now almost out of flak range ... thud, thud, thud. Three times we are hit by flak ripping into* Doc *in my area. Lt. Kaczaraba requests all battle stations report in. All report in OK. For twelve more minutes the flak continues. We take at least ten additional hits in the fuselage, nose, left wing, both stabilizers, and the tail. It stops as suddenly as it began. At last, we clear the defensive zone below.*

"Bremen, below and slightly behind, billows with black smoke rising as evidence of the formation's bombing effectiveness. This, combined with the German smoke pots that surround the ancient city, presents a picture of total destruction in the target area. (Smoke pots are used by the Germans to obscure targets and to make positive identification difficult.) Through occasional breaks in the smoke and around the fringes the streets appear deserted, like a dead city.

"I start to relax ... just a little ... wham! At least 200 German fighters come out of the sun quite unexpectedly. They form up in battle groups of four on the rear of the formation where the 384th is flying. It seems the Germans have sent up their damned entire Air Force — consisting of Ju88s, Fw190s, and Me109s. They have completed their

assembly and are in battle positions to attack the 384th rear. To make matters worse, Doc has lost one engine from low oil pressure and another is struggling without the supercharger. This will cause us to lose speed and the ability to maneuver to escape the fighters. I swing my ball turret toward the German fighters in readiness for their attack."

From his top turret position Sam narrates the attacks and a helping hand to friends:

"Here they come, four abreast, attacking in waves. Cannons and machine guns blink their deadly lights, searching for each and all of our crew. We are determined this time to give more damage than we receive. Our guns are firing from the tail, both waists, and my top turret.

"The ball turret is silent! I wonder if Shorty is wounded, dead, or are his twin .50s out of service? I worry about Shorty but things are too hot now to check on his condition.

"We are taking many hits from the German fighters, mostly in the tail and stabilizers. Countless hits are tearing into Doc but in spite of the heavy flak and fighter attacks, he is still healthy and fit for duty.

"Another B-17 is hit and spirals downward. Four of the crew are spotted bailing out, and will live, the other six will die. Friends are dying and the battle rages on!

"A brief lull in the attacks allows Gilly to determine the status of Shorty. He rotates the ball-turret until the guns are in a vertical position, which allows him to communicate with and determine the condition of Shorty. It is evident by the thumbs up from Gilly that Shorty is uninjured and cocky as ever.

"'How's a guy supposed to get any sleep around here?' Shorty quips. He informs us that his guns are malfunctioning, 'I can only fire after I remove the back plate and manipulate the trigger bar with my left thumb. I just want to let the bastards know I'm still in my ball-turret so they won't attack from my position.' He can only fire a few rounds until his left thumb is hurt, then he uses a screwdriver to fire. This is a very dangerous and unorthodox method of firing a machine gun.

"It now becomes apparent to me why we are having the brief interlude in the attacks. Two B-17s of our group are crippled and have drifted back several hundred yards to our left. These are B-17s of our squadron, the 547th. One of the cripples is A/C#9870, Tough Shit, Lt. Kauffman's ship. This crew trained with us for the last four months and we are close friends. The brief interlude is because the German fighters are forming up for the kill on the two crippled B-17s. The cripples are

alone at the seven o'clock position,[2] about 800 yards back. Me109s and Fw190s are slicing between the cripples throwing a hail of lead into them but the crippled forts aren't quitting. One fort has two engines out, the other two props are straining away, and her guns are still blazing. She's still in the air in that hell back there.

"The crippled forts continue to fight back as the fighters belch fire upon them. Four times the fighters attack. The cripples continue to limp home. Four more times the fighters attack the lagging planes. They can't last for long. The Fort's gunners are no longer firing, they remain still as the enemy fighters jockey for the kill. Our hearts are touched with pain as we witness the 25–30 German buzzards gathering for an easy feast."

The events that follow are evidence of uncommon valor, above and beyond the call of duty. To put it simply, the love for their friends will force this crew to disobey a known Eighth Air Force standing order and go to the aid of their comrades in distress.

The standing order is that no aircraft will leave a formation to aid others that can't keep up. The reasoning being that any B-17 leaving the formation would weaken the protective firepower of the entire formation. All airmen in the Eighth Air Force are aware of this order. In this unusual, particular case, however, the Germans have no intention of attacking the formation. This is obvious as the 25–30 fighters gather for the kill on the two lagging B-17s.

There is a major difference between risking one's life when given an order to do so by a ranking military superior and doing so voluntary. The first is due to rules governing one's military conduct and the latter is for purely selfless reasons. The crew chose to place their lives on the line for their friends. This is the true meaning of courage.

With suppressed tears drowning their hearts, one crew member finally says aloud what all are thinking: We must go back and help!

Lt. Kaczaraba then questions the crew, "Is that what each of you want to do?" All answer in the affirmative.

Lt. Morgan communicates to the 384th Bomb Group's lead aircraft commander, Major Maurice Dillingham. He flatly states, "Aircraft 525 leaving formation to aid our two stragglers." Lt. Morgan did not request permission, nor did he expect it. He merely stated the crew's intentions.

Gilly relates the return to aid the stragglers:

"Lt. Kaczaraba immediately throttles back, banks left to form-up with the cripples and to offer what protection we can. We are all well aware that we will attract the hostile fighters like flies to honey. The

enemy fighters know that both of the stragglers can be disposed of at their leisure once we are knocked out of the sky. By disposing of our ship first, the other two would still be easy prey.

"We have now attracted the 25–30 fighters and our gunners are firing almost without pause trying to ward them off. The attacks come mostly from the rear of Doc.*"*

Gibby becomes gainfully employed defending *Doc's* tail position against enemy fighters:

"Fighters, high at six o'clock ... coming in four abreast. The fighters are within range and I sense that Sam is rotating his top turret around for a clear shot at them. The top turret opens fire causing Doc *to shake from nose to tail.*

"I am also firing and my bullets are tearing into the right wing and fuselage of a Fw190. Black smoke burst from the fighter as he banks right, up and over the nose of our aircraft.

"Shorty is still having problems with his twin .50 caliber machine guns. He must continue to use a screwdriver to fire short burst. A Me109 coming up from under our B-17 for a belly attack makes an unsuccessful pass, shoots past Doc *and stalls out on my left as if he has lost power. This proves to be a fatal error for the young German pilot. Sam, tracking him on his approach, opens up on the fighter with a hail of lead from his deadly twin .50 caliber machine guns. The fighter is no more than 50 yards away as it explodes into pieces and falls away burning and smoking. Lt. Kaczaraba's voice on the interphone is calm, 'Great shooting, Sam.'*

"The attacks on Doc *continue with a renewed fury. The fighters still number 25 or more and are concentrating on my tail position. The two cripples can only watch this lopsided duel between* Doc *and the 25 fighters."*

Again, from Sam's top turret battle station, he relays the vicious fighter attacks:

"The fighters are coming in on us with what seems like a vengeance for the two we have destroyed. We are flying west trying to get to the North Sea. The attacks are continuous and fierce. We start evasive action to keep from being a steady target for the many Me109 and Fw190 fighters. They bear in from the eleven and three o'clock high positions, then from six o'clock straight on. Most of the attacks contin-

ue to be from the six o'clock position, our tail section. We are determined to protect our two cripples or die with them.

"One lone Me109 makes a one o'clock head-on attack and comes so close to us before banking that Lt. Kaczaraba pushes down quickly on the stick sending the aircraft into a momentary dive. We are tossed about like rag dolls but recover as *Doc* levels off.

"By now the fighters are so thick that Wilber gives up his radio duties and is calling out fighter positions as fast as he can. He looks out to the left side of *Doc* and spots ten Me109s lined up for the attack. 'Fighters at nine o'clock high,' he shouts. Down they zoom, heading straight for us. I am sure I will feel a bullet penetrate my body before the attack is over.

"Pete is firing into the attacking fighters with effective short bursts. Bullets are ripping into his area (the left fuselage) in great numbers. Pete stands like an old war horse in battle and continues to pour lead into the attacking Germans. A fighter explodes from Pete's accurate fire and another is smoking as it begins its deadly descent."

Gilly is also busy with fighters. He speaks of his close encounter with a Me109:

"Four fighters at three o'clock low. Up they climb at a slight angle for the attack. I can see the blinking of the fighter's guns searching for me. I wait, wait, wait for the fighters to get within range. Thud, thud, thud … bullets are tearing into *Doc's* skin searching for our crew. The fighters are now within range and I open up with my single .50 caliber machine gun firing in the cone pattern taught in gunnery school. Four fighters continue to bore in on me. I try not to flinch as bullets tear into the fuselage around me. My .50 caliber continues to respond, hitting one on the underside. It explodes. Scratch one Me109 and one Hun from the German war machine.

"The three remaining fighters streak under *Doc* so near that I can clearly see the familiar black cross insignias on their wings and the pilots in their cockpits. The fighters are now forming up for another attack on our rear. Relieved that they did not cause delivery of a telegram of death to my family, I relax for a minute."

Gibby is now the main target of the enemy pilots. He must fight off wave after wave of fighters as they commence their attacks from the rear of *Doc*:

"During all this time, I have been more than busy protecting our tail section. The main thrusts of the German attacks are on my position.

Their attacks have gone on for two hours. I am concerned as my ammo is getting low. The fighters attack in waves of four consisting of Fw190s and Me109s. My two .50 caliber machine guns square off with the fighters' 16 machine guns leaving me greatly over matched in firepower. This does not deter me. I do what must be done. During one of the many attacks on my position, I destroy two fighters on a single pass. They both explode close to my tail section. One sprays oil on the tail Plexiglas, further reducing my vision of the oncoming attacking fighters.

"Shouting, 'Four at six o'clock high,' however, I know I cannot get much help from the crew due to the German attack strategy. They approach the tail section at a slight angle and roll beneath our aircraft. This allows neither the top turret or waist gunners a proper line of fire. It normally provides our ball turret a clear shot, however, Shorty's guns are still basically out of action. I fight off wave after wave of fighters, scoring three more single kills, each engulfed in flames as they plummet toward the patchwork countryside far below."

Suddenly the trio of B-17s find themselves completely alone in the sky. The two cripples, now three, are doing the best they can to limp home. Other fighters along the route home stage sporadic attacks on *Doc* but each time the crew gives more than they receive in the exchange of fire.

Around 1400 hours, Gibby reports that both his guns are burnt out. The ball turret is basically out of action and the remaining battle stations are low on ammunition. Consequently, there is no firepower in the tail section, little more in the belly area and the remaining guns will soon be out of action in the waist and top turret positions.

The running battle with the German flak and fighters has lasted for over three hours. It started at the Initial Point of the bomb run on Bremen, then on the return to and over the North Sea. Even over the North Sea the fighters continue to try to place their stamp of death on the gallant little group of three.

At last the fighters finally bank and return to Germany. They are probably low on ammo or fuel. The crew prays a silent prayer for their deliverance.

The English Channel comes into view and is a welcome sight. They are greatly relieved to see its waters below. It means no more flak or fighters trying to send them to their Last Retreat.

Sam gets us back to Grafton-Underwood, home, sweet, home:

"Over the channel, we have one more hurdle to overcome before we can all breathe easily. I report to the crew that our fuel supply is low as a result of the evasive flying and the necessity to maintain airspeed

with two ailing engines. On hearing this bad news, Lt. Morgan decides to ease up on engine power and more or less try to coast to our base. The crew is ordered by Lt. Kaczaraba to throw all unnecessary equipment overboard. This we do, as machine guns, ammo, any remaining, boxes, etc. all take a dunking in the English Channel.

"*Coasting into Grafton-Underwood we experience quite a breeze blowing through hundreds of holes in the punctured fuselage, courtesy of the enemy fighters and flak. We land late and taxi to our assigned parking space. The gas gauge indicates about 60 gallons of fuel left in the tanks. (This is comparable to about a quart of gas remaining in the family car.) Talk about "coming in on a wing and a prayer." I have gained a new appreciation of what this old air force song implies.*"

Their second mission complete, the crew is relieved to be back on the ground safe and sound. Quickly exiting the aircraft through the nose and waist hatches, they gather around *Doc* to inspect the damage. Their beloved *Doc* is suffering with over 250 holes by either fighters or flak giving it the appearance of a sieve. There are holes in the waist, nose, left wing, both stabilizers, and tail, however, *Doc* had meted out more punishment than it had received. The crew claimed, in addition to its successful bombing raid, the destruction of nine enemy fighters and the probable destruction of one other. The two crippled B-17 crews later corroborated these claims.

In a daze from the ordeal of their three hour battle, the crew slogged to the debriefing room. For an hour they talked to the debriefing officer, relating all pertinent information of the long nine hour mission to Bremen. They discuss every minute of the mission from the time guns were checked out over the English Channel until the return landing. Refreshments are offered, but declined.

This mission was traumatic and the crew will never forget this nightmare called Bremen. All total, the crew fired over 5,000 rounds. Gibby burnt up both of his guns firing over 2,500 rounds.

It is almost 1700 hours and the crew is very hungry since breakfast was almost twelve hours ago. Somehow they manage to trudge to the mess hall and get a little something down. Rest is really all they desire. Friends from the two crippled B-17s insist on the crew joining them at the Officers' and Zebra Club for a celebration. The two crippled B-17 crews are more than grateful for they would certainly have been shot down over Germany if the *Doc* crew had not come to their aid. All would have been killed in action (KIA), missing in action (MIA), or prisoners of war (POW). At the Officers' and Zebra Clubs, glasses are lifted. Someone asks, "What should we toast to?" The answer is obvious … "Let's toast to friendship."

While the rest of the crew members are lifting their glasses in a festive mood, Lt. Kaczaraba is experiencing quite the opposite. He is ordered to report to the squadron commander's office. The commander speaks as Lt. Kaczaraba stands at attention:

"Lt. Kaczaraba, today you and your crew disobeyed the rule of formation flying by going to the aid of two crippled bombers. I could, and should, have you court-martialed, however, in view of the fact that your crew saved the lives of 20 airmen and two aircraft, I am giving you a verbal reprimand only. Enemy fighter kills claimed by your crew may not be allowed by higher command. I will inform you of their decision. While I respect and admire your actions privately, to condone them publicly would send a signal to the other crews to break formation when they believed it necessary."

Lt. Kaczaraba protested the non-recognition of his brave crew's actions but offered no excuse or justification. As he left the commander's office his only regret was that his crew would not receive the heroes' acclaim they so richly deserved, but, instead would receive a hero's reprimand. In his heart, however, he knew that they had done the right thing.[3]

Anguish after Anklam

After the trials of yesterday's Bremen mission, last evening's celebration of survival and a night yielding precious little sleep, the crew was in no mood to receive an early morning caller. Yet here he was, that pesky little operations clerk with a southern drawl, rousting them from their short-lived slumber for another strike mission. As usual, Sol cracks a joke, "Is it legal to kill a clerk?" Though everyone laughs the notion seems strangely appealing to all.

Sam relates the upcoming raid:

> "At dawn we are awakened to take off once more. It is damp and chilly this Saturday morning of October 9, 1943 as we dress for our third foray on Der Fuhrer. How disgusting it is to get up at this time of day!
>
> "We manage to get through breakfast without falling asleep. Then we stumble, only half awake, to the briefing room. The briefing officer informs us where and what we will bomb on today's raid. 'The target for today is Anklam, Germany. This will be a deep penetration that will carry us into eastern Germany, northwest of Berlin. Our strike will be at a major source of enemy air strength, the aircraft factories at

Anklam. Major Raymond Ketelsen, flying Patches II *will lead the 384th. Expect to meet stout enemy resistance to and from the target. Are there any questions? No? Good hunting!'*

"*Takeoff is scheduled for 0630 hours. We are delayed for a few minutes due to minor changes from wing headquarters concerning the mission. We will not be flying* Doc *because of the extensive damage it received yesterday. We depart for our assigned B-17. Arriving at the hardstand, it is still semi-dark; however, I can make out the A/C serial number on the tail … 9927, nicknamed* Homesick Sal. *This B-17 was transferred from the 96th Bomb Group on September 23, 1943 and will be* Homesick Sal's *first mission in the 384th aircraft inventory.* Doc *was shot up so badly from the day before maintenance indicates it will require almost a month to get him air-worthy again.*

"*After the horrifying experience of Bremen yesterday, I hope* Homesick Sal *will grant us a nice, short, uneventful raid to France or "Happy Valley."*[1] *Then we might sneak in undetected on Adolf, quickly deliver our bombs, and scoot back home for some well-desired rest.*

"*We are wrong, as usual. This mission will be a deep penetration, almost to the Russian front. It will mean in excess of nine hours flying time over flak infested territory with fighters lying in wait to attack all along the mission route.*

"*After finally getting airborne, the next two hours are spent forming up over England. As briefed, we assembled and climbed to our combat position as the high group. Soon we approach the central coast of Denmark, and while crossing at 14,000 feet, we are jumped by 10 to 15 fighters at approximately 1055 hours. The formation exchanges lead with the fighters for about ten minutes. The fighters peel off and head for home. Not much fight in them on this day.*

"*The flight to the target is unimpaired by flak or fighters. Bombs away and as we are leaving the target area Lt. Horsky shouts, 'It was perfect bombing under perfect conditions. If there's still a target in the vicinity it's buried underground. There's a lot of smoke and fire.'*

"*It is approximately 1200 hours as we leave the target area. In the distance I spot many dots from the south. As the dots approach the formation to within a quarter of a mile, I shout over the interphone to the crew, 'Bad guys, more than I can count, nine o'clock high, here they come.'*

"*The enemy fighters formations consist of Focke Wulfe (Fw190s), Messerschmitt (Me210s) and Junkers (Ju88s). (Later confirmation at debriefing would estimate approximately 200 enemy aircraft). We fight off several head-on and upper fuselage attacks. These attacks are not as bad as the day before as the fighters do not attack four abreast in waves. I don't know why, I just thank God for our good fortune. Only one close call is experienced when an enemy fighter almost hits Sal on its way down after being shot up by another B-17 in our formation. We are under constant attacks for over two hours. I had a probable kill. It was on fire and smoking as it left the battle area.*

"Winging it home, we are approximately 60 miles west of the Frisian Islands. Again, we are intercepted by a formation of Fw190s approximately 30 minutes after the first attack. Most of these attacks are directed at the wing following our 41st Combat Wing.

"The rest of the mission is quiet. Encountering low clouds all the way into the Grafton-Underwood area and the persistent overcast over our base necessitates an instrument landing down through the clouds. Spotting the control tower the windsock is standing straight out, like some kind of a symbol of triumph. The weather breaks near the field, we circle the base once, and land at 1500 hours."

The crew is hustled off to the debriefing room where debriefing officers are waiting like expectant fathers. During the session, these officers usually act as secretaries and let the combat crews speak at random. Lt. Morgan speaks of the fighter attacks:

"There must have been 200 fighters on us today. They picked us up right after we left the target, Focke Wulfes, Messerschmitts, and Junkers. They stayed with us for more than two hours.

"I don't think a single bomb went into the river. There was lots of smoke, it was difficult to see the ground. We encountered a lot of fighters and a lot of shooting, but they didn't attack in large waves."

Lt. Kaczaraba on Sam's probable kill of a Me210:

"T/Sgt. Honeycutt got a probable kill but we couldn't see if it went down, I believe it did. It was smoking badly."

Shorty speaks of the crew's near collision with a Me109:

"It was a bull's eye. The smoke was a reddish black. There was fire in it, lots of fire. One of our planes shot up a Me109 and it almost hit us as it went down out of control."

It had been a history-making day for the Eighth Air Force. Some bomber formations had penetrated the German defenses as far east as Danzig, not too far from the general area of the Russian front. The 384th effort carried the group some 1,600 miles.

The debriefing ends on a sad note. The officer informs the crew that two 384th B-17s are missing from this journey of 1,600 miles. Forced down at sea was the *Dallas Rebel* of the 544th Squadron. The other craft that failed to return was the *Philly-Brooklyn* of the 546th Squadron. It was later confirmed that twelve crewmen were killed and eight captured.

The deaths of twelve friends and the capture of eight more fill the crew with anguish after Anklam. They are saddened by these losses. They knew them as friends as well as comrades in arms. The crew didn't know it then, but this would be the first of many.

Summary of 384th Missing Aircraft and Crew Status
Anklam Mission (October 9, 1943)

A/C#	Name	Pilot	Squadron	Crew Status
42-29814	*Dallas Rebel*	1st Lt. John T. Ingles	544th	10 killed
42-29712	*Philly-Brooklyn*	2nd Lt. Mark B. Cainon	546th	2 killed
				8 prisoners

Total = 12 killed, 8 prisoners

In Memory
544th Squadron
1st Lt. John T. Ingles, Pilot; 2nd Lt. Harry M. Pratt, Co-pilot; 2nd Lt. Charles L. Ruman, Navigator; 2nd Lt. R.L. Fish, Bombardier; S/Sgt. Lawrence W. Smith, Radio Operator; T/Sgt. Clarence E. Morrison, Engineer; S/Sgt. John F. Farley, Ball Turret Gunner; S/Sgt. Alfred T. Brescia, Tail Gunner, S/Sgts. Carl W. Janes and Charles A. Spaulding, Waist Gunners.

546th Squadron
2nd Lt. Mark B. Cainon, Pilot; 2nd Lt. V. D. Barnes, Co-pilot; 2nd Lt. T. H. Kusler, Navigator; 2nd Lt. L.C. Hasler, Bombardier; T/Sgt. B. B. Patterson, Radio Operator; S/Sgt. J. D. Rolleri, Engineer; S/Sgt. S. Lopez, Ball Turret Gunner; S/Sgts. J. A. McGettigan, Jr. and R. N. Henrickson, Waist Gunners; S/Sgt. C. G. Lenorie, Tail Gunner.

8

Holy Terror

By this time the air wars strategic picture is beginning to take shape. It is apparent that the 384th is in the middle of an all-out battle against the German Air Force, first by attacking their aircraft industry and second by challenging them to battle in the air.

The production of enemy fighter planes has reportedly doubled in the last six months under the impetus of reorganization and new assembly line methods. According to intelligence the enemy's production plans call for 2,000 single engine fighters per month by August of 1944 and 3,000 per month by March, 1945. The time to strike is now — even though the group's bombers would have to fight their way in and out of Germany and the occupied countries without a friendly fighter escort.

The 384th is playing its part in this strategic plan. Harassed by terrific fighter opposition and unprotected by their own fighters, they are attacking factories deep in the heart of Germany. It is costing a lot of planes and men, but already it is beginning to have an effect. Headquarters tells the group that Germany's single engine fighter production has been cut to less than half the planned rate.

Trying to catch-up on their sleep from two nights ago, the crew is sound asleep on this Sunday morning, October 10, 1943. They look forward to a quiet Sabbath. Suddenly, their favorite private, the operations clerk with his southern drawl wakes them at 0400 hours for a 0530 hours briefing. This will be the third consecutive day of forays into the dangerous skies over Germany. Lt. Morgan relives this unusual mission:

"The briefing officer informs us of where our target will be for today's raid. 'Today's mission is the railroad junction city of Munster, Germany. Railway traffic from Munster serves the ports of Bremen, Hamburg, and Emden to the north and feeds Dartmund, Hamm, and the industrial Ruhr valley to the south.' Then he speaks, almost in a reverent tone. 'Unlike all previous military and industrial targets attacked to date by the 384th, today will be different, very different. Today you will hit the center of the city, the homes of the working population of these marshaling yards. You will disrupt the German citizens' lives so completely that morale will be seriously affected. Their will to work and fight will be substantially reduced. Bombs away is at 1200 hours. Your aiming point will be the steeple of the Munster Cathedral.

"'Should the primary target be obscured by cloud cover or industrial haze, the secondary target is Hamm, located in the Ruhr Valley, and as a last resort, any industrial town in Germany. Major Thomas Beckett, piloting Patches II *will lead the 384th. Good luck!'*

"There is dead silence. Reaction does not register for a while. We are shocked to learn that we are going to bomb civilians as our primary target for the first time in the war and that our aiming point is to be the steeple of the Munster Cathedral at noon on Sunday, just as mass is completed.

"The high command must have had second thoughts on the timing for we are informed later that orders were changed so that bombs away will be scheduled for 1300 hours when the cathedral will be less populated. It is no accident that we are to bomb on Sunday with a church for a target. What better method to shatter the civilian morale than to destroy their church and disturb their worship on the Sabbath.

"The briefing over, we proceed to the hardstand where our assigned B-17 is waiting. We huddle at the nose of the aircraft for last minute instructions from our aircraft commander. At this time the NCOs are not aware of today's target. Lt. Kaczaraba repeats to the NCOs the revelation he has just received. The crew is then asked, 'What is your reaction?'"

Shorty speaks immediately and with passion:

"I am, and I think most of you are, aware of the killings and sufferings the Nazis have committed against the Jews throughout Germany and Europe. I believe the German people are also aware of these killings. Some of you may have misgivings about using the center of the city and the cathedral for our aiming point, but not me. I think it's great." (Shorty is of the Hebrew religion.)

Sam gives his opinion of this church-bombing mission:

"I have been raised as a Southern Baptist and am very reluctant to fly this mission but I know that the Germans have been killing innocent people all over Europe for years. But let's face it, we're in an all-out fight! Our bomb group has suffered almost 100 percent losses in the last three months. Our job is to beat the hell out of these Nazi bastards. Let's go do it. (Sam Honeycutt, six weeks ago, had been scolded by his mother for daring to use the word 'damn' in her presence.)"

The rest of the crew offers little resistance and seems to have no second thoughts about the mission. Lt. Kaczaraba, on purpose, waits last to express his viewpoint:

"We have tried to concentrate our efforts, in the past, on military targets in an attempt to destroy the German war machine. I believe the civilian population that serves this war machine shares some of the blame for the killings and suffering in Europe. We need to break their will to serve the Nazis and cause them to doubt the Nazis' capability to win this war. I'm planning to fly this mission today because I know that by doing so it will save innocent lives."

Lt. Morgan continues to narrate this unusual mission:

"It is still dark. Some of the crew stands around smoking cigarettes. I enjoy a good cigar as I watch B-17s roar down the runway ahead of us. We climb aboard and taxi out to the perimeter track. At 0840 hours, we start our roll and slowly build up speed as Homesick Sal roars down the runway into the mist of this Sabbath morning.
"Our B-17 is loaded with ten 500 pound bombs and fully fueled with 2,600 gallons of 100 percent octane gasoline. We finally lift off the runway and experience prop wash[1] from the B-17 in front of us.

The wash throws Homesick Sal *sideways and the left wing dips very close to the ground. Lt. Kaczaraba corrects it in the nick of time as we clear the trees, ever so slightly, at the end of the runway.*

"*The 547th climbs to assemble with our sister squadrons, the 544th, 545th, and 546th as briefed. The 384th Bomb Group is assembled without difficulty. The rendezvous is accomplished with the 41st Combat Wing over our first navigational fix, Molesworth, through the use of flares. Molesworth is departed on time and we start climbing at Kyebrock, our second navigational fix. The other two groups in the combat wing fall into close rear-end position. The 41st Combat Wing formation proceeds, on course, toward our target. Just ahead is the Danish coast. The 384th is the high group and in combat formation position at 14,000 feet. Minor fighter attacks are encountered just before leaving the Danish coast toward Germany.*

"*Lt. Horsky informs us that we are five minutes from the IP. Lts. Horsky and Wirth now recognize the Aw Lake, which leads to the target. Lt. Kaczaraba maneuvers the B-17 to position us for an undisturbed run on the target (Image 8.1). Immediately after we turn on the IP, and until over the target Lt. Kaczaraba has excellent control of the ship. Bombs away!*

"*Upon leaving the target, the 384th must catch up the distance lost at the IP. This time is made up and the 384th rejoins the wing in proper formation position approximately five minutes later. Immediately after rejoining the wing, our formation is attacked from the front and rear by fighters that number 20 to 25, growing larger in number as our course progresses home. The formation remains tight throughout the fighter attacks. We are lucky, there are no enemy fighter attacks on* Homesick Sal. *The flight the rest of the way out of Germany and to the English coast is uneventful. We encounter low clouds just off the English coast. This forces our group to let down through the thin overcast and continue on to home, sweet home. Our B-17 touches down at 1558 hours.*"

It is almost 1600 hours and the crew has flown for over seven hours. Hungry and tired, they head for debriefing. The crew begins recounting and the debriefing officer starts to write. Lt. Wirth speaks of the destruction of the target:

"*Before we got over the target the whole area was already thick with smoke from the bombs of the lead formation, but I could still see the target fairly easily. First our demolition bombs hit and then the incendi-*

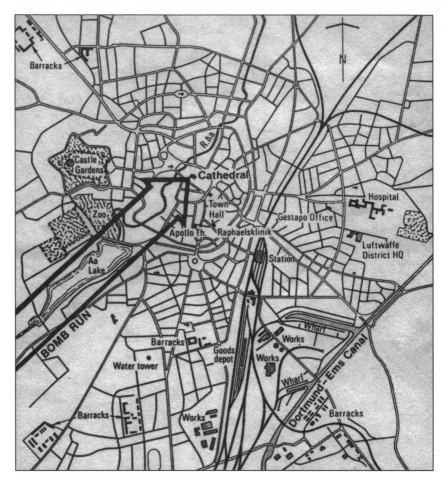

Image 8.1: Bomb run on Munster, Germany, October 10, 1943.

aries burst over the same area. The burst pattern ran from one end of the city and walked right over the target. Our bombs were right on target."

Shorty tells of the fighter attacks:

"The enemy fighters wove in and out of our formation. From my ball turret, I had a grandstand seat at the show. I saw three Me-210s go down right in front of our B-17."

Sam believes God guided this mission:

"The weather cleared up just before we reached the target as if God's hand had pushed the cloud cover away."

Today, all the 384th planes returned safely, although one had to ditch in the channel and several others landed at alternate fields. Lt. William Wilson's crew had to abandon their B-17 over the channel. The crew parachuted to safety after the pilot set the ships course back toward enemy territory.

On this Sunday, October 10 the 384th was not able to keep the Sabbath holy, instead their enemies received holy terror from them.

The 384th later received commendations for the raids inflicted on Bremen (10/8/43), Anklam (10/9/43), and Munster (10/10/43) (Image 8.2). The commendations are from Prime Minister Winston Churchill; Air Chief Marshal Portal, Chief of Staff, RAF; General Marshall, Chief of Staff, U.S. Army; General Arnold, Commander General, Army Air Force; Lt. Gerald Eaker, Commanding General, Eighth Air Force; Brigadier General Anderson, Commanding General, VIII Bomber Command; Brigadier General Williams, Commanding General, 1st Bombardment Division and Colonel Julius K. Lacey, Commanding Office, 384th Bombardment Group. The commendation from Colonel Lacey is to T/Sgt. John S. Honeycutt, however, all air crew members of the 384th Bomb Group received identical commendations.

10 Downing Street
Whitehall.

<u>PRIME MINISTER TO GENERAL DEVERS:</u>

I shall be obliged if you will convey to General Eaker and his Command the thanks of the British War Cabinet for the magnificent achievements of the 8th Air Force in the Battle of Germany in recent days culminating in their remarkable successes of last week.

In broad daylight the crews of your bombers have fought their way through the strongest defense which the enemy could bring against them and have ranged over the length and breadth of Germany, striking with deadly accuracy many of the most important hostile industrial installations and ports.

Your bombers and the fighters which support them in these fierce engagements have inflicted serious losses on the German Air Force, and by forcing the enemy to weaken other fronts have contributed notably to the successes of the Allied arms everywhere.

The War Cabinet extend their congratulations also to the ground crews of the 8th Air Force without whose technical skill and faithful labor these feats of arms would not be possible.

I am confident that with the ever-growing power of the 8th Air force, striking alternate blows with the Royal Air Force Bomber Command, we shall together inexorably beat the life out of the industrial Germany and thus hasten the day of final victory.

Initials —W.C.

INCOMING MESSAGE
HEADQUARTERS EIGHTH AIR FORCE

IN REPLY CITE: A 105   DATED: 11 OCTOBER
1943

FROM: AIR MINISTRY WHITEHALL

TO: AWW

Personal for General Eaker from CAS

I should be grateful if you would pass to your squadrons an expression of my deep admiration for their splendid achievements over Germany during them last few days.

I know I am speaking for the whole of The Royal Air Force in offering you our heartiest congratulations and expressing our full confidence in evergrowing success for your command in the future.

PORTAL

Image 8.2: Commendations to the Eighth Air Force. (Retyped for legibility.)

COPY   COPY

INCOMING MESSAGE
ETCUSA

FROM: AGWAR   REF NO.   R-
4219

TO: ETOUSA FOR ACTION   DATED: OCT 111545Z

Interior Addresses: To :   DEVERS

                        For :   EAKER

                        From :   MARSHALL

During the past few days the series of brilliant punishing blows which the crews of the Eighth Air Force have been delivering far into the interior of Germany are producing a devastating effect on German military power and the morale of the German people. Please give my congratulations and personal thanks to your gallant flight crews.

INCOMING MESSAGE
HEADQUARTERS EIGHTH AIR FORCE

IN REPLY CITE: R 4218   DATED: 11 OCT

FROM: AGWAR

TO: AWW

Internal Address: From: ARNOLD

                         For: EAKER

Long mission into Baltic and attacks on distant German objectives in Poland shows the world your growing ability to hit the enemy wherever you choose.

Well done.

The employment of larger bombing forces on successive days is encouraging proof that you are putting increasing proportion of your bombers where they will hurt the enemy.

Good work.

As you turn your effort away from ship building cities and toward crippling the sources of the still growing German fighter forces the air war is clearly moving toward our supremacy in the air.

Carry on.

Image 8.2 continued. (Retyped for legibility.)

HEADQUARTERS
EIGHTH AIR FORCE
APO 633   12 October 1943.

SUBJECT: Commendations
TO   :   Commanding General,   VIII Bomber Command,
                    "   "   VII Fighter Command
                    "   "   VIII Air Support Command

1. Enclosed herewith are copies of commendations received from the Prime Minister; Air Chief Marshall Portal, Chief of Air Staff, RAF; from the Chief of Staff, U.S. Army, General Marshal; and from the Commanding General, Army Air Forces, General Arnold. In my opinion, every officer and man of the Eighth Air Force who participated in the great air offensive which has been waged during the past ten (10) days should be fully advised of these estimates which the highest Government and Military leaders place on their work. If it is administratively possible, I think that every participating combat crew member should receive a letter from his Commander stating that he participated in these great air battles and that, therefore, he is entitled to a personal copy of these commendations.

2. Last Sunday, October 10th, after seeing the pictures of the effort of the preceding Saturday and particularly the destructive effects on the German fighter factories at Anklam and Marienburg, I sent a cable to General Arnold, from which the following is a quotation:

"Marienburg undoubtedly destroyed. It will be a better example of pin-point bombing, better concentration even than Regensburg. It looks like a perfect job. Believe you will find October 9th a day to remember in the air war. The Prime Minister is sending message to crews."

Subsequent examination of photographs supports this estimate.

3. Convey to all your officers and men my unbounded admiration for the courage and boldness with which they pushed their attacks into enemy territory and the accuracy and skill with which they disposed of their targets. They have, by their effort, won the respect and admiration of the air leaders of Britain and that great band of fighting men, the Royal Air Force. They have outfought a tough, experienced and battle-tried enemy. Their success has altered the course of the war and hastened its favorable conclusion.

/s/ IRA C. EAKER
Lieut, General, U.S.A.,
Commanding.

4.Incls.

1st Ind.
HEADQUARTERS VIII BOMBER COMMAND, APO 634, 13 October 1943.

TO: Combat Personnel of the VIII Bomber Command.

1. It is my privilege to be the instrument of bringing directly to you as individuals the comments and commendations from these distinguished sources.

2. Such expressions of appreciation of your efforts are extremely gratifying.

F.L. Anderson

F.L. ANDERSON
Brigadier General, U.S. Army
Commanding

4 Incls.

Image 8.2 continued. (Retyped for legibility.)

2nd Ind.   A-A/G-3

HQ, 1ST BOMB. DIVISION, APO 634, 16 October 1943.

TO: All Personnel, Air and Ground, of the 1st Bombardment Division.

My hearty congratulations on these well earned commendations.

                              ROBERT B. WILLIAMS,
                              Brigadier General, U.S.A.,
                              Commanding.

4 Incls
   n/c.

3rd Ind.

HQ, 384TH BOMBARDMENT GROUP (H), AAF, APO 634, U.S. ARMY, 23 October 1943.

TO: T/Sgt. John S. Honeycutt, 33220825, 547th Bombardment Squadron, 384th
Bombardment Group (H), AAF. Top Turret Gunner on a B-17F airplane No. 42-29927
on a mission over Anklam, Germany on 9 October 1943.

1. Attached hereto are commendations from Prime Minister Winston Churchill; Air Chief Marshal Portal, Chief of Air Staff, RAF; General Marshall, Chief of Staff, U.S.Army: General Arnold , Commanding General , Army Air Force: Lt. General Eaker, Commanding General, Eighth Air Force; Brigadier General Anderson, Commanding General, VIII Bomber Command; and Brigadier General Williams, Commanding General, 1st Bombardment Division.

2. I am proud to give you these commendations as I realize more than anyone else what you went through to earn them and that they were honestly earned and earned the hard way.

                              J. K. LACEY
                              Colonel, Air Corps,
                              Commanding

Image 8.2 continued. (Retyped for legibility.)

★ ★ ★

CHAPTER

9

London, Later Lament

The U.S. Army Air Corps decided the *Doc's* crew was in need of some well-deserved and desired rest after three consecutive raids. During these raids, they were engaged in a total of 23 air combat hours. In appreciation for these tough missions, three-day passes were granted. The crew decided to use their three days off on a trip to London.

"Rest, relax, and forget the war for a few days," the crew is told. When Lt. Morgan heard the words, forget the war for a few days, his memory flashed back to an incident in his quarters a few nights before. He remembered that particular night because it was after the terrible Anklam raid where twelve of his buddies were killed and eight captured. The realization of the air war came home to him that night. Lt. Morgan takes us back a few nights:

> "It was the night of October 9,1943. Someone shook me awake. It was another crew's navigator and he was frightened. He asked me if I thought he was going to be scheduled to go on a mission the next day. As he spoke, both of us could hear bomber engines in the maintenance area being run in and checked out; a certain indication that we were

going on a mission in a few hours. My friend, the navigator, had been walking the floors all night and was almost in a state of hysteria. He tried but was unable to keep his fears and anguish inside. He had to express his fears, but at the same time he couldn't let go of them.

"Was he any less brave than the rest of us? I doubt it. He just couldn't hide his fears as well. Later on, he couldn't function as a combat officer and was transferred to a less demanding non-flying position.

"I understood his fears for we are all under constant pressure and dreading the next raid. No matter what we are doing or where we may be, always hidden in the back of our minds is the nightmare that we will be going over again and again until the job is done."

The crew departs Grafton-Underwood on Wednesday, October 13 for London, which is about an hour and a half by train. The next three days they plan to check out the sights by day and the pubs by night.

Upon arrival they discover that London is a tale of two cities. In the daytime, it is a business-like city. There is an appearance of calm on the surface, but tension is hidden within her people. During the day, the crew tours all the normal historical landmarks. Westminster Abbey, St. Paul's Cathedral (with one side damaged from a German bomb), London Bridge, the Towers of London, Big Ben, and all the other sights that the crew had only read about.

Londoner's fear sundown as the nightly roar of German bombers will soon be heard overhead, once again. Her parks are barricaded and filled with anti-aircraft guns that continuously flash in an attempt to shoot down the hated German bombers. Being in London is as close as the crew will get to the feeling of the civilian war because of the nightly air raids by the Germans. The noise of the air raid sirens, the flashing anti-aircraft guns, and the explosions of the bombs along with the fires cause them to appreciate the nightly terror the English experience. The crew learns very quickly to scurry with the civilians into the air raid shelters. "Forget the war for a few days," they had been told.

At night, in total darkness, they wander about London's darkened streets, feeling their way in and out of pubs and enjoying the nightlife. It is a new and exciting experience. The three days in London seems to relieve and revive the crew and the trip temporarily takes their minds off the combat flying that lays ahead of them.

Back at Grafton-Underwood on Friday, October 15, they discover that the 384th went on the longest and toughest penetrations to date into the southern part of Germany — the ball-bearing plant at Schweinfurt. It was to become known as the infamous "Black Thursday" raid of October 14, 1943.

The 384th had taken off for Schweinfurt in a thick haze at 1030 hours and the field was still blanketed by haze at 1600 hours when the group was supposed to return. Only the lead ship, carrying Major George Harris as Air Commander, returned at the appointed hour.

Three other ships crashed in the surrounding countryside and the remainder were forced by damage and weather conditions to land at emergency fields. One, which had landed at a nearby base was able to return to Grafton-Underwood a little before midnight but the others were gone for the night.

Crews of the B-17s piloted by 1st Lt. Edmund Goulder, 1st Lt. William Price, and 2nd Lt. Erwin Johnson, bailed out over England. One airman on Price's crew had his leg broken, the B-17 crashing near Corby, a few miles north of the base.

Two of the 384th's original B-17s, *The Natural* and *The Joker*, ended their combat careers as their crews parachuted to safety. The other B-17 that came down without its crew was the *Windy City Avenger*. The aircraft's elevator had been shot up, but remained in a locked position despite the loss of the control cables. As the aircraft was coming in for a landing the elevator completely malfunctioned and at a scant 150 feet above the ground the crew prepared to bail out. The pilot was able to coax the less then responsive B-17 up to 1,000 feet before giving the order to "hit the nylon."

Major Harris, whose lead ship *Battle Wagon* also displayed the wounds of battle, reported that 200 to 300 enemy fighters struck in waves at the formation. The battle went on continuously for almost four hours.

When the survivors finally limped home the mechanics counted up the damages. There were 218 holes in Lt. Bedsole's, 147 in Lt. Carter's, and so on. One B-17 had to have a new wing, engine, and ball turret.

Nine more planes lost, 60 more airmen. It is little wonder that by this time airmen of the 384th had developed the idea that it would be impossible to complete a full tour of duty. It is now an accepted fact that you would be shot down eventually.

The 384th had entered combat four months ago with a combat flying strength of 363 officers and men. Already the group had lost more than it started with back in June. The group was just as strong, due to replacements that continually came in, but there were few originals left. In just 116 days the 384th had lost 371 airmen over enemy territory.

The Schweinfurt raid was a maximum effort by the Eighth Air Force because it was the maximum number of aircraft put up and the maximum range of the bombers. Eighth Air Force bombers shot down were 60 out of 250 dispatched, a 24 percent loss in one day.

The 384th Bomb Group suffered greatly on this raid as nine bombers of 19 dispatched were shot down or lost, a 47 percent loss. Three 384th B-17s had to ditch in the channel because they ran out of fuel. That is one experience the *Doc* crew had thought of many times coming from Germany all shot up and barely able to make it back to base.

The 547th Bomb Squadron's losses were even deadlier as three of four bombers dispatched were shot down, resulting in a 75 percent loss. The nine plane toll is the greatest the 384th had sustained, while the loss of six crews equaled the number missing from the Hamburg raid of July 15, 1943.

The crew, in a daze, sat on their bunks the evening of October 15,1943 and gazed at the empty bunks and lockers of the crew of Lt. Giles Kauffman, whom they had trained and partied with. These friends were either killed, taken prisoner, or trying to evade capture somewhere in Germany. Saddened, with hearts heavy — somehow they must go on.

Summary of 384th Missing Aircraft and Crew Status
Schweinfurt Mission (October 14,1943)

A/C#	Name	Pilot	Squadron	Crew Status
42-29800	*Me & My Gal*	1st Lt. William Harry	546th	2 killed 8 prisoners
42-29867	(No Name)	2nd Lt. Walter E. Williams	544th	10 prisoners
42-29870	*Tough Shit*	1st Lt. Giles Kauffman	547th	10 prisoners
42-30196	*Sad Sack*	2nd Lt. Lawrence L. Keller, Jr.	546th	6 killed 4 prisoners
42-31059	(No Name)	1st Lt. Donald P. Ogilvie	547th	1 killed 2 prisoners 7 evaded
42-3216	*The Joker*	2nd Lt. William Kopt	547th	7 prisoners 3 evaded

Total = 9 killed, 41 prisoners, 10 evaded or escaped capture.

In Memory
544th Squadron

No Name   2nd Lt. Walter E. Williams, Pilot; 2nd Lt. Belford B. Candler, Co-pilot; 2nd Lt. Carl W. Abels, Navigator; 2nd Lt. Thomas C. Breen, Jr., Bombardier; T/Sgt. Clyde T. Bush, Engineer; T/Sgt. Thomas P. Hanrahan, Radio Operator; S/Sgt. William R. Genette, Ball Turret Gunner; S/Sgt. Albert Wickline, Tail Gunner; S/Sgts. Michael R. Henneberry and James W. Deese, Waist Gunners.

546th Squadron

Me & My Gal   1st Lt. William R. Harry, Pilot; 2nd Lt. Ivan L. Rice, Co-pilot; 2nd Lt. David H. Black, Navigator; 2nd Lt. Charles P. Mannka, Bombardier; T/Sgt. Edward F. Simpson, Radio Operator; S/Sgt. T. B. Wheeler, Engineer; S/Sgt. John C. McKenna, Ball Turret Gunner; S/Sgt. Leroy Parent, Tail Gunner; Sgts. Howard M. Parks and Julius M. Markus, Waist Gunners.

Sad Sack   2nd Lt. Lawrence L. Keller, Jr., Pilot; 2nd Lt. Marion D. Odell, Co-pilot; 2nd Lt. Jerome F. Hart, Navigator; 2nd Lt. Kenneth E. Gross, Bombardier; S/Sgt. Wallie H. Vansandt, Radio Operator; S/Sgt. V. Jacoby, Engineer; S/Sgt. Harold K. McClean, Ball Turret Gunner; S/Sgt. C. A. Jellings, Tail Gunner, S/Sgts. P. C. Motiaytis and J. E. Maloney, Waist Gunners.

547th Squadron

The Joker   2nd Lt. William E. Kopf, Pilot; 2nd Lt. Alfred W. Scott, Co-pilot; 2nd Lt. Toscha M. Massey, Navigator; 2nd Lt. Eugene W. Connor, Bombardier; S/Sgt. Heervert E. Yeryar, Radio Operator; T/Sgt. Hugh Mauritho, Engineer; S/Sgt. Clyde Smigh, Ball Turrett Gunner; S/Sgt. Elton W. Buddemeyer, Tail Gunner, S/Sgts. Anthony R. Perroni and Leroy Bernard, Waist Gunners.

Tough Shit   1st Lt. Giles F. Kauffman, Jr., Pilot; 2nd Lt. George Molnar, Co-pilot; 2nd Lt. Frank Pogerzelski, Navigator; S/Sgt. David D. Dannaman, Nose Gunner; T/Sgt. Jules T. Beck, Radio Operator; T/Sgt. William Jarrell, Engineer; S/Sgt. Jacob M. Martinez, Ball Turret Gunner; S/Sgt. Stanley T. Reuben, Tail Gunner; S/Sgts. Peter Seniawsky and Paul Spodar, Waist Gunners.

No Name   1st Lt. Donald P. Ogilvie, Pilot (one of the group's oldest crews and one of the original crews); 2nd Lt. Robert B. Kilmer, Co-pilot; 2nd Lt. Everett Childs (544th Squadron) Navigator; 1st Lt. William H. Wilson, Bombardier; T/Sgt. James R. Murray, Radio Operator; T/Sgt. Emmett A. Hood, Engineer; S/Sgt. James W. McKeon, Ball Turret Gunner, (the most decorated man in the group); S/Sgt. Louis L. Ratkiewicz, Tail Gunner, S/Sgt. William E. Marti

★ ★ ★

CHAPTER

10

Double Duren

It is hard getting back to combat on this Monday, October 18, 1943 after the three-day pass to London. The pall continues to linger with the crew as a result of the 384th losses on the Schweinfurt raid. Still in sorrow and shock, the crew must fly their assigned missions.

Sam recalls today's difficult raid:

"Thanks to the unpopular operations clerk, we are up again at 0400 hours. Rumors indicate we are going to bomb a city in Germany by the name of Duren. Our Doc is still out for repairs due to the extensive fighter and flak damage suffered during the Bremen raid, so today, we will, again, be flying A/C #927, Homesick Sal.

"The briefing officer, Major Dolan, begins, 'Major Gilmore will lead today's mission. Our target will be the marshaling yards at Duren, Germany. The weather officer indicates we can expect poor flying conditions locally and all the way to the target.'

"With briefing complete, weapons/ammo issued, we proceed to the hardstand where Homesick Sal *is waiting for another crack at the nasty Nazis.*

"The usual procedure for takeoff is followed and, once again, we are airborne. The local weather is extremely poor and the fog as thick as soup. We are airborne but ... we can't find our group. In about five minutes there is a slight improvement in visibility. We now spot 384th aircraft slightly ahead and to our left.

"The 384th, in turn, is having great difficulty forming up with the 41st Combat Wing and 1st Air Division. This is understandable in this lousy weather. The bad weather, combined with the great number of B-17s in the vicinity, the methods of takeoff employed by the Eighth Air Force and the frequent late takeoffs make this type of snafu impossible to avoid.

"We fly around, under difficult conditions, for the next 40 minutes trying to form up with other groups from our wing and division. Finally, we are in combat position at 1000 hours. At 1030 hours we pass over the enemy coast. I observe considerable flak but no damage is inflicted on our B-17. A recall[1] message is now received from Headquarters for the entire division to abort due to adverse weather conditions. The 384th formation returns to base, with some difficulty, but lands safely at approximately 1200 hours.

"The bad news is that we do not get credit for this mission toward the required 25. The good news is that today four new crews arrive for duty with the group. These crews are badly needed to replace the losses from the Anklam and Schweinfurt raids. My squadron, the 547th, is at half strength. We welcome the new men.

"It seems that the brass[2] really wants Duren destroyed as it is our target again on Wednesday, October 20th. I am surprised we are scheduled for a mission as there is a heavy overcast and generally bad visibility in the area.

"Nevertheless, the base public address system announces a standby alert for all personnel. Within an hour the mission is planned and the necessary preliminaries complete. Our ship is readied with 1,800 gallons of fuel, and bombs loaded to the extent of four tons. Whining revolutions of our B-17 props begins at 1000 hours. At 1038 hours, lift off is complete and we climb to 1,000 feet. We form up with the rest of the 384th, the 41st Combat Wing, and the 1st Air Division with great difficulty due to the piss poor weather conditions.

"Just as two days earlier on our aborted mission to Duren, we pass into Germany. This time, however, the Jerries meet us with heavy fighter opposition. We engage them for about ten minutes; then, as before, we receive a recall message from headquarters.

"*The bad news is that we are compelled to turn back again without dropping our bombs due to the weather, not the enemy. The good news is that this snafu is chalked up as a mission and there are no aircraft losses or casualties, with the exception of Gibby, who suffered frostbite on his feet in the −43°C temperature at 29,000 feet altitude. Five missions down, 20 to go.*

"*On Saturday, October 23, we welcome six new combat crews to the 384th. With these additions, our 547th Squadron is back to full strength — six aircraft and 60 airmen. Watch out, Huns!*"

★ ★ ★

CHAPTER

11

Brown Bomber

For the last 14 days, the 384th Bomb Group has been in a status of stand down.[1] The group has not flown a mission because of damaged aircraft in need of repairs and missing crews that needed to be replaced. The Group had received replacement crews over the last two weeks, however, they require at least two weeks of ground training and local flying before they are combat ready. But today, the 384th is fully combat ready and eager to spit in the Fuehrer's face, once again.

Gilly describes the mission called Brown Bomber:

"We awake on this Wednesday, November 3, 1943 at 0400 hours for a 0515 hours briefing. By now Shorty has verbally abused the operations clerk so badly that he tip toes into our barrack and gently taps our shoulders to awaken us. Shorty is convinced that a couple more verbal abuses and he will have this boy serving us breakfast in bed.

"We proceed to the mess hall where I notice Shorty eating a large breakfast of eggs and shit on shingle (SOS).[2] Next, we stumble to the briefing room. Briefing commences at 0515 hours, as scheduled, with crew assignments to aircraft and flight positions. The briefing officer

pulls back the bad news curtain[3] and says: 'The port areas and naval installations at Wilhelmshaven, Germany are your targets for today. You can expect the target to be hidden by a solid overcast. We will bomb with the use of the Pathfinder method.[4] Today the 384th will put up a total of 24 bombers. This will be the greatest number of B-17s to go out on a mission. You can expect fighter escorts to and from the target. Major Harris will lead today's mission. Questions? No? Let's have a safe mission.'

"The pilot for this mission will not be our aircraft commander, Lt. Kaczaraba. He must attend an awards ceremony to receive the Air Medal for completing five missions. Lt. Kaczaraba has flown one more mission than the rest of our crew, therefore, is the first to receive the well-deserved Air Medal.

"Today's mission pilot will be 2nd Lt. T. L. Carter. (Lt. Carter was promoted from the Canadian Air Force rank of Flight Officer to the U.S. Army Air Corps rank of Second Lieutenant with an effective date of October 18, 1943.) He is known to be an excellent pilot and steady under pressure. We have full confidence in him.

"The briefing over, weapons/ammo issued, we board jeeps and trucks and head out to the hardstands where B-17s are awaiting their crews. Preflight checks are still in progress as Lt. Carter relays the highlights of the briefing to the rest of our crew.

"While waiting to board the plane, I notice that Lt. Morgan and Shorty are protecting a fully packed duffel bag. Gibby inquires as to its contents.

"'This is part of a secret weapon and it will destroy the backbone of the German people,' replies Shorty, half laughing. That is all the information the two tightlipped crewmen would divulge. Our curiosity runs wild, but we inquire no further.

"The preflight is complete, and, at last, we board the plane. I notice that Lt. Morgan is very careful loading the duffel bag through the forward nose hatch. He places it slightly behind and between his and the pilot's seat.

"The engines are started and we taxi out to the active runway. Here we wait for the green flare to signal us for takeoff. At 0930 hours, we proceed down the runway at increasing speed until tires release their grip. Our B-17 is airborne. Assembly with the rest of the 384th over the field is complete as with the 41st Air Combat Wing over Kings Lynn, our first navigational fix. The weather is lousy; however, the group and wing are now assembled and in good combat position. From *an altitude of 11,000 feet the formation departs the second naviga- tional fix, known as 'The Wash.'*

"*The next hour we are continuously on alert for possible midair col- lisions. As we depart the English coast the weather improves some- what. The cruising speed of the formation, after leveling off over the North Sea is too fast and the 384th is having a hard time keeping up.*

"*We are flying directly to our next navigational fix, Baltrum, locat- ed in the East Frisian Islands. The formation will make its approach to Wilhelmshaven from there. Climbing to 23,000 feet, the formation proceeds into Germany. 'At 23,000, crossing enemy coast,' Lt. Horsky announces over the interphone.*

"*Continuing a southeasterly route, the formation is experiencing sharply defined solid clouds running north and south. This prevents making our planned approach to Wilhelmshaven. The Pathfinder air- craft, piloted by Major Harris, informs the formation, 'We will make a different bombing approach to the target, follow me.'*

"*The formation follows the Pathfinder ship as it swings to port and circles around to make its attack northwesterly across the target. Following this route, the formation starts the bomb run. Each of us lis- tens for the Pathfinder to communicate to the rest of the formation when to release bombs. Still in a dense overcast, midair collisions are a real possibility.*

"*'Bombs away,' Major Harris orders and the formation's bombs are dropped in unison on the Wilhelmshaven naval base below. Smoke screens and cloud conditions make it difficult to assess damage but we have confidence that the dock areas are hit. Leaving the target area we experience minor flak but no opposition from German fighters.*"

Lt. Morgan continues with the narrative:

"*Now that we have dropped our regular weapons (vis-à-vis bomb load) the time is ripe to deliver our secret weapon. Lt. Carter, today's pilot, had been briefed before we left base about our plan. He stated the required conditions needed to deliver our secret weapon. 'Our B-17 must not be under enemy fighter or flak attack and the entire crew must be informed of the secret weapon prior to delivery. Both condi- tions are met when I speak to the crew over the interphone.'*

"*As you know, on our milk run to Emden, I suffered great physical damage to my Superman comic book. (It is normal for Lt. Morgan to read comics on missions when he is not busy. On the Emden mission, with his window slightly open, flak metal came through the window and cut his comic in slivers.) This pissed me off. In addition, Sgt. Craden's people have suffered for many years under the Nazis. Today, Sgt. Craden and I will deliver a secret weapon to pay the bastards back. Sgt. Gilrane, help Sgt. Craden get out of the ball turret so he and I can prepare to deliver our weapon.*

"The crew's attention is now concentrated on the actions of Shorty. With the help of Gilly rotating the ball turret guns into the vertical position, Shorty is able to exit the ball turret. He immediately removes his flight suit and quickly drops his pants to his ankles. He must hurry for we will be out of German airspace in less than 15 minutes. He now struggles forward about eight feet to the open bomb bay area. He has eaten the largest breakfast of his life this morning and his 5'1", 105-pound body is fully loaded for the excruciating task ahead of him.

"'Lt. Morgan, get your duffel bag ready. I am ready to deliver my part of the secret weapon on the German people. On the count of three, we will release our secret weapon.'

"Now cued, I unsnap the duffel bag, hold it closed by hand and place it just outside my window. Shorty positions his body so that his butt is directly over the open bomb bay doors. He has his chest chute on. Gilly and Pete are holding on to his arms for dear life for we are at 23,000 feet. It is 45 degrees below zero. Shorty, trying not to laugh, begins the suspenseful count down, 'three, two, one ... turds away.'

"Concurrently with his release, I open the duffel bag and the vacuum created by our B-17s 150 MPH airspeed sucks hundreds of unraveled sheets of toilet paper out of it. The toilet paper is sheered by the inboard engine prop into thousands of small pieces and continues aft to the bomb bay area where it combines with Shorty's 'brown bombs.' Both are flushed downward to some unsuspecting and surprised Germans far below. The entire episode lasts about three minutes.

"The deed now complete, Shorty hustles back to his turret to observe his payload on the way down to some unlucky Germans. From the ground, the Krauts must be highly confused for it appears that the Americans are out of normal bombs and have resorted to using frozen turds."

Shorty is concerned that his payload may have missed Germany:

"'Lt. Horsky, Are we still over Germany?' 'Our position is about 13 miles north west of Wilhelmshaven. We are still over Germany,' replies Lt. Horsky. 'Lt. Wirth, do you think we hit the target?' 'Based on our

airspeed, altitude, direction, and your highly accurate anal bombsight, Sgt. Craden, I'd say we walloped Wilhelmshaven,' answers Lt. Wirth."

Lt. Mike Morgan and S/Sgt. Solomon Craden smile with deep satisfaction knowing that their secret weapon delivery system had worked perfectly. The crew is in good humor as they make for the North Sea. Fighter opposition is nonexistent, flak is meager and mostly inaccurate as they leave the German coast and head for home.

This mission was a good one for the 384th Bomb Group as 24 B-17s were dispatched and all returned safely after releasing their bombs on the target. The group had only two crewmen wounded when flak burst in the nose of their B-17 and shattered an oxygen bottle, the fragments of which struck two crewmen. The wounded were 2nd Lt. John B. Kennedy, co-pilot, and 2nd Lt. Carl A. Hedin, navigator, on the B-17 piloted by 2nd Lt. Walter R. Carpenter.

The crew exits their B-17, and heads for the debriefing room. This is a short session because they inform the debriefing officer that it was a routine mission with very little flak and no enemy fighters to speak of. No mention is made of the secret weapon and its delivery system.

The day's activities are not quite over for Shorty. There is one little problem. He has suffered frostbite on his butt while it was exposed over the bomb bay. He must report to the base dispensary to have the frostbite treated. The medical officer examines the area in question and advises him to keep it warm for a few hours and it will be as good as new.

The medic, however, did have a question, "This is the first case that I have treated a frostbitten butt. Did you piss in your pants because of the combat excitement which froze and caused the frostbite?"

"No, Sir," Shorty replies, "I can only tell you that our crew was responsible for a top secret mission, therefore, I can't discuss it with you." Needless to say, the Germans failed to surrender because of Lt. Morgan and Sgt. Craden's secret weapon. By the way, the medic's diagnoses was correct, in a few hours Shorty was the same old witty asshole he had always been.

★ ★ ★

CHAPTER

12

Happy Valley

Just like a popular western song of the era entitled, *Ride Away to Happy Valley*, today, Friday, November 5, 1943 the 384th Bomb Group is briefed to *Fly Away to Happy Valley*. The Ruhr industrial valley is known ironically to Eighth Air Force crews as Happy Valley. The reason is obvious, as the Ruhr industrial valley is one of the most heavily defended areas in Germany. Bombing missions to this area have resulted in many crews being shot down.

Briefing starts at 0615 hours. It is short with all but the essentials left out. This will be one of the 384th Bomb Group's longest missions to date. The days are getting shorter, therefore, there will be more time flying in darkness. The briefing officer starts:

"Today the Eighth Air Force will put up over 600 bombers with combined air strikes by the USAAF[1] and the RAF[2] to smash important targets at Gelsenhirchen in the center of the Ruhr industrial valley. The 384th will put up 21 aircraft and our specific target will be the marshaling yards at Gelsenhirchen. The secondary target is any city in Germany with military targets. There are no targets of last resort. You can expect intense flak within a ten-mile zone of the target. Colonel

William Buck in A/C #527 will lead today's mission. Are there any questions? No? Dismissed!"

Lt. Kaczaraba tries his hand at pronouncing the German target:

"As I leave briefing, I am thinking: Why can't HQ pick a damn target I can pronounce? The crew is going to ask what our target is and I won't be able to pronounce it. I am also thinking how proud I am to be a part of such a large strike force. (This period in the war was long before the time of the thousand-plus aircraft raid.)

"Gathered at the nose of our B-17 with the other crew members, the first question is, 'Cap, what is our target for today?' I couldn't pronounce the target but I knew that Sgt. Peifer, a naturalized German could, so I had attempted to pronounce it to him on the way to our plane. Slightly flustered, I look to Sgt. Peifer who clearly states, 'Gelsenhirchen, in the Ruhr Valley.'"

Today the 384th Bomb Group will carry high explosives and incendiary bombs. Nineteen aircraft will be carrying 42X65 M47 A-1 type high explosive bombs, one aircraft will carry 36X65 M47 A-1 type high explosive bombs, and one aircraft will carry 36 incendiary and six parachute bombs.

After the usual assembly of groups, wings, and divisions, the formation departs the English coast at 1145 hours. Due to the late departure, it will probably be dark when they get back.

The formation is now over the German coast and Sam spots A/C #0033, Lt. Vanderhaughen's crew, turning back because of oxygen failure and the number 3 engine not operating properly. As A/C #0033 turns back, its crew spots a target of opportunity, a 30 to 50 enemy ship convoy. A large ship is leading, heading south, about one mile off shore. The crew unleashes its bomb load on the convoy. Results of the bombing could not be determined due to an 8/10-cloud[3] cover.

At 1305 hours, the formation is about 30 miles north of the target. There are no signs of enemy fighters. This is due to the P-47 escorts that literally blacken the sky. This raid is of immense proportion as there are at least 250 B-17s ahead of the 384th Bomb Group's formation and at least that many behind.

Position of the formation is now approximately ten miles north of the target. The Germans are attempting to screen the city with smoke pots. The smoke screen is not successful as the wind is blowing it south of the target. Lt. Wirth will not have his aim spoiled today.

Lt. Morgan narrates at this point in the mission:

"*Thud, thud, our B-17 is being pelleted by an intensive shower of flak. Our fort catches two major flak hits in the fuselage but flies on. On the bomb run, Lt. Kaczaraba demonstrates excellent control of our B-17. The lead ship is now dropping its bombs ahead of us. Lt. Wirth depresses the switches to release our bombs. High explosives and incendiaries descend to earth. These type of bombs are used respectively to explode on the target and also to set fire to the target and the surrounding area.*

"'*We have a mechanical failure, I have indication the bombs did not drop,' shouts Lt. Wirth.*

"'*I'll go back and manually release the bombs,' responds Sam. Sam leaves his top turret position and enters the extremely cold bomb bay area. The bomb bay doors are open, wind is entering the area with a major force. It is a −55 degree environment at 28,000 feet. Hanging on for dear life, he attempts to kick the bombs loose. Sam reports his lack of success.*

"*Lt. Kaczaraba decides to make another pass, makes a short left turn and banks to line up for a second bomb run. The flak is even more intense over the target area on this second run as the aircraft lifts and rolls violently from the deadly blanket of flak. Once again, we are over the target.*

"'*Bombs away!,' Shorty shouts to Lt. Wirth. 'Our bird has laid ten eggs, Sir. Lets get the hell out of here, I think the Jerries are mad at us.'*

"*Now out of the flak area, I notice that our gauges indicate we have less than two hours of gas left. This is because we had bucked strong head winds all the way to the target and made two passes over the target. I inform Lt. Kaczaraba that we will have to cut back on cruising speed enough to keep us flying and try to glide back to England.*"

Sam takes us back to Grafton-Underwood:

"*The unwelcome news of our low fuel condition gets the crew's attention. Due to our reduced speed it is necessary to leave the formation. Homesick Sal is all alone and an inviting target for enemy fighters. I pray we will not encounter any that may either shoot us down or cause further consumption of fuel. I spot four fighters in the distance but no attacks are initiated. My prayers are answered; enemy fighters fail to put in an appearance.*

"*Visibility is excellent so weather is not a problem. We are flying at less than cruising speed and gliding when possible. I leave my top turret and go forward to monitor fuel consumption. The base is now in sight, however, at this time I announce more unwelcome news to the crew by advising them to prepare for a crash landing. There is approximately 20 gallons of fuel left. We might not make the runway.*

"The crew assembles at their designated areas. Gunners go to the radio compartment, all other crew members remain on station. Lt. Morgan informs the control tower of our fuel situation. We are assigned a straight in approach. Then the squawk of our bird's rubber hits the runway and my prayers are answered, once again. Thank you Lord for watching over us, I softly whisper to myself."

Lt. Kaczaraba applies full brakes as *Sal* speeds down the runway. He avoids overshooting the exit and starts to taxi to the crew's assigned parking area. Just as *Sal* turns onto the exit, all engines go silent. *Sal* is out of gas.

Shorty couldn't miss this opportunity as he half laughs to relieve his fears. "Hey, this is supposed to happen with a good looking gal, not with nine ugly guys."

Then Lt. Morgan, also relieved, contacts the control tower. "Control, this is 927, we need some roadside assistance to tow us to our parking area."

While the crew waits they continue to make small talk to relieve their tension. *Sal* is hooked up to the tow truck and they head for their parking area. Happy and relieved, they have tucked another mission, the seventh, under their belts.

As missions go it had been a good one. There is minor battle damage to *Sal*. The crew found only two flak holes about the size of silver dollars in the left fuselage, aft of the waist gunner's window. But they had plenty of excitement prior to their bird getting back into its nest.

Debriefing is next and the debriefing officer opens up the session. Lt. Kaczaraba is confident of the bombing results:

"The Germans tried to put up a smoke screen around the city but it failed to spoil the aim of Lt. Wirth. We couldn't miss. The group dropped bombs in the area for at least ten minutes. I saw clouds of reddish smoke indicating a chemical plant had been hit. We had no problem with fighters but the flak was intense to unbearable. As we made our turn from the target, I could see that it was covered with black smoke from our bombs."

Gibby is also confident of the bombing results:

"I've seen smoke screens before. It was easy to tell smoke from the pots and the kind our bombs kick up. Most of the smoke was from our

bombs. I saw no enemy fighters. My guns were silent all during the trip, that's how dull it was over Happy Valley."

Shorty had the best view of the target and speaks next:

"A large, long row of dark brown smoke came up as our bombs hit and made a vivid contrast to the black smoke pots. We must have pretty well destroyed the target. There were so many Forts up there they looked like those flocks of birds heading south back home this time of year. It was an easy job for the Ruhr, lots of flak but no fighters. It was cold though, about 40 below."

Lt. Morgan speaks last:

"The clouds broke over the city. It stood out clearly, an easy mark. Smoke gushed up after the bombs landed. Enemy fighters were as scarce as ours were numerous. I saw four or five German fighters but our P-47s kept them at a respectable distance."

The day ended on a happy note as all 21 of the 384th Bomb Group's aircraft returned to base, and, with the exception of A/C #0033, Lt. Vanderhaughen's crew, bombed the primary target, with good results.

More good news. Eight new combat crews reported in today, two for each of the four squadrons. One of the crews assigned to the 544th Squadron is the crew of Lt. Ralph Connell. One week later on an aborted mission, tragedy would strike this crew. See notation for Saturday, November 13, 1943, this chapter. Of these pilots, only three will survive to reach double figures of missions and between all eight, they will only fly 63 missions with none completing their tour.

Exhausted, the crew heads to the chow hall[4] for a late supper, then to the barracks for rest before the next mission. The crew wasn't too exhausted. They managed to provide the new crews with war stories to welcome them aboard.

On Saturday, November 13th a B-17 piloted by 2nd Lt. Ralph J. Connell of the 544th Squadron, flying its first mission, crashed in England claiming the lives of nine members of the crew. Following is the information given to the intelligence officer by T/Sgt. Alan B. Purdy, the radio operator and sole survivor of the crash:

"At approximately 0910 hours, flying at 10,000 feet, the aircraft began to vibrate badly, but maintained a forward course. At that time, myself, the bombardier, tail gunner, ball turret gunner, and the right

waist gunner were in the radio room. The bombardier had just returned from the bomb bay, where he had pulled the safety pins from the bombs. None of us had parachutes on, but all had the harness adjusted, except the bombardier.

"Shortly after this the plane began to vibrate, and went over sharply on its left wing and then abruptly over on its right wing, then into a very tight spin. Just as it went into the spin, I snatched my parachute and hooked in onto my chest. As the plane went into a spin the previously mentioned crew members rushed into the waist of the plane. I was thrown to the floor of the plane because of the force of the vertical spin. My feet were injured at that time. The plane was finally pulled out of the spin, and as it leveled off it broke completely in half in the center of the radio room. I managed to get to the open end away from the tail and bailed out. I estimate we were at an altitude of between 800 and 1,000 feet when I bailed out.

"In my opinion the plane broke in half because of the force exerted as it pulled out of the vertical spin. I did not know the plane was on fire until spectators on the ground informed me. There was an interval of between 80 and 90 seconds between the time I noticed anything wrong with the plane and the time I bailed out. During this interval no other crew member had time to express an opinion as to what might have gone wrong. I have no explanation and can give no reason for the plane going into the spin."

In Memory

2nd Lt. Ralph J. Connell, Pilot
2nd Lt. Albert M. Doman, Co-pilot
2nd Lt. Lawrence M. Angthius, Navigator
2nd Lt. Claude I. Gober, Bombardier
T/Sgt. Harvey A. Wick, Engineer
S/Sgt. Robert C. Bryant, Tail Gunner
S/Sgt. Ellsworth F. Calder, Ball Turret Gunner
S/Sgt. William M. McCully, Waist Gunner
S/Sgt. Kenneth Barr, Waist Gunner

Sam sadly reflects on this tragic accident:

"This crew had only been with us for a week. We had developed a loose friendship with them during this short time. We have been taught, the hard way, not to develop strong friendships, especially with new crews."

★ ★ ★

CHAPTER

13

Needle in a Haystack

Three days after Sergeant Purdy's miraculous escape in the crash at Wargrave the 384th is alerted for a raid to Norway. The group will be going after one of the smallest and most concentrated targets ever attacked by the Eighth Air Force, a molybdenum mine and its ore processing plant at Knaben, important to Germany's steel production. The target, in addition to being small, will be well protected by natural and artificial camouflage. The raid will call for expert navigation and precision bombing.

It is dark at 0400 hours when that damn persistent operations clerk stumbles into the NCO's barracks on Tuesday, November 16, 1943. He yells those ill-fated words that have already sent too many good airmen to their last retreat, "Get up, y'all are flyin' today."

Shorty gently shoves him out of the hut and remarks, "Don't let the door hit you in the ass on the way out."

Today, and for the last few days, Lt. Morgan is not feeling well. He is suffering from severe stomach cramps and doubts his potential performance on today's mission. He gets up anyway, dresses, and has only a cup of coffee for breakfast. Proceeding into the cold, damp air to the briefing hut, his stomach is in knots. His stomach orders his brain to inform Lt. Kaczaraba that he can't fly this mission but his brain disobeys the stomach. He knows the crew is counting on him and his dedication won't allow him to let the crew down.

It is 0530 hours by the time the crew settles into the briefing room. Today's briefing is for a new type of target:

"Today our bombers will span the North Seas as we will shift our attacks from German targets to Norwegian ones. Today we will blast the molybdenum mine known as Knaben II and its ore processing plant at Knaben, Norway. Your secondary target will be an airdrome in Oslo, Norway. The target is situated in the lake region of south central Norway approximately midway between the west coast and the capital city of Oslo. It will be one of the smallest and most concentrated targets ever attacked by the Eighth Air Force. Due to its size and the natural and artificial camouflage, it will present a problem in expert navigation and will call for exactness in precision bombing. Your target today constitutes one of the most important industries in Norway to the Germans because molybdenum is used in the manufacturing of steel. You will bomb from 12,000 feet, but be careful, a 10,000 feet balloon barrage[1] with wire is stretched across the valley in which the mine is located, protecting the target from low level bombing. Any questions? Good! The group will be led by Colonel Lacey, our Commanding Officer."

Colonel Lacey addresses the group to discuss today's armament:

"We will put up 21 aircraft. Thirteen will carry 12X500 general purpose (GP) bombs and eight will carry 6X500 GP bombs. I will be flying with Lt. Frink. Any questions? No! Good hunting, men."

The briefing complete, Lt. Morgan heads over to discuss the weather conditions with the meteorologist. The weatherman informs him to expect heavy clouds up to about 2,500 to 3,000 feet, then clear skies all the way to Norway and return. These will be words that will haunt Lt. Morgan on this mission.

Sam describes this mission called "Needle in a Haystack":

"The trucks are now outside to take us to our waiting B-17. It is almost dawn as we pull up to the hardstand. Could it be? Yes, it's Doc, all patched up and fit for duty. I am so glad to have Doc back. We all feel better, even Lt. Morgan. I am not quite complete with my preflight

checks as I inspect the airframe to confirm the repair work just recently completed on Doc. The rest of the crew's preflight checks are finished, so they will have to wait on me.

"While waiting, the rest of the crew is sitting on the concrete hard-stand and those who smoke, do so. The weather is heavily overcast and we began to discuss how rough the mission might be. Lt. Kaczaraba interrupts us, 'Just do your jobs like you were trained and we will fly a good mission and get home safely.'

"I give the crew the thumbs up indicating my preflight checks are complete. We climb aboard, and assume takeoff positions. Lt. Kaczaraba taxis Doc off the hardstand and onto the perimeter track. We taxi to the main runway. Most of the other B-17s in the group have already taken off as we wait for the green light for takeoff at the head of the runway. The green light is flashed and we start our roll at exactly 0731 hours. The four 1200 HP Pratt & Whitney engines are roaring as they hurl Doc down the runway. Once airborne, our right wing dips slightly but Doc lifts easily as we head straight for The Wash, our first navigational fix, to catch up with the 384th at the departure point. Our departure from Grafton-Underwood is late and we must cut all corners to catch the 384th as soon as possible.

"At 0845 hours, after flying above The Wash for about ten minutes and dodging scores of other aircraft, I spot the 384th and inform the crew that Triangle P² is at one o'clock, approximately half a mile ahead. Lt. Morgan slides us nicely into our assigned formation slot. We now head off to do a little mining using bombs instead of picks.

"At 0900 hours the 41st Combat Wing joins the 1st Air Division. The 1st Air Division is now assembled and departs on course and on time from The Wash. We are climbing to an altitude of 12,000 feet to get above the weather front. Instead of breaking out of the overcast at 3,500 feet (as predicted by the meteorologist) we must climb to 20,000 feet to get over the weather front. The wind shifts at this altitude and the formation is slightly ahead of schedule.

"About midway over the North Sea, the lead B-17 initiates a 360-degree turn to slow us down. As we are turning, I spot one of our aircraft turning back. It is A/C #560, Lt. Jorgenson's aircraft. He is turning back due to a loose oil line on the propeller governor.

"We cross the enemy coast (Norway) on time and are flying toward the target, Knaben, Norway. No flak or fighter opposition so far.

"The briefing officer was correct with his information. The mine complex is well hidden in a remote spot in the mountains. Our formation *flies over the area searching, searching, and searching. We search for over an hour with no visual sighting of the mine. Colonel Lacey, our Group Commander, realizes that we have gone beyond the target area and orders the formation to return to the coastline. From there, we will try and get our bearings.*

"*After orienting ourselves, we head back, picking up landmarks along the route. Convinced we are over the target area the formation makes two test runs before we spot the mine entrance on the side of a mountain. On the third run, Lt. Wirth announces bombs away. The formation had been in the target area for almost two hours before the target was definitely identified and the successful run made.*

"*As we turn for home, Lt. Horsky remarks, 'That was like looking for a damn needle in a haystack.' Again, we must climb back to 20,000 feet to get over the weather front for our return to England. We have been flying close to nine hours when we land back at Grafton-Underwood.*

"*Due to the weather and excess fuel consumption, three of our returning 20 planes are forced to land at other bases. A/C #440, Lt. Merritt's crew, lands at Catfas; A/C #058, Lt. Herbert's crew lands at Oaston and A/C #828, Lt. Jacob's crew lands at Lisseth.*

"*Sixteen of our aircraft returned to base safely and in formation. The primary target was bombed with good results. A/C#5838, Mad Money II, Lt. Frink's crew, had to salvo their bombs in the vicinity of the target due to a faulty bomb release mechanism.*

"*It is 1615 hours, almost dark, as we exit* Doc *and head for the debriefing room, hoping for a quick recounting of the day's events. After an extremely cold mission of 800 miles, we are in need of rest and warmth.*

"*At the debriefing we do not offer any noteworthy information such as enemy fighters or flak. We did not experience either as the Germans were too smart to be out in the pea soup we had just experienced. We did provide our opinions on the bombing results.*"

Lt. Morgan expresses his concern about the balloon barrage:

"*The mine was located on the side of a valley and we were careful to make sure that this was the target before we let our bombs drop. There were no enemy fighters around so we could have taken all day. I was more concerned about the balloon barrage and wires stretched across the valley at 10,000 feet and our fuel consumption.*"

Gilly speaks of his observations of the bombing:

"Our bombs seem to walk right up the side of the valley and across the mine. I could see the blast and even hear the sound bursts."

Gibby speaks about the extreme cold in his battle station:

"It was the coldest mission I've ever been on. The outside temperature was 45 degrees below zero. It must have been 65 degrees below in my tail section. I almost wished for some fighters to come up just to warm me up a little. What I remember is nothing but snow, ice, and rock. It's going to be a cold winter in Norway. The last thing I remember was the unpleasant task of eating my lunch and realizing just how cold it was. My sandwiches were frozen."

Another mission completed, the eighth, is now in the books. It was also the last mission to be flown with the 384th by Col. Julius K. Lacey before he was replaced as commanding officer. Most skip supper and go straight to check on mail from home. Mail is never left unchecked. It is their lifeline to sanity.

On Wednesday, November 17, the 384th receives two new combat crews. One is assigned to the 544th Squadron, 2nd Lt. William Lotz, Jr.'s crew and one to the 546th Squadron, 2nd Lt. Charles E. Dedhe's crew.

There is still some hesitation by *Doc's* crew to become friends with new crews. They have learned the hard way to keep their circle of friends small for death is ever lurking with a penchant for green crews.

Birmingham Bamboozled

On the weekend following the mission to Knaben, Norway, Lts. Morgan, Wirth, and Horsky decide to visit one of the nearby towns for a little fun and games. They select Birmingham because it offers a wide variety of activities that have potential for mischief, adventure, and dirty deeds.

It is important to remember that Shorty Craden is the NCO's joker. His counterpart in the officer ranks is Lt. Marvin Horsky.

Lt. Morgan details the mischief, adventure, and dirty deeds for this weekend:

> "We three, Ted, Marvin, and myself, after a trip of about an hour, check into a hotel in Birmingham and hastily get ready for a fun weekend. A play and then a few nightspots are scheduled on our weekend agenda.
>
> "Hopping into a taxi, we are soon in a queue (line) at the theater. The lobby is packed. When we are about two positions from the ticket cage, the Joker, (Marvin Horsky) spots a poster on the wall giving admission prices in pounds, shillings, and pence. In a very loud voice so all in the lobby can hear, the Joker shouts, 'I don't know if I can pay these high

prices to see this play or not. It's going to cost me a whole week's pay and I'm almost broke. That poster says three pounds, five shillings. Let's see, that equals $21.25.

"Everyone in the lobby is looking at us while Ted and myself are trying to find a hole to crawl into. The woman in the ticket box tries to explain that it is five shillings — not five pounds, which is only $1.30 instead of $21. The Joker acts as if he doesn't understand. She tries to explain again. Finally, after a few tries, the woman gives us the tickets free as the line behind is quite long by now. In addition, an elderly gentleman, feeling sorry for the poor GIs, slips the joker a five-pound note as we go into the theater.

"Inside the theater Horsky doesn't understand why we are upset with him. He boasts, 'Hell, I got you guys in free and bamboozled five pounds for the pubs later on.'

"That night we had lots of fun with the Irish civilians that are brought to England to supplement the English labor force. In the pubs, with little effort, we get a group of them to sit with us and drink bitters (beers). They get half-crocked and want to sing, and of course, we encourage them. We all had a good time, playing the piano, singing, and drinking bitters.

"Later that night, after many pub visits and feeling no pain, the Joker is spoiling to pull just one more prank before calling it a day. Returning quite late to our hotel he notices the shoes of the guests are lined up outside each room, all the way down the hall. (It is a custom for the English, when retiring for the night, to leave their shoes outside their rooms so the maid can have them shined.) The Joker laughs, 'Let's have a little fun and change everyone's shoes to a different door and to a different floor.' Ted and I decide to go along with him.

"The next hour is spent rearranging every shoe to effect maximum confusion among the unsuspecting owners. Now having finished the dirty deed with all the shoes once again in neat rows along the corridors, albeit thoroughly shuffled, Ted and I retire for the night, (with our shoes securely under our beds, of course). The Joker is staying in another room with an English captain.

"About 0900 hours the next morning, we hear loud, unusual noises up and down the hall. Doors are slamming, guests are yelling back and forth accusing each other of taking their shoes. We are in our room laughing our heads off when Horsky walks in. He says, 'The captain in my room said some bloody bloke exchanged all the shoes and it would take hours to find his.' What did you say?, I asked. 'I looked him *straight in the eye and told him, I agree with you, it takes a low down bloke to play a dirty trick like that.' When we checked out the next day the case of the wandering shoes had still not been solved.*

"The shoe exchange and half-crocked Irish were the topics of conversation that gave us many laughs back on the base. This is one way we try to get away from the specter of war."

Monday, November 22, the 384th Bomb Group welcomes 24 new combat crews. The crews are assigned to the four squadrons equally as follows:

544th Squadron

(1) 2nd Lt. Anthony J. Gredido's crew. (2) 2nd Lt. John E. Crayton's crew. (3) 2nd Lt. Raymond L. Austin's crew. (4) 2nd Lt. Sheldon I. Vernon's crew., (5) 2nd Lt. Warren F. Donoven's crew. (6) 2nd Lt. James J. Brown's crew.

545th Squadron

(1) 2nd Lt. Scott A. Briley's crew. (2) 2nd Lt. Hugh E. Burch's crew. (3) 2nd Lt. Robert A. Butler's crew. (4) 2nd Lt. Sidney L. Bush's crew. (5) 2nd Lt. Martin P. Bachicha's crew. (6) 2nd Lt. Paul M. Beler's crew.

546th Squadron

(1) 2nd Lt. John L. Aegeter's crew. (2) 2nd Lt. Harold L. Bertram's crew. (3) 2nd Lt. Walter S. Bawel's crew. (4) 2nd Lt. Ralph E. Couremanche's crew. (5) 2nd Lt. James F. Carne's crew. (6) 2nd Lt. John J. Corcoran's crew.

547th Squadron

(1) 2nd Lt. Greeley Gay's crew. (2) 2nd Lt. Carlton F. Dow's crew. 2nd Lt. Loren A. Inman's crew. (4) 2nd Lt. Charles Stearn's crew. (5) 2nd Lt. Norman F. Defree's crew. (6) 2nd Lt. George H. Bean's crew.

On Tuesday, November 23, Colonel Dale O. Smith, assumed command of the 384th Bomb Group succeeding Colonel Julius K. Lacey, Commanding Officer since early September. Colonel Smith is a graduate of the United States Military Academy, Class of '34. The new CO is easy to find in a crowd due to his great stature; he is easily six feet, seven inches in height. Col. Smith had been stationed at the New York based AAF anti-submarine command before arriving in England where the commander of the 1st Air Division, Brigadier General Bob Williams, sent him to Polebrook to get blooded. With the 351st Bomb Group at Polebrook, he had flown just two missions to Wilhelmshaven, Germany and Knaben, Norway, both as an observer.

The 384th, although eager to take charge and win the war, did not welcome Col. Smith with open arms. The group had been taking a deadly beating with the two Schweinfurt raids and several other maulings. In addition, the group had lost their beloved commander, Col. Budd Peaslee, who had built the group from scratch and taken them to war. As the Eighth Air Force grew in size, Col. Peaslee had been transferred to higher duties where his experience was needed.

The truth, however, is that the nature of combat command is to achieve victory over the enemy, and this in the eyes of the Combat Wing Commander, Brig. Gen. Robert Travis, and the Air Division Commander, Maj. Gen. Bob Williams, had not been achieved by the 384th. So their beloved commander, Col. Budd Peaslee, who had led some of the roughest missions, had been relieved of command.

There wasn't a man who had served under Col. Peaslee who didn't consider his relief an injustice. Now this lanky beak-nosed stateside Colonel with very little combat experience was taking his place. Col. Smith could not truly assume command until he had gained more combat experience — he would have to get blooded with them before being accepted by the officers and enlisted men of the 384th.

The Hitchhiker

On a gloomy Friday in late November, three days after Colonel Smith took over the 384th Bomb Group, the group is alerted for another raid on Bremen. Once again, 384th airmen will discover how desperately the Germans will attempt to thwart any meddling with their U-boat pens at Bremen.

It is Friday, November 26, 1943, 0400 hours, when the operations clerk with a southern drawl "gently" taps on the barracks door to get the crew out of bed. Shorty definitely has this boy trained after only eight missions, no more yelling and shaking beds, just taps on the barracks door. This is the first mission since the Birmingham weekend and getting up this morning takes longer and requires an extra effort for Mike, Ted, and the Joker. The crew downs coffee and toast for breakfast (they have learned not to eat a large breakfast before a mission) and heads to the briefing room.

Major W. C. (Pops) Dolan, the S-2 Intelligence Officer, briefs the 384th crews on what they can expect on this mission in the way of enemy flak and fighters. It is not good news:

"Today our bombers will participate in the greatest mass flight of Flying Fortresses from bases in England to drop heavy explosives and

incendiaries upon the great and often bombed German port of Bremen. The attack will be made in heavy overcast, which will completely shield the target from observation above, therefore, we will drop our bombs by the Pathfinder (PFF) method. Expect to encounter in excess of 200 fighters and at least that many AAA batteries over the target. The group today will be lead by Major Raymond Ketelsen, Commanding Officer of the 545th Squadron. Colonel Dale Smith, our group's new commanding officer, will be along on this mission in the number two ship piloted by 1st Lt. Maguard Thomson, Jr."

Gilly remembers the last raid on Bremen back on October 8th and the trauma the crew suffered. He already knows from experience what Bremen will be like. He recounts the mission:

"After the briefing, we proceed by jeep out to Doc where we start preparations for our ninth mission. The crew chief and his mechanics are just about complete with engine inspections and other last minute checks of Doc. Fuel tanks are topped off and we climb aboard. The crew has completed their on board preflight checks such as mounting weapons, radio checks, and other required preflight duties.

"Engines are started at 0630 hours, as scheduled. Prior to taxi, Lt. Kaczaraba revs the engines up to full power. It is 0640 hours as we roll out to the perimeter track for takeoff.

"Today the 384th will put up 17 B-17s. Each will takeoff in approximately 45-second intervals. We wait for five minutes while B-17s in front of us takeoff. Now it's our turn. At 0648 hours, Doc is positioned on the takeoff runway. Lt. Kaczaraba applies full brakes and revs up the engines. I look for the green flare go signal ... off we go.

"For this mission, Doc is carrying a 1,000 pound bomb under each wing and a heavy gas load. Doc has no trouble clearing the runway. We are airborne.

"Lt. Kaczaraba is trying to form up with the rest of our group. The 384th assembly is complete and we head for our rendezvous and assembly with the 41st Combat Wing. The 384th rendezvous with the 41st is complete but is having great difficulty in assembling with the wing.

"The 2nd Air Division, which consist of B-24s, is in the 384th traffic pattern due to some time hack[1] instructions. B-24 bombers are cutting through our traffic pattern. The 384th formation is trying to get around the 2nd Air Division. This is a scene of utter confusion. B-17s and B-24s are crossing over and under each other from all angles.

There are several near misses, but somehow, Major Ketelsen leads us around the 2nd Air Division.

"*Proceeding toward our assembly with the 41st Combat Wing, we are having trouble getting into position due to cloud layers and the second element of our low squadron in our lead group lagging behind. Doc becomes separated from the 384th due to heavy clouds. Our crew is over the North Sea struggling between two formations, one ahead and one behind. The formation behind is approaching and Sam recognizes them as B-24s. The B-24 aircraft is faster than the B-17, therefore, we would burn up too much fuel trying to keep up, so we decide to let them go by and wait for the next formation.*

"*As the next formation approaches, Sam informs us, 'They are B-17s from the 91st Bomb Group. They have a white A on the tail with a black background.' (Each bomb group has its insignia on their aircraft's vertical tail section. The 91st Bomb Group, flying out of Basingbourn, England has a large black triangle background with a white A.) We decide to hitchhike on to the end of the 91st Bomb Group formation and fly the mission with them.*

"*The channel is behind us now. The tops of the clouds are at Doc's present altitude, however, the 91st Bomb Group pulls up above the clouds to allow their low squadron to proceed without flying through the clouds. We follow and just as we reach this new altitude, we are immediately set upon by enemy fighters, approximately 50 in number.*

"*Again, because we are hitchhiking, we are flying the undesirable tail-end Charlie position. Sam shouts, 'There are 30 to 40 yellow-nosed fighters (these are Goering's elite squadron) forming up for the attack. They are lining up, four abreast, from the nine o'clock position.*

"*Lt. Kaczaraba, on hearing this bad news, immediately pushes the throttles forward. We are in a speed formation and performing evasive action to spoil the fighter's aim. I look up and spot a Me109 coming through our formation head on with guns blazing directly at us. The Me109 zooms under and past our left wing by about two feet and immediately hits the B-17 behind and just below us. The tremendous impact tears the nose completely off the B-17. The bombardier and navigator never had a chance. The damaged B-17 is unable to stay airborne. It starts a deadly spiral earthward. Spellbound, I watch as a total of eight chutes blossom in the wake of the doomed ship.*

"*Then something unusual happens, the German fighters do not attack again but pair off in typical fighter combinations. Next, they start an air show of sorts. They perform circles, loops, figure eights, and other aerobatics, all just outside the range of our guns. This is confusing, seeing the enemy so near especially since our formation is without fighter protection. But still they do not attack. The Germans have always attacked an unprotected formation, especially us, as we are the unfortunate tail-end Charlie B-17. They must have a reason!*

"*This unusual aerial display continues at the nine o'clock position for about ten minutes. Then suddenly the Me109s stop their air show and make a short radius turn to come in from the rear of our formation. Concurrent with this flanking maneuver to our rear, an attack is commenced from our ship's three o'clock position. Doc is under attack from the six and three o'clock positions simultaneously by 30 Me109s and Fw190s. This attack pattern allows the top and ball turrets, both waists and tail guns to be in action. The* Doc's *total of eight guns must answer their 120.*

"*The first wave of fighters approach from the three o'clock position. All our guns concentrate on these as they are the closest, about 400 to 500 yards out. They peel off for their attack. The leading fighter, a Me109, is barrel rolling in at two o'clock high. The German pilot is firing with good effect. Me109 slugs are ripping into* Doc *a few feet on each side of me.*

"*Suddenly, I hear an explosion in my right ear, violently snapping my head back, immediately followed by brief dizziness and a stagger. Regaining my senses, I resume firing short, effective bursts at the German pilot closing rapidly. The lead Me109 careens past our slower bomber and roars back to join the other German fighters.*

"*I now attempt to communicate to the crew that I am not hurt but my interphone is not functioning. I place a hand on my right earphone and realize a bullet that almost bore my name has shattered it. Death was only inches away. (This is visit number two to Gilly by the Grim Reaper, but again, the deadly reaper must leave with empty arms. The little guy on Gilly's shoulder is still watching over him.) I expend many more rounds of lead at the next German pass but no fighters go down.*

"*The fighters' third pass results in several hits that rip into the skin of* Doc. *On this pass, Sam is tracking the oncoming enemy fighters but does not fire his twin .50 caliber machine-guns until they are within 300 yards. Now the lead Me109 is within range of Sam's guns. This will prove to be a fatal move on the part of the German pilot. The lead Me109 continues to bore in. Sam is pouring hot lead into it. His twin .50s inject a lethal dose of 40 to 50 rounds into the lead Me109's fuel tank and lines. The enemy fighter starts to smoke badly, indicating a fuel rupture. He loses altitude rapidly, bursts into flames and explodes. This German pilot will never again fly for his Fuehrer.*[2]

"*The kill is confirmed by me as I observe the fighter exploding. The battle continues for over 30 minutes. It only stops when we are near the target and the flak so heavy and intense that the enemy fighters break off.*

"*We settle down for our primary job of dropping bombs on the Bremen shipyard below. Over the target, we encounter intense, accurate flak. It is 1120 hours. Our altitude is 28,000 feet. There is a solid undercast below us.*

"*Lt. Wirth reports that flares are lit up ahead designating the IP. He opens the bomb bay doors. The 91st Bomb Group drops its bombs by salvo*[3] *on the deputy leader of the wing. We do likewise. The results are unobserved as clouds are 10/10 over the target. Lt. Wirth believes the target is hit, according to Lt. Horsky's dead reckoning method of navigation.*

"*Intense flak continues to be encountered. The crew reports at least ten more hits. None serious, no crew injuries. We are turning off the target and I can't believe what I see. The 384th is cutting the 91st out of position by crossing in front at the same altitude. We quickly decide to slide in behind our group. Lt. Kaczaraba guns Doc to close the distance and we catch up to the 384th in a few minutes. Now we must pull Doc into our flight position in the 384th formation. Suddenly, a large puff of black flak smoke appears right in the center of our assigned flight position in the formation. If we had been in position a few seconds earlier, we would have taken a direct hit. We are now in our original assigned formation position and we settle in for the trip home.*

"*The 384th formation spots the 41st Combat Wing and assembles with it. Our fighter escort shows up as we leave the target area. They cover several stragglers down below all the way back to the North Sea. The flight from the target to Cromer (a navigational fix on the English coast) is made in trail of the lead group of the 41st Combat Wing. From Cromer, the 384th breaks off and returns to base. Doc touches down at Grafton-Underwood at approximately 1310 hours.*

"*Once out of Doc we survey his damage. The survey reveals two large flak holes, about the size of grapefruits under the bomb bay and 62 bullet and flak holes in the stabilizers and fuselage.*

"*Our ninth mission complete, we are exhausted after our day's work of having served with two bomb groups (91st and 384th). Shorty* remarks, 'Hey, we should get double pay for this mission, one from the 91st and one from the 384th.' This humor relaxes us as we head for the debriefing."

The debriefing begins with Lt. Kaczaraba:

"We had German fighters on us all the way to the target. We would have had them on the way out but our escorts finally showed up to abort their attack."

Shorty speaks next of the possible target damage:

"We hit it all right, but we were attacked by so many enemy fighters that I didn't have time to check for bomb bursts. We damn sure hit Bremen, how bad I don't know."

Gibby tells of too many fighters:

"We were pretty busy, but I think we hit the target all right. The enemy fighters were swarming all over us from the three and six o'clock positions but we tooled right along. Our fighters picked us up on the way back and we didn't see any more opposition."

Lt. Wirth relates the near miss:

"There was flak all right, but not as much as the last time. For a while we had plenty of German fighters. There were battles going on all over the sky. Our aircraft was almost hit by a Me109. It struck another B-17 just behind us, and it went down. I saw eight chutes. The navigator and bombardier never had a chance."

Pete remembers the coldness of the raid:

"It was a cold trip. Lt. Morgan said the mercury went as low as it would go. It hit the stop at 46 below. Almost everything froze, including my gun."

Sam claimed a kill:

"An Me109 came to within 300 yards of us. I fired many times and finally smoke started pouring from his engine. He lost altitude rapidly and then burst into flames."

The crew's debriefing ends with the knowledge that four aircraft are missing from this long and dangerous mission to Bremen. One of the four, the *Barrel House Bessie*, A/C#42-5051, piloted by Major William Gilmore of the 544th Squadron floundered in the channel. The ship was riddled by shells and flak, a quarter of the nose was shot away, there was a twelve-inch hole in the right wing, the leading edge of the wing was shot up, the horizontal stabilizers were full of holes and the oxygen system in the waist was destroyed. Over the channel, one by one the engines quit. But *Bessie* struggled to within 40 miles of the English coast before Major Gilmore crashed into the icy waters.

"We began losing altitude when the number three engine was set on fire by fighter attack," said Major Gilmore in recounting the episode after he had returned to base. "The fighter attacks continued and a fire started on the left side of the cockpit. Sgt. Henry put it out, although he was sick and vomiting from the acrid smoke."

By that time *Barrel House Bessie* was lagging far behind the formation so Major Gilmore headed for the protection of a cloud bank. That put an end to the fighter attacks, but the ship was losing altitude rapidly and was at a scant 6,000 feet when it broke out of the clouds. Almost immediately it was engaged by flak, but Major Gilmore was able to get it out to sea. By this time he had started the right inboard engine again and was getting spasmodic power from it. Then the outboard engine on the same side quit and he was unable to feather the propeller. He couldn't tell from the instrument panel just how much power the engine was producing as all engine instruments were inoperative. He couldn't send out a SOS because the electrical system was shot out.

"All this time Sgt. Henry was an example to the entire crew," said Major Gilmore. "He quit the defense of his post only long enough to extinguish the cockpit fire. He destroyed one enemy aircraft and undoubtedly damaged others. Only his efficient performance of his duties as engineer enabled us to get as far back as we did."

Finally both engines on the left side quit and Sgt. Henry assembled the crew in the radio compartment and prepared them for ditching. Off to the right Major Gilmore could make out the wake of a boat, so he turned in that direction. But all engines were inoperative by that time and *Bessie* couldn't reach the surface craft.

When the B-17 ditched, water gushed into the bomb bay and the ship broke in half.

"It was Sgt. Henry who directed the crew's exit," said Major Gilmore, "and seconds before the ship went under he exited with the emergency radio. Maybe if he could have let himself forget the radio ...."

In about ten minutes the rescue boat arrived and the seamen picked two airmen out of the water and found six in the aircraft's dinghy. Sgt. Henry, and the radio he had assumed the responsibility for, was not found.

Two high awards came out of this episode. T/Sgt. Maurice V. Henry, for his valor, was posthumously decorated with the Distinguished Service Cross. His pilot, Major William F. Gilmore, was decorated with the Silver Star.

The other three aircraft that failed to return were the *Chaplain's Office* of the 545th Squadron, the A/C (*No Name*), piloted by 2nd Lt. Leslie Amundsen and the A/C (*No Name*), piloted by 2nd Lt. John B. Holland of the 547th Squadron.

The two crews of the 547th Squadron, Lts. Holland and Amundsen, had only been assigned to the 384th since November 5, a little over two weeks. This was their first, last, and only mission. The deaths of six friends and the capture of 26 more are losses that will be with the crew for the rest of their lives. But at the same time it stiffens their resolve to fight on until they have defeated those who inflict pain and death on their friends.

Summary of 384th Missing Aircraft and Crew Status
Bremen Mission (November 26, 1943)

A/C#	Name	Pilot	Squadron	Crew Status
42-5051	*Barrel House Bessie*	Major William F. Gilmore	544th	2 killed 8 rescued
42-37762	*Chaplain's Office*	2nd Lt. Charles A. Zitnik	545th	1 killed 9 prisoners
42-29987	(*No Name*)	2nd Lt. Leslie O. Amundsen	547th	2 killed 8 escaped
42-31042	(*No Name*)	2nd Lt. John B. Holland	547th	1 killed 9 prisoners

Total = 6 killed, 18 prisoners, 8 escaped, and 8 rescued.

In Memory

544th Squadron

The deaths on the *Fortress* piloted by Major Gilmore, which crashed in the English Channel, were T/Sgt. Maurice V. Henry, Engineer and S/Sgt. James E. Bucher, Waist Gunner.

545th Squadron

2nd Lt. Charles A. Zitnik, Pilot; 2nd Lt. Richard G. Tesvan, Co-pilot; 2nd Lt. Rodney R. Helms, Navigtator; 2nd Lt. Frank A. Pelley, Jr., Bombardier; S/Sgt. Lewis E. McNett, Jr., Radio Operator; S/Sgt. Anthony J. Roberts, Engineer; S/Sgt. Robert H. Rimmer, Jr., Ball Turret Gunner; Sgt.

Clarence R. Lehmann, Tail Gunner; and Sgts. Florian S. Pretasiewicz and Edgar Strauss, Jr., Waist Gunners.

547th Squadron

2nd Lt. John B. Holland, Pilot; 2nd Lt. Frank A. Procopie, Co-pilot; 2nd Lt. Charles T. East, Navigator; 2nd Lt. Thomas G. Witt, Bombardier; S/Sgt. Walter J. Lazars, Radio Operator; S/Sgt. James H. Winfree, Engineer; S/Sgt. Lennon C. Lisenby, Ball Turret Gunner; Sgt. Julian Britt, Tail Gunner; S/Sgts. Stanley Duzynski and Angus L. Newman, Waist Gunners.

2nd Lt. Leslie O. Amundson, Pilot; 2nd Lt. William T. Marcelle, Co-pilot; 2nd Lt. Frank Faragasses, Navigator; 2nd Lt. Robert V. Coughlin, Bombardier; S/Sgt. Murray M. Howard, Radio Operator; S/Sgt. Lawrence F. Lord, Engineer; Pvt. James Cullety, Ball Turret Gunner; Sgt. Cecil W. Brown, Tail Gunner; and Sgts. Frank A. Chairet and Charles E. Zesch, Waist Gunner.

★ ★ ★

CHAPTER

16

Frozen Flyboys

As Lt. Morgan lay awake in his bunk on the cold Monday morning of November 29, 1943, he is thinking of the crew's first nine missions: Emden, Bremen (twice), Anklam, Munster, Duren, Wilhelmshaven, Gelsenkirchen, and Knaben. It is 0230 hours and he is unable to sleep knowing he is scheduled to fly again today. He desperately tries to block all thoughts from his mind while praying the target assigned won't be Bremen again. He thinks back to the first Bremen mission on October 8th and still feels the trauma of that mission. He painfully remembers the four crews shot down who were either killed or captured on the second Bremen mission of November 26th just three days past. He knows that any mission to Bremen will be as bad as the last one, for Bremen is in the heart of industrial Germany and the most heavily defended of all German cities.

Lt. Morgan is experiencing combat fatigue after nine hard missions. The fear and the anticipation of being shot down, killed, or taken prisoner is with him every minute of his conscious hours. He shelters these fears without any outward appearance to others. Under constant pressure, he dreads the next mission, for no matter what he is doing, always in the back of his mind is the nagging fact that he will be flying over the channel again and

129

again, until the job is done. These fears however are not peculiar to Lt. Morgan; they also reflect the hidden fears of the entire *Doc* crew. Finally, from sheer mental exhaustion, he drifts off into sleep.

In what seems like only an instant, as Lt. Morgan recalls it, he is abruptly awakened:

"At 0400 hours the OD (Officer of the Day) yells to us. 'Get up, this crew is flying today!' After dressing, Lts. Kaczaraba, Wirth, Horsky, and I proceed to mission briefing in the dark. On the way we have breakfast of toast and coffee, and then head over to the briefing hut. The briefing starts at 0530 hours as scheduled.

"'Today the 384th will go back to Bremen. We are not satisfied we did the job on the 26th, three days ago. The strike pictures indicate our bombs were slightly off target. We will drop high explosives and incendiaries again. You can expect a solid overcast in the target area. The wing will be led by our Commanding Officer, Colonel Smith, in Captain Algar's aircraft. Expect to experience bitter cold at your bombing altitude of 28,000 feet. Any questions? No? Good!'

"I am shocked when the target for today is announced as Bremen, again. This will be the third raid for us on Bremen!

"After the briefing, we gather combat gear and head out to Doc on the hardstand. On this, my tenth mission, I am so battle weary I can hardly function. I must fly this mission and do my duty. Maybe, subconsciously, I wish it would be over, one way or another. After two months of combat there have been six B-17s shot down from our squadron. A 100 percent turnover. Our luck has got to be running out.

"We receive our pre-mission briefing in a heavy fog in front of Doc from Lt. Kaczaraba. After some major moaning from the crew, we climb aboard. Our gunners are placing their gun barrels in sheaths to protect them from the moisture of the fog. Others are checking oxygen masks, gloves, goggles, electric switches, and steel helmets. The crew is still complaining when we complete our preflight checks about having to experience the hell of Bremen again in less than three days.

"The green flare is spotted. We run up engines and taxi for takeoff. Lt. Kaczaraba advances the throttles to full boost and we are roaring down the runway. Lift off is easy and Doc makes a gentle turn to the right to assemble with our group. Doc is now positioned within our squadron, however, the air turbulence is rough at the assigned altitude that we circle the field. The group is having a hard time staying in

position as we orbit the base. Several circles of the field are required before the 384th is finally assembled.

"Finally, with the 384th assembled, we proceed to Molesworth (a navigational fix in England) which we reach on a heading of 300 degrees. At Molesworth we pick up two additional bomb groups and continue on to Splasher #4 (the next navigational fix). Here the formation starts its climb. The groups hold together in tight formation on the climb.

"The climb to our assigned altitude of 24,000 feet is complete. It is a −45 degree Celsius day and all the Forts are trailing long and persistent vapor trails. They look pretty but present a rough ride for trailing aircraft. They also provide an excellent visual path for enemy fighters to follow.

"Approaching the enemy coast, the formation takes a heading of 150 degrees from the North Sea. Moving inland the formation receives only light, intermittent flak along the bomb route. As we near the target area however, the flak begins in earnest, heavy and accurate as it buffets and pelts our lumbering bomber. Welcome back to the hell of Bremen! Turning onto the IP, the lead division shoots a red flare indicating a new heading of approximately 60 degrees to the target. Approaching the target, we do not drop our bombs on the bomb run. Why did the lead B-17 not order 'Bombs Away?' We proceed slightly past the target.

"'Oh my God,' shouts Sam, 'the lead B-17 just took a direct hit in the nose section and it's blown completely off.' I know, in my heart, that the bombardier and navigator are dead. The entire front of the damaged B-17 was blown completely off and is falling down almost on top of us. We bank Doc sharply to avoid the nose section from hitting us. Human body parts, aircraft metal, and other debris litter the sky. Blood partially covers our cockpit window making visibility difficult. I am in shock — nine missions and now this. Lt. Kaczaraba is having such a hard time coping with this scene that even flying Doc is a challenge. My nerves are shot as we attempt to rejoin the 384th formation. At last, we manage to move back into our assigned position just as the group is about to make its second bomb run.

"We start our second run on the target in about the same vicinity as before. I check the gas gauges over the target and discover that there is less than two hours of fuel left. No matter how hectic the battle around me I never neglect my instrument monitoring duties. This will be a problem on the way home as flight time back to base at normal cruising speed is a little over two hours.

"There are now approximately 75 enemy fighters in the target area. They are attacking from below the flak, firing rockets. It is strange to have enemy fighters over the target where there is a heavy concentration of flak. Once more we are over the target. The shipyards and docks are directly below. It's bombs away and Doc's bombs, in concert with many others, descend on Bremen.

"WHAAAM" ... a direct rocket hit explodes in our number two engine. BOOOM ... a flak burst hits our tail section and Doc lurches upward violently. Pete and Gilly are thrown against the top of the fuselage, then slammed to the floor, which is now littered with spent .50 caliber machine gun shell casings. With our number two engine destroyed, I attempt to feather its useless propeller (prop). (Feathering involves adjusting the pitch of the prop blades via a servo-motor in the engine to minimize wind induced rotation. This windmilling effect could cause destructive wing vibration.)

"Sam, who can easily observe the engines and both the left and right wings, reports, 'We have a large hole in the number two engine and the cowling is blown completely off. The right stabilizer also appears to be damaged.'

"We are in serious trouble. Doc will burn excessive fuel trying to get us home with the number two engine shut down and the remaining three operating at a higher RPM to maintain altitude.

"Now the Fw190s are attacking, again. One comes very close and almost hits us as it rises up past our left wing tip and appears to stall. Sam is waiting and cuts loose on him. The Fw190 is no more than 30 yards away. I observe the horror on the enemy pilot's face as his fighter seems to hang in mid-air. The deadly force of Sam's slugs rips into the Fw190 and it immediately explodes. I feel the shock wave and heat from the explosion. Lt. Kaczaraba shouts, 'Good shooting, Sam.'

"The German fighters continue the attacks. This time their passes are towards our right waist gunner's position. Gilly is ready, leads a Ju88 and fires his .50 caliber machine gun. He fires with good effect as smoke erupts from the German fighter, however, it continues to fire its deadly 20mm cannon shells into Gilly's area. Suddenly, Gilly shouts that his gun mount is jolted as if struck by a giant hammer. He is too busy to determine what struck the gun mount as he continues to fire at the attacking fighters. The Ju88 streaks past and heads for home.

"Leaving the target area, Bremen is below and slightly behind. We observe, through occasional glimpses of the ground, billows of black smoke, evidence of our bombing, and the smoke pots around the city.

"Lt. Kaczaraba turns on a new heading of north, toward the sea. Trying to stay up with our group, we must limp home with one engine out of service and a badly shot up Doc. The bigger problem, however, is that the attacks have knocked out Doc's heating system. We are flying at an altitude of 26,500 feet. The outside air temperature is –55°C.

"When the heating system is functioning you are constantly cold, but when it is out of service your body feels a lower temperature than the outside air. The crew aft of the radio compartment (waist gunners, tail gunner, and ball turret) request permission to leave their battle stations and assemble in the radio compartment where it is a little warmer. Lt. Kaczaraba, on the belief that we will no longer be subject to fighters and flak, grants permission for them to leave their battle stations.

"As Gilly is leaving his station, he notices a strange object wedged between his gun mount and the piece of armor plating that is used to provide some degree of protection for the waist gunner. Shocked, he discovers that a live 20mm cannon shell is lodged only inches from where he stands to fire his gun. He decides to leave it and let the ground crew remove it. (The Grim Reaper had come for his third visit to the fightin' Irishman, but again was disappointed! Gilly's little guy on his shoulder scores another victory over the Reaper.)

"For the next hour-and-a-half we suffer with the terrible coldness as it consumes our body heat. Lt. Wirth must remove his oxygen masks every 15 minutes and clear the ice from his eyebrows. Oxygen mask hoses are freezing and we must break the ice up every few minutes to keep the passage free. After about 15 minutes, our hands and feet are hanging lifeless. It is as if these limbs are not attached to our bodies. Lt. Kaczaraba and I can barely manipulate Doc's controls.

"We leave the formation over the Dutch coast, and immediately cut back on cruising speed to 125 MPH, just enough to keep us flying. This should reduce fuel consumption, hopefully enough to get our damaged Doc back to base.

"I know Doc will not stall out at a low air speed, even as low as 120 MPH. We will try to glide back to England. The lift provided by Doc's huge wings is quite evident when forced to fly with reduced horses. Doc has an excellent glide ratio (for every foot of descent the aircraft moves forward so many feet) provided by the enormous airfoils. Doc should have no problem holding altitude with one engine inoperative.

"The English coastline now comes into view. We continue to glide back to Grafton-Underwood. Soon the field is sighted. As we enter the landing pattern I inform the control tower of the loss of our heating *system and low gas situation. Doc breaks through the undercast at 300 feet. We land under this ceiling that covers the field like a blanket.*

"*Taxiing off the runway, the remaining three engines go silent. We are out of gas, again. A tow is requested and soon Doc is hooked up and under tow to his hardstand.*

"*Shorty remarks, 'Hey, this is getting to be a habit.' Chuckles echo throughout Doc. Even under these cold circumstance the crew still has a warm sense of humor. Raid number ten is now history.*

"*As we stand outside of Doc our bodies are quite numb from the severe cold temperatures experienced on the flight home. Fingers and toes are black on most of the crew. We have a difficult time standing because of the numbness in our legs and feet. We are a pitiful sight as ten frozen fly-boys struggle to climb into the ambulance to take us to the base infirmary.*

"*At the infirmary we are examined by the medic and informed that we have a bad case of frostbite on our hands and feet. He assures us that we will not lose any limbs and also informs us that he would recommend to the medical officer that we be given a week off to recoup. Next, we stumble to debriefing.*

"*In the debriefing room, with several other returning crews, we warm up somewhat and start to get a touch of sensation back into our bodies. At an adjoining table, I overhear 1st Lt. Francis Witt, "Jr., Co-pilot, say: 'I won't thaw out for six months. It was cold, bitter cold, about 55 below. I've never been so cold in my life.'*

"*From another table, we learn that several other fliers had been overcome by the combination of the cold and frozen oxygen systems. However, they were all revived, with the exception of S/Sgt. Kuspa, a ball turret gunner, who was a member of 1st Lt. Sidney Taylor's crew. He died from asphyxiation when his oxygen mask became frozen. His condition was discovered too late to allow resuscitation.*

"*From a different table, another crew member overcome was S/Sgt. Vernon Kaufmann, ball turret gunner, on the fortress piloted by 1st Lt. Earl Allison.[1] Sgt. Kaufmann's condition was discovered when he failed to respond over the interphone system. He was lifted from the ball turret by T/Sgt. William Clements, the engineer and top turret gunner, and placed in the radio room where he was revived.*

"*From another table, 2nd Lt. Darwin Nelson, Pilot said, 'They used to say it was cold back home in Minnesota but that was mid-July weather compared to what we went through today on that long raid to Bremen.'*

"*As we complete the debriefing, our bodies are still half-frozen, however, we receive some heartwarming news ... none of the crews were missing.*"

CHAPTER

17

English Gentlemen

The medic kept his word and the medical officer approved a seven-day leave in a rest home for the crew to recoup. They were not too happy about spending a full week in a rest home (referred to as the Flak Farm by Eighth Air Force airmen) with little to do and no real excitement. Since they were already booked, they decided to go, check in, and then sneak out the next day.

The plan was to sneak away to London and spend the rest of the week there, however, after arriving they discovered it wasn't a bad place and decided to give it a try. After the first day the crew is hooked and wished they could spend the duration of the war at the Flak Farm.

The Flak Farm is actually a rich Englishman's estate taken over by the U.S. Government to be used as a rest and recuperation (R&R) center for Eighth Air Force crews. The R&R Center is run by a 1st Lieutenant in the ground services division and two civilian women attached to the Red Cross organization who act as hostesses. The rest of the staff run the household and are part of the estates' domestic help. There is a butler, housekeeper, cook, and two maids.

Lt. Morgan fondly reflects on the pleasant week the crew spends at the Flak Farm:

"Our day starts at 0800 hours as Mike Flynn, the butler, wakes us and serves a glass of orange, grape, or grapefruit juice. Next he draws our bath and lays out our clothes. Then, he announces breakfast will be served in one hour. Breakfast consists of real, honest to goodness eggs, fresh bacon or ham, potatoes, pancakes, or toast. After breakfast a variety of activities are available for participation including tennis, skeet, badminton, and billiards.

"The first day starts off with a real English fox hunt complete with horses, hounds, and a couple of Englishmen to lead us. We are excited about the hunt. There are twelve horses and at least 14 hounds. I just happen to be the last to leave the stables with one of the hostesses, who is my partner. We accidentally get lost from the rest of the crew and end up on top of a hill overlooking the valley. From this location we observe the hunt as it begins with the hounds running, the horses jumping over the fence rows, running over the fields and into the woods.

"The lost hostess and I, in a couple of hours, catch up with the hunting party after they have holed the fox. The crew accuses me of chasing my own fox. All and all it was a fun day and something that I will always remember because I will never ride after the hounds again in England or at home. Finally, we are back at the rest home. I am rather tired from riding all day, which I am not used to. I imagine how sore my butt will be later this week.

"We get back to the estate in time for tea, which is scheduled at 1600 hours each day. Tea is a relaxing hour. Everything comes to a stop and everyone congregates in the living room. The maids roll in a large two-wheel cart stacked high with cookies, rolls, fresh butter, and jelly, and of course, hot steaming tea. I am already fond of tea so I do not have to acquire a taste for this popular English drink. The goodies are rich and tasty, and, of course, a topic for good conversation. Tea is served three times a day, 1000 hours, 1600 hours, and 2300 hours just before retiring for the night.

"After tea we relax with a game or two of billiards or ping-pong. Around 1730 hours we go to our rooms to get ready for a formal dinner at 1900 hours. A hot bath is the next order of business, Class A uniforms are donned, and then a return to the bar for cocktails before dinner. Dinner is in a formal dinning room that is larger than most of the other rooms. It is over 30 feet long and 20 feet wide. The large, long table, at least 15 feet long, accommodates about 20 people *including the two hostesses who dine in formal evening gowns. The large overhead chandeliers are dimmed and dinner is by candlelight. The formal dinner lasts over two hours. About 2100 hours we retire to the living room for tea or coffee and enjoy a full-length movie seated in overstuffed chairs. After the movie, around 2300 hours, tea and cake is served again before retiring at 0030 hours.*

"The next several days have the same relaxing routine with only a few changes in our planned activities. However, tea and dinner are the same time each day along with cocktails at 1830 hours and a movie at 2100 hours.

"It is sweet irony to realize that here we are, in the midst of a great war, living like royalty. We enjoy a very delightful seven days of rest, but of course, at the end of the week we must go back to war."

During the crew's stay at the Flak Farm, the 384th Bomb Group flew two combat missions, one to Germany and one to France. On Wednesday, December 1st the group suffered the loss of three B-17s and as many crews in the attack on the Ruhr Valley city of Solingen, Germany. Their bombs were dropped with unobserved results, as the target was hidden by a solid overcast. One of the B-17s that failed to return was the lead plane, *Little America*, piloted by Major Maurice Dillingham, the 547th Squadron Commanding Officer. It is believed that mechanical failures were responsible for the loss of the three B-17s that did not return. These mechanical failures forced the crews to break formation and in doing so became easy prey for enemy fighters, which singled out the stragglers and shot them down resulting in four KIAs, 22 POWs, and four evaders.

Summary of 384th Missing Aircraft and Crew Status
Bolingen, Germany (December 1, 1943)

A/C#	Name	Pilot	Squadron	Crew Status
41-24557	*Damn Yankee*	2nd Lt. Bruce G. Sundlun	545th	4 killed 5 prisoners 1 evaded
42-29768	*Winsome Winn*	2nd Lt. Darwin G. Nelson	547th	8 prisoners 2 evaded
42-30033	*Little America*	Major Maurice S. Dillingham	547th	9 prisoners 1 evaded

Total = 4 killed, 22 prisoners, 4 evaded.

In Memory

545th Squadron

2nd Lt. Bruce G. Sundown, Pilot; 2nd Lt. Elmer L. Smith, Co-pilot; T/Sgt. Joseph H. Harrison, Navigator; 2nd Lt. Sam E. Drake, Bombardier; T/Sgt. Curtis Easley, Radio Operator; T/Sgt. Vincent Gregorich, Top Turret Gunner; S/Sgt. John Turner, Ball Turret Gunner; S/Sgt. Albert Brewer, Tail Gunner; S/Sgts. Francis M. Seager and Antonio Gomez, Waist Gunners.

547th Squadron

2nd Lt. Darwin G. Nelson, Pilot; 2nd Lt. Andrew J. Boles, Co-pilot; 2nd Lt. Reine O. Jylkka, Navigator; S/Sgt. George C. Hayes, Bombardier; T/Sgt. Charles L. Snyder, Radio Operator; T/Sgt. William M. Ramsey, Top Turret Gunner; S/Sgt. Chester P. Snyder, Ball Turret Gunner; S/Sgt. Frank Lekas, Tail Gunner; and S/Sgts. Mike J. Cppelletti and Harry F. Cologne, Waist Gunners.

547th Squadron

Major Maurice S. Dillingham, Pilot; 1st Lt. Edmund S. Goulder, Co-pilot; 1st Lt. Arthur C. Harris, Navigator; 1st Lt. William Beenhower, Bombardier; T/Sgt. William F. Sears, Radio Operator; T/Sgt. Edward Thomason, Top Turret Gunner; S/Sgt. Claude R. Leslie, Ball Turret Gunner; 2nd Lt. Ernest H. Boyes, Jr., Tail Gunner; S/Sgts. Michael J. Vedike and Paul R. Saunders, Waist Gunners.

Also on Wednesday, December 1, a training film company arrived at Grafton-Underwood to begin work on the heavy bomber scenes for the motion picture *Target for Today*. This film is being produced by the Eighth Air Force as a sequel to the RAF produced *Target for Tonight*. Lt. Col. Keighley, a Warner Brothers studio director before the war, heads the unit. The film company is visiting various bases for shots of medium bomber and fighter plane activities. The shots to be made at Grafton-Underwood will cover the heavy bomber phase of the film.

On Thursday, December 2, Colonel Dale Smith presented 1st Lt. Lester Hegstad, the Distinguished Flying Cross in recognition of 25 combat missions. Lt. Hegstad, who has completed his operational tour of duty, will go to Northern Ireland to serve as a navigational instructor.

Capt. Dayle R. Schnelle, Group Chaplain, was transferred to the 33rd Station Complement. Lt. Method Billy, Catholic Chaplain, is detailed Group Chaplain and 1st Lt. Donald H. Brown was named Assistant Group Operations Officer.

On Friday, December 3rd, the base received a copy of a letter to the 384th Bomb Group Commander from 1st Lt. Wayne L. Wentworth, navigator on the plane piloted by 1st Lt. Frank G. Mattes, which was shot down on the Schweinfurt raid on August 17, 1943.

> *Dear Sir:*
> *This is the first chance I've had to write since being shot down. Haven't seen any of the crew as yet. Have been in three different hospitals. Expect to go to prison camp soon. Pilot killed in action, for whom I request the DFC. Am uncertain of bombardier, engineer and first radio operator. Regards to all there. Good Show! Good Show!*
>
> *Wayne*
>
> *Give to the Red Cross. Take care of my personal articles. Send same to Eastman.*

The letter was dated October 14, 1943, the date of the infamous Black Thursday raid on Schweinfurt, Germany, in which the 384th Bomb Group lost 47 percent of its aircraft dispatched.

On Sunday morning, December 5th, 384th bombers in company with vast numbers from other bases headed for the southern half of France but were compelled to turn back twelve minutes from the target. The target was a German fighter plane base a short distance inland from LaRochelle. A dense overcast covered area, and in keeping with the policy of not bombing promiscuously in occupied countries, the bombers returned to England. The formations were fired upon by anti-aircraft defenses, although no enemy fighters were encountered, thus, the mission was credited as an abortive-sortie, which is equivalent to a credited mission.

The following crews arrive on Monday, December 6th, for combat duty with the group:

545th Squadron

2nd Lt. Farris O. Heffley's crew.

547th Squadron

2nd Lt. Walter E. Garner's crew, 2nd Lt. Kendall Daskey's crew and 2nd Lt. James B. Taylor's crew.

CHAPTER

18

Easy Emden

"Lt. Kaczaraba, get up, you are flying today." The Officer of the Day repeats again, "Lt. Kaczaraba, its 0400 hours. You are scheduled to fly today!" Lt. "Bill" Kaczaraba is dreaming of the seven relaxing days he and his crew had recently enjoyed at the Flak Farm. But it is Saturday, December 11th, 1943 and time to go back to work for Uncle Sam. This is the first mission since his return from the Flak Farm, and he is something less than eager to get started.

Lt. Kaczaraba recalls the upcoming mission:

"My crew has breakfast consisting of only coffee and proceeds to the briefing room for a 0530 hours briefing. The briefing officer begins by announcing today's target:

"'Emden is our target for today. You can expect ideal weather conditions for precision bombing. We should be able to bomb by visual observation. The Eighth Air Force will put up 320 B-17s, with the 384th putting up 22 of these. Expect the Germans to have all of their smoke pots out. They will try to have a smoke screen over the city to

spoil your aim. Major Raymond Ketelsen will lead the 384th today. Any questions? No? Good hunting!'

"Crews are notified at the briefing that today's bomb load will consist mostly of incendiaries and high explosives. I draw a good flight position in the lead of a high element. Everything seems to be going our way for a change. The weather is excellent for flying, unlimited visibility, calm winds, and no clouds. I am optimistic that this mission will be a Milk Run.

"It is 0630 hours as we take off on schedule. We assemble the 384th, 41st Combat Wing, and 1st Air Division with little difficulty. By 0830 hours, we have completed the forming up and are departing England from The Wash navigational fix, just north of London. The entire British coastline is visible from 15,000 feet. The green North Sea is below and fully in view.

"Doc is now positioned as the lead aircraft in the high element and because of the colder temperatures is giving off vapor trails. At 15,000 feet I witness the most beautiful sunlit scene imaginable. As far as the eye can see B-17s and B-24s are emerging into view. It is a tremendous, awe-inspiring sight. Even after eleven missions I am still filled with great amazement and pride to witness such an achievement of several hundred aircraft flying in perfect formation.

"Climbing on course we reach our bombing altitude about 20 minutes before crossing the German coast. At our assigned altitude the East Friesian Islands and the German coast are quite visible. The formation is flying parallel to the coast prior to turning inland to the primary target, Emden, the German city gateway to the sea.

"The 384th is now being led by Captain Floyd Edwards, who assumes command of the formation when the original group leader, Major Ketelsen, is compelled to abort. Below are about 50 P-47s, our escorts. They fly past our formation on the way to the front of the 41st Combat Wing. More follow and these stay with the 384th.

"Twenty miles from the target we turn onto the IP for the bomb run. The target is now in sight and putting up a lot of smoke, however, the wind is blowing most of it away from the city, which provides perfect visibility for bombing. Lt. Wirth flips his switches and releases our bombs. They are visible as they fall all the way to the ground. Large billows of smoke and fire erupt from the port area of the city. Our bombs are right on target. So far we have experienced little flak and few fighters.

"*The flight back to Grafton-Underwood is uneventful. We land at 1415 hours. Our milk run lasted under seven hours. This mission is just what the* Doc *ordered following the crew's week long Flak Farm R&R vacation. Mission number eleven is now behind us. I hope the next 14 will be easy Emdens.*"

The crew eats a little lunch and then proceeds to the debriefing room. The debriefing begins with Lt. Horsky:

"*The Germans tried to throw a protective smoke screen over the city, but it failed to prevent us from finding and hitting the target. Fires polka dotted the area, however, the target was clearly visible through the smoke. Each succeeding group left new fires behind until flames had spread throughout the entire city.*"

Sam provides his observation of the bombing:

"*I could see the target clearly in spite of the smoke screen they threw up. The group ahead of us had already dropped its bomb load and by the time we arrived at the target smoke was already reaching up a couple of thousand feet. It was a great mass of fire.*"

Pete provides his opinion:

"*It was uneventful for us. Our P-47s were everywhere. There wasn't anything to stop us or to slow us down.*"

Lt. Morgan is quite satisfied with the bombing results:

"*It appears that the bombs hit the target squarely on the nose judging from the explosions and dense smoke rising above the smoke screen. It was an effective job. We were unmolested as far as enemy fighters were concerned. Our escorts filled the sky, milling around looking for a fight that never materialized.*"

Gilly shares his secret on how to end the war quickly:

"*We hit the target okay, plowed right over it in perfect visibility. If we could have conditions like we had today on each mission, we'd get this war over in a hurry.*"

Shorty summed it up best for the crew, when he said:

"*It was a good day, all of our planes returned safely.*"

CHAPTER 19

Bremen Is Blazing

The Officer of the Day's voice suddenly cuts into the silent darkness, "Kaczaraba's crew in here, briefing at 0530 hours." It is 0400 hours, Monday, December 13th, 1943.

Lt. Horsky remembers the crew's mission for today and prays it isn't Bremen again.

> *"We get up, have toast with coffee and proceed to the briefing room. This will be our twelfth raid and somehow the fame and glory seems to diminish with each mission. Crew flight positions are posted on the mission bulletin board and we draw the low formation. This is bad news and not considered a good draw as the German AAA batteries can determine range, altitude, speed, and direction with deadly accuracy at low altitudes."*

Major Alfred Nuttall, Commanding Officer of the 544th Squadron, will lead the low group and is also the briefing officer:

> *"Today your target is Bremen. This is the third trip to Bremen in the last three weeks. We are determined to obliterate the Bremen shipyard*

and today the Eighth Air Force plans to smash this great German sea port. Strike photos indicate that previous raids did not do the job on the docks and piers. Today we will drop our bombs by the Pathfinder method due to the extended overcast over the target. The 384th will put up its largest force ever, 40 B-17s. Colonel Romig will lead our 41st Combat Wing in one of the two Pathfinder ships, with 1st Lt. Robert Leoates as pilot. That's it. Questions? No? Good hunting!"

Disappointed that his prayers were not answered, Lt. Horsky continues describing the upcoming mission:

"The weatherman is next and he informs us of the nice conditions at our assigned altitude and temperatures of only –35°C. No problem with frostbite today — sure! Next, we are given the usual bad news about what to expect into, over, and out of Bremen. Combined with the nice conditions described by the weatherman, it wasn't exactly comforting to my already jittery nerves. From experience on previous Bremen raids I know we could tangle with as many as 250 enemy fighters and also experience an equal number of heavy AAA guns over the target.

"Next, the lead navigator outlines the course for the mission. We perform a time adjustment of our watches (known as a hack) and are dismissed to our individual briefings. I proceed to the group navigation room to prepare all the necessary information for the flight. Preparation consists of the flight plan, which indicates the route and ETA (estimated time of arrival) for all checkpoints along the flight path. ETAs for formation arrival times at navigational points such as Molesworth and Spaulding over England, departure point from the coast of England above London known as The Wash, arrival at the enemy coast, IP (Initial Point), and target times are calculated. I complete my preflight navigation tasks and head for the dressing room along with Lts. Kaczaraba, Wirth, and Morgan.

"As we dress out, each of us tries not to show his anxiety by making small talk, mostly about what we may experience on today's raid. Our crew has been to Bremen three times and we know the hell we can expect. We complete our dressing in blue electric suits, gloves, shoes, and lastly, coveralls. The transport trucks arrive to take us to Doc. We jump aboard with our baggage. With eleven of our required 25 missions completed we are eager to rack up yet one more today.

"The ground crew has already warmed up the engines and Doc is topped off with fuel. The oxygen truck is plugged into and charging the

aircraft oxygen system with our lung fuel. The NCOs, already at their posts, are busy setting up their guns and ammo belts. The officers climb aboard. It has been four-and-a-half hours since getting out of our bunks and at last we start engines. By 0845 hours, all Doc crew members are in their respective takeoff positions. We wait while Lts. Kaczaraba, Morgan, and Sgt. Honeycutt run the engines up for the last time before takeoff.

"At 0900 hours, we taxi out to the perimeter track and follow the B-17 ahead of us to the active takeoff runway. Full brakes are applied, our 1200 HP Pratt and Whitney engines are revved up to a mighty roar. We wait for the green flare to signal takeoff. Once the flare is spotted, we roll down the runway until reaching V speed[1] and Doc breaks free of the runway at 0920 hours. All 40 of our group's B-17s take to the air between 0902 and 0942 hours.

"With the entire group now formed up over the field, we climb through the overcast and regroup on top at 5,000 feet. Assembly of the 384th is excellent and accomplished on time at 0945 hours.

"The formation is now proceeding to Molesworth navigational fix for assembly with the 41st Combat Wing. Sam spots a 384th B-17, A/C #9935, Lt. MacPhail's crew, turning back over Molesworth at 0950 hours. The copilot indicates a rough running engine, which had to be feathered. The assembly with the 41st Combat Wing is complete at 0959 hours at an altitude of 5,000 feet. The 41st Air Combat Wing now proceeds to Spaulding for assembly with the 1st Air Division. Assembly with the 1st Air Division is complete over the Spaulding navigational fix, as briefed, and on schedule at 1033 hours.

"The 1st Air Division formation is proceeding to the North Sea. Suddenly, we receive a WT[2] message to delay the formation for half an hour to allow the 3rd Air Division to catch up with us. We are about midpoint of the North Sea and the lead group is flying S patterns at an altitude of 10,000 feet to delay the 1st Air Division for half an hour.

"Sam spots two more 384th B-17s in trouble. A/C #9826, Lt. Fioretti's crew, turns back at 1207 hours. The copilot reports number four engine fuel pressure is low.

"A/C #4578, Lt. LaVorn's crew, leaves the formation at 1247 hours. The engineer reports the number four engine leaking oil badly, number three super-charger inoperative at 20,000 feet (unable to pull over 15 inches), number two prop ran away at 24,000 feet (and had to be feathered), and the oil line is split in number two engine. I observe Lt. LaVorn's bomb load being dropped on an enemy held island after turning right when leaving the 384th.

"After this delay, we continue on to the enemy coast which is reached at 1300 hours. We are at our assigned altitude of 25,000 feet and proceeding into Germany. The 1st Air Division encounters cirrus clouds that disrupt the formation somewhat. Likewise, due to the −55°C air temperature there are heavy contrails, which causes severe air turbulence to the formation.

"The 41st Air Combat Wing is in a tight formation as we turn onto the target IP. We are about ten miles from Bremen and the visibility from here to the target is unrestricted except for a low overcast. The 384th is making its turn for the bomb run at 1322 hours. Lt. Wirth observes the formations' lead group dropping its bombs and our aircraft does likewise. At 1323 hours bombs are away from 25,000 feet. Over the target, flak is moderate to intense. Knock on wood, we have not observed any enemy aircraft.

"The flak now becomes intense and extremely accurate. Inky black bursts carpet the sky like a checkerboard and all seem to be searching for us. I duck as each explodes. Jagged spikes of flak rip into Doc. Sam reports, 'Flak damage to the left wing!' Our B-17 is rugged and continues to fly normally with this damage. For twelve more minutes, the intense flak pelts us. Doc absorbs the damage without any loss of control. No wonder we love Doc, he may not be a fortress but he's a tough old bird.

"Gibby speaks from his tail position as we leave Bremen below and behind, 'The target is smoking, I see black smoke and Bremen is blazing with a reddish glow.'

"Good luck rides with us as the formation does not attract any German fighters after leaving the target. This is in spite of the only fighter escorts we spot — three squadrons of P-47s and one squadron of P-51s observed at 1345 hours after leaving the target. They apparently are on their way back to their base.

"About ten minutes after leaving the target, Sam reports an enemy aircraft at the six o'clock position. 'He's coming up very fast, making his turn into us and leveling off. It looks like a Me210.' This is the first time our crew has seen the Me210, which is a much faster aircraft than the Fw190s or Me110. "Lt. Kaczaraba starts evasive action to spoil the enemy fighter's aim, then levels off to give our gunners a shot at him. Shorty gets the fighter in his sights and delivers a perfect shot. The Me210 explodes and goes down consumed in flames.

"Was this a lone enemy fighter? I got my answer about 30 seconds later when another Me210 attacks us from the six o'clock position.

"Gibby requests of Lt. Kaczaraba to 'Hold it steady, Sir, so I can get a good shot.' The fighter peels off, circles around again, to come once more within range. Gibby gives him a long burst. The Me210 over shoots Doc and comes within the waiting gun sights of Sam. His twin .50 caliber machine guns spit out a deadly stream of lead into the Me210, which is approximately 250 to 300 yards out. The Me210 is spinning as it goes down in flames. No chute is seen. The crew erupts with shouts of 'Atta boy, Sam.'

"The route back again takes us through cirrus clouds and except for stragglers our formation remains fairly intact. We experience meager to moderate, and mostly inaccurate flak in two or three locations on the way out of the target area and over the enemy coast. Our group remains with the 41st Combat Wing until arriving at Splasher #6 navigation fix.

"At Splasher #6 the formation makes two circles. The lead group and high group then peel off and initiate group let downs[3] followed by our low group. Individual aircraft accomplish let down on a course of 300 degrees over the Molesworth navigational fix according to Standard Operating Procedures (SOP).

"Our crew, along with several others, are experiencing considerable difficulty in locating Grafton-Underwood after let down because of very poor visibility. Other aircraft are heading for alternate landing fields but we are determined to make it through the poor visibility and take Doc home.

"A/C #7924, Lt. Stears' crew, heads for Alconbery. A/C #4525, Lt. Boosha's crew, heads for Wyton. A/C #7801, Lt. Martin's crew, heads for Polebrook and A/C #9735, Lt. Cosontine's crew, crash lands at Gettishall. (Later confirmed this B-17 was a total wreck but none of the crew was injured.)

"Wilber requests and receives a heading from the radio center to guide us to Grafton-Underwood. I believe we are now where our base is supposed to be. The visibility is less than 50 feet ahead and 75 feet below.

"At one end of Grafton-Underwood there is a church with a high steeple. We are lucky for we barely miss it. We plan to use the church steeple to provide a reference point in relation to the runways. (The crew had practiced many hours landing on their arrival at Grafton-Underwood and this allowed them to remember the relative position of the steeple to the runways.) From the steeple Lt. Kaczaraba lines up for a pass but misses the runway. On our second pass the base personnel *are shooting flares and turning the runway lights on. The flares are faintly seen as we pass over the field. I'm sure Sam, as usual, is silently saying his favorite prayer.*

"The next turn to the runway is now complete and very suddenly the ground comes into view. Lt. Kaczaraba chops the engines, lifts the wings and pulls back on the wheel.

*"*Doc *misses the runway and hits the ground hard. A big bounce, another, and one last bounce.* Doc *rolls to a stop at the end of the field. It is 1535 hours.*

"Thank God we are safe. All sigh in relief as Sam aloud completes his prayer.

"It was a long day and we were lucky to survive another mission. We exit Doc *and start to inspect it for damage. Sam reports two grapefruit size flak holes in the left stabilizer and one large baseball size hole in the left wing. There are too many small pellet size holes to count (see Image 3.5).*

"Our twelfth mission is complete, only 13 to go."

A jeep picks up the crew for delivery to the debriefing room. The session begins and Gibby is first to speak:

"There were three or four large clouds of smoke. They spurted up through the ground smoke pots, heavy and dark black. We hit some flak and had some damage but Doc *got us home."*

Lt. Morgan gives his view:

"Enemy fighters were as scarce as extra ration points today but we did see and were attacked by two Me210s. Our two turrets took care of both of them. Other than those two, we didn't see any other enemy fighters."

Lt. Kaczaraba is critical of the enemy:

"We've been over Bremen three times before, but this job was the easiest of the lot. The Jerries have softened up, judging by their performance today."

Later in the day, Colonel Dale Smith, Commanding Officer, in a brief speech over the public address system, commended the group for its splendid performance, adding that this organization is ranked fourth in efficiency of 26 bomber groups in the Eighth Bomber Command. The crew survived another mission and received an "atta-boy" too. What a day!

★ ★ ★

CHAPTER

20

Code Users

After their last mission to Bremen on December 13th, 1943, the crew is scheduled for two weeks of off duty time. Most of the crew uses this time for personal activities such as writing home to loved ones and getting ready for another Christmas away from home.

On Friday, December 17th, the 384th Bomb Group recognizes the crew with a Presentation of Decorations Ceremony. Colonel Dale Smith presents each crew member with the Air Medal and Oak Leaf Cluster in honor of ten combat missions flown. Sgts. Parker and Gilrane are awarded the Air Medal for destroying one enemy plane. Sgts. Honeycutt and Polley are awarded the Air Medal with an Oak Leaf Cluster for two enemy planes destroyed.[1]

It is during this period that Lt. Ted Wirth and Sgt. Sam Honeycutt are ordered to report to London. Neither is informed as to the purpose of the trip. Ted is unaware that Sam is to report and vice-versa.

Both are privately transported, on different days, to London for secret briefings. These briefings were the first time either had any knowledge of an organization known as MIS-X. Both Ted and Sam receive information about this organization on a need to know basis only.

Early in 1942, a secret unit was created within the military structure of the War Department. Known only by the initials MIS-X, this unit was responsible for initiating and overseeing all escape and evasion (E&E) efforts of the United States. It was so covert that the Congress of the United States and the military leadership knew nothing of its existence.

MIS-X Headquarters is located at Fort Hunt, Virginia, some 20 miles south of Washington, DC. Fort Hunt had once been a Civil War and World War I military post, however, all that remained in 1942 was a World War I Coast artillery gun emplacement bunker, an officer's quarters that served as the ground-keeper's residence, and the name Fort Hunt. Unoccupied and surrounded on all sides by dense rows of trees, in 1942 it was being used by the citizens of nearby Alexandria, Virginia, as a picnic area and lover's roost.

Fort Hunt, however, made an ideal site for sending and receiving information and E&E materials to POWs, as its proximity to Washington allowed sensitive information to be transmitted quickly to the General Staff. The Fort was leased from the Interior Department for the duration of the war plus one year. By April 1942 the recently quiet site of Fort Hunt, Virginia, had returned to its former military cast. Quarters, supply, mess, and administration buildings had been erected and a full complement of Army personnel was on hand.

Neither the citizens of Alexandria nor the members of Congress knew that inside Fort Hunt the Military Intelligence Service known as MIS-X was carrying out some of the most covert and sensitive activities of the war. The Commanding Officer of the fort, was aware of MIS-X, but had no direct knowledge of what this unit was all about. Neither did anyone else in the United States in late 1942 — for the remaining events leading toward MIS-X's operation would take place abroad.

MIS-X was officially established in October 1942 as an ultra-secret agency under the Prisoner of War Branch. Its finances and activities were scrupulously concealed even from government and military inquiry. MIS-X was given the following missions:

a. Indoctrinate Air Force Intelligence (A-2) officers who will, in turn, instruct air crews in the various Theaters of Operations on evasion or capture when forced down or captured in enemy territory.

b. Instructions on escape — including the instilling of escape psychology in combat airmen and communicating plans for escape to American prisoners of war by means of secret codes.

c. Instruction in proper conduct after capture and to inform intelligence officers of the rights of prisoners of war under international law.

d. To secure information from American or allied escaped prisoners of war on their return to allied territory.

e. To obtain by means of secret codes from prisoners of war still in captivity information concerning locations of prisoners, conditions of imprisonment, opportunities for escape, reason for failure in attempts to escape, and other pertinent intelligence.

f. To assist in the preparation and distribution of kits, emergency kits containing maps, money, and other necessities to be furnished aircrews on missions and to incorporate new ideas and improvements in such equipment.

g. Plan and carry on correspondence with prisoners of war by means of secret codes, which will be taught to select trustworthy personnel from each squadron.

In World War II American POWs would not be considered passive victims, grounded and inoperative. Every POW was briefed and trained to understand that, if captured, he was to consider himself an active resistor, and to constantly occupy and distract his captors through escape efforts. He was to strive by any means possible to relay information to his commander, carrying on the war behind barbed wire. The POW must think of barbed wire as his new front.

MIS-X was a daring program, and its success or failure depended primarily on the quality and quantity of communication that airmen received from their bomb groups prior to combat. It would be of no avail to establish MIS-X if air force crews were not effectively apprised of the new role of POWs. It would also be of no avail for the MIS-X technical section back at Fort Hunt to develop ingenious escape and evasion devices. There was no way to determine whether those devices ever reached the POWs. Plus there was no way to alert POWs to be on the lookout for the arrival of these devices inside a camp. Communication was therefore the cornerstone of any escape and evasion activity. The quality of communication that each airman received, the initial briefing, would determine the success of everything else MIS-X did.

While training air force crews in E&E tactics and procedures, certain selected MIS-X staff briefers were additionally secretly selecting two men from each squadron. These men were taught the secret letter codes used by the MIS-X correspondence sections building. This building was also referred to by its code name, 1142 — its post office box number in Alexandria.

The two men selected as Code Users (CU) for the 384th Bomb Group, 547th Bomb Squadron were Lt. Ted Wirth and Sgt. Sam Honeycutt. Each was given training, a code name and instructed that, if captured, he was to advise his camps Allied Commanding Officer that he was a code user and possessed the means of maintaining contact with the U.S. War Department.

Using the prevailing U.S. mail system, Lt. Wirth and Sgt. Honeycutt would write conventional letters to family members and conceal within it a coded message. They had no knowledge how or by whom that coded message would be intercepted, only that somehow it would reach the proper authorities in the U.S. government.

Knowledge of these codes was the only secret information to which the MIS-X staff briefers were privy, and so guarded was this information that not every briefer was taught the codes by MIS-X, only those who were considered most trustworthy and competent.

Amazingly, MIS-X personnel were able to maintain greater secrecy than those associated with the atomic bomb project.[2] A primary reason for this secrecy was the assistance of an additional department within the U.S. government — the U.S. Office of Censorship.

The U.S. Office of Censorship was established under the War Powers Act on December 18, 1941. Located on the 15th floor at 90 Church Street in New York City, the censoring department's sorting office oversaw all mail to or from POWs in Europe. Letters to POWs in Europe were identified by the camp address on the envelope and the red or purple German postmark identified letters from POWs with the accompanying swastika.

MIS-X obtained a dozen censor's stamps and arranged to have a list of the names and addresses of all known POWs who were code users posted in each of the 24 cubicles at 90 Church Street, where sorters picked though hundreds of thousands of letters daily. Should the name of a CU appear, the sorter passed the envelope to the supervisor, who would then direct it to the head censor. It would then be put in a sealed pouch placed aboard a daily military shuttle to Bolling Air Force Base, Maryland, via courier plane. A MIS-X officer then picked up the bags and brought them to 1142. The code users who decoded the letters were all stationed in the same room in the Creamery, seated at a table that was 20 feet long. Fourteen cryptoanalysts worked at this table, seven on each side, with a wooden partition separating them to ensure privacy. In addition to decoding incoming mail, each of the code users wrote letters to about 20 POW CUs, pretending to be girlfriends, wives, fathers, siblings, or just friends. They each had their own distinct stationery to avoid arousing the suspicion of the German censors.

Once the mailbags arrived in the Creamery, the chief cryptoanalyst would unlock the bags and separate the coded letters from the rest of the POW mail. Each coded letter was then steamed open and the message decoded.

Then the letter was resealed and returned to the mailbags, which were relocked one to two hours after receipt. The bags were then sent to the post office in Alexandria where an informed supervisor slipped the letters back into the postal system for normal delivery. All coded letters were immediately decoded and directed to the head of the MIS-X program with a copy going to the Pentagon via daily couriers.

The friends, lovers, wives, and families who were the recipients of these coded letters had no idea that the letters they were receiving from a POW had been opened or that the text contained a secret message. To them, the letters looked like ordinary mail from a loved one held behind barbed wire.

Both Ted and Sam hope that they will never get a chance to use their code user skills as POWs. Only time and lady luck will tell.

★ ★ ★

CHAPTER

21

Targets of Opportunity

Wednesday, December 22, 0400 hours, and the unpopular operation's clerk (Private Hick as Shorty has dubbed him) tugs at the crew's bunk covers.

He speaks softly, "Get up, y'all are flyin' today." Shorty informs him, in a not too gentle manner that, "This crew is off duty until December 27."

Private Hick replies, "Operations said to tell y'all that this dang crew is flyin' as a spare today."

Shorty threatens Private Hick and he quickly leaves in fear of his life. Before leaving, however, he informs the NCOs that he has a special Christmas gift for this dang crew." Shorty tells him to keep his gift and just leave or he might not make it to Christmas. The NCOs are upset, for being a spare means that they will be flying the vulnerable position of tail-end Charlie, which is usually reserved for rookie crews.

Briefing comes at 0615 hours. It is very brief with all but the essentials deleted:

"The 384th will put up 22 B-17s today, including three spares. The 384th will bomb on the 482nd Bombardment Group PFF ship. We will mass with the 3rd Air Division and bomb targets of opportunity in the

154

Osnabruck area. The primary target for the 384th bombers will be the marshaling yards and steel shops at Osnabruck. Secondary targets are any military targets in the area. Questions?"

Lt. Kaczaraba raises his hand and asks,

"Sir, I request that my crew be designated as a part of the regular formation and not as a spare. We are supposed to be off duty, in addition, we are a seasoned crew with 12 missions.
"'See the operations officer and have him re-assign your crew to regular formation,' answers the briefing officer."

Even for the non-superstitious there is an unsettling quality about the number 13. The 13th mission for the *Doc* crew is no exception in this regard. Sam recounts it this way:

"This is good news, as we will not be tail-end Charlie. It makes us feel much better. For some reason on this day the normal preflight activities drag on for almost four hours. We take off late at 1110 hours and join the formation at the Chesterfield navigational fix at 1216 hours at an altitude of 15,000 feet. The group departs the English coast at 1253 hours, at an altitude of 21,000 feet, slightly north of the navigational fix Cromer.
"The lead ship, on approaching the enemy coast, loses its number two supercharger and the copilot's oxygen system. At 1320 hours, at an altitude of 23,000 feet, the lead ship, commanded by Lt. Colonel William Buck, Wing Commander, PFF, signals us that he is aborting and that the 384th must take over the lead.
"I spot A/C #792, Lt. Cosentino's ship, turning back at 1322 hours, altitude 23,000 feet. The copilot reports supercharger number two going up to 60 inches which forced him to feather the number two prop.
"The formation reaches the enemy coast at 1323 hours according to dead reckoning.[1] Our formation now slips in behind three combat wings of B-17s and two combat wings of B-24s. We do not know whether they are going to Munster or Osnabruck. The three B-17 combat wings turn left indicating they are heading for Osnabruck. Our formation is about two minutes behind these wings when we get into trail behind them. We intend to drop on their PFF once over the target.
"The formation enters the target area. We look for flares from the leading wing's PFF ship to signal the rest of the wing to salvo bombs.

No flares are sighted but knowing that we are over the target area the 384th salvos their bombs at an altitude of 26,000 feet.

"We have been lucky, as flak has been meager along the entire route from the enemy coast up to the point of bomb release. During bombs away flak is observed off to our left about two miles. Shorty reports a few bursts in our vicinity after bombs away. Enemy fighter opposition is meager, only eight to ten enemy aircraft are seen. They consist of Fw190s, Me109s and Me210s. No attacks are made on our formation.

"On the route out of the target area our formation follows the leading wing on a course approximately as briefed. The wing ahead is 'S-ing' (formation flying an S pattern) to get all aircraft back into a tight formation, which, according to Lt. Horsky's dead reckoning, forces us slightly off course. We cross the enemy coast at 1450 hours at an altitude of 25,000 feet on a magnetic heading of 235 degrees.

"The English coast is coming into view and we cross it at 1530 hours three miles north of the navigational fix, Great Yarmouth, at an altitude of 16,500 feet. On to Splasher #5 navigational fix, where we experience dense clouds. We cut right and pass seven or eight miles from the Kings Lynn navigational fix. From Kings Lynn we fly directly to Grafton-Underwood and land at 1614 hours.

"How strange, I thought. This being our 13th mission, I had imagined that something awful would happen, that we would be shot down; however, this mission has turned out to be a routine one for us. I am not disappointed, just thankful to God to be back at our home station. We didn't even have any flak or bullet holes to count in Doc *after this mission. Next, we proceed to debriefing."*

Shorty starts the debriefing:

"The smoke rolled up as high as our formation. It was jet-black and we could see it about 50 miles away."

Lt. Morgan was happy with the fighter escort:

"Those P-47s were making it hot for anything that came close to us. I saw a Me210 go down with five or six P-47s on its tail. He was smoking and finally the Kraut bailed out."

Lt. Kaczaraba tells of a strange event:

"On the way back I saw something unusual. One of our fortresses did something that's supposed to be impossible (this B-17 was from

another group). It was in trouble but before going down it did some fancy acrobatics, including a barrel roll. I saw six chutes."

During debriefing, the crew receives bad news from the debriefing officer:

"The primary target for our bombers was the marshaling yards and steel shops at Osnabruck, however, some doubt exists as to whether the intended point was bombed. The reason for the doubts are that when our Pathfinder (PPF) ship aborted and we were forced to bomb by dead reckoning, the precision was reduced considerably. It is believed that this group dropped its explosives on a village marshaling center northwest of Osnabruck, with results that cannot be immediately assessed. In other words, we are not quite sure where our bombs landed."

It had been a good mission to begin the upcoming peaceful Christmas holidays. The crew will try and enjoy their remaining days off until December 27th, when they go back on duty.

★ ★ ★

CHAPTER

22

Private Hick's Revenge

By the end of the year the Eighth Air Force is attempting to destroy some highly secret targets, the emplacements from which Germany is launching her vengeance weapons against England. Such a target is assigned to the 384th to take place the day before Christmas, 1943. The mission will be to fly to Croisette, in the Abbeville area of France.

The *Doc* crew plans on sleeping in with three remaining days of their official off-duty time. By Christmas eve, Friday, December 24, 1943, the men are content as each has completed gift buying long ago and sent presents stateside to families and loved ones.

Shorty remembers this Christmas eve:

"It is 0800 hours and could it be, yes, it is, a rap on our hut door. It is none other than Private Hick.

"Fearfully he utters the words that no one wants to hear, 'Get up, y'all are flyin' today.'

"Once again, I inform him that we are off duty until December 27th.

"He replies in his worst southern drawl, 'Y'all better get up now, y'all gonna be a spare again today.'

"Once more, I bestow verbal abuse upon Private Hick. As he turns to leave our hut, he unexpectedly stops at the door and proclaims, 'Here is that special Christmas present I promised y'all last time.' He then reads from a handwritten piece of paper:

'Twas the Day Before Xmas

'Twas the day before Xmas
and all through the hut,
Not a sergeant was stirring,
not even Honeycutt.

Yawl's Doc is parked
on the hardstand with care.
In hopes that this dang crew
soon would be there.

Each sergeant is nestled
all snug in his bunk,
With visions of three day passes
all tucked in his trunk.

When all at once there arose
such a clatter, that
everyone knew Private Hick
twas the matter.

When, who to your sleepy eyes should appear,
but that lowly private,
that ya'll loathe so dear.

Y'all get up, so lively and quick!
Y'all knew in a moment
it was little old Private Hick.
Y'all cuss me to leave,
but back I came,
to whistle and shout,
and call y'all by name:

Now Shorty, now Pete,
now Gibby and Gilly!
On Wilber and Sam!
To the briefing, to the runway!
Now, fly away, fly away,
fly away, y'all!

"By now we are fully awake and amazed that, not only can Private Hick read, but he can write poetry as well. We are all dumbfounded, and for once I have no retort."

Still in disbelief, but as directed by Private Hick's poem, the crew proceeds to the briefing room. The briefing officer begins:

"Our target for today is Croisette, France. It is of utmost importance. Croisette is a small village about 15 miles inside of France. It is home of one of the secret weapons sites used by Hitler to fire rockets against England in retaliation for the destruction of German cities. This raid will call for precision pinpoint bombing because of its minute size. The 384th will put up 30 aircraft, including three spares. Bombs away will be from a very low altitude, 12,000 feet.

"Operation's planning has been waiting for good weather for several weeks and today we have perfect weather in all respects. S-2, has been trying for months to find the German rocket site and Croisette is it. Their job is done, now its up to each of you to destroy the site. Major Raymond Ketelsen will lead the group. Questions? No? Dismissed!"

Shorty continues to narrate the mission:

"Briefing now finished, we proceed to our assigned B-17 for last minute checks and crew briefing. Lt. Kaczaraba informs us that we will be flying as a spare which means flying the tail-end Charlie position. He didn't protest in this instance for two reasons. We will only be over enemy territory for 15 minutes and he didn't want to force operations' plans to be revised. We understand and no one questions his judgment; he continues to have our full confidence.

"The bomb crew is still loading our assigned aircraft so we have a little spare time on our hands. Gilly informs our officers of Private Hick's 'Twas the Day Before Xmas poem. They are amazed that he could compose such a poem and all enjoy a good laugh.

"When the bomb loading is finished and we have completed our preflights, we climb aboard for our 14th mission; only eleven to go.

"The targets today are scattered all over northwestern France with concentration on the Pas de Calais area. In addition to the 384th, the rest of the Eighth Air Force will be bombing on those targets. I suspect

the Germans will defend these strategic sites with everything they can muster.

"The 384th takeoff time is scheduled late this morning, (from 1100 to 1200 hours), in keeping with the brevity of the raid. Around 1220 hours, the 384th is assembled over the field without difficulty. Rendezvous with the 41st Combat Wing and 1st Air Division is made at the briefed time.

"We are now climbing, on course, from the navigational fix Molesworth to Leamington at a normal rate of speed. The formation departs the English coast at 1306 hours at an altitude of 12,000 feet near the navigational fix Beachy Head.

"Suddenly a voice over the interphones anxiously announces: 'Lt. Kaczaraba, our oxygen system is malfunctioning. The system pressure is below minimum. I recharged it to 250 pounds but it again dropped to 120 pounds in less than 15 minutes.' It is Sam.

"Lt. Kaczaraba, on hearing this warning, notifies the lead aircraft that we must turn back. We do so at 1308 hours over Beachy Head at an altitude of 11,000 feet.

"Today we are flying the assigned A/C#7924 as a spare. We did not know all the details of this B-17 as we did Doc, however, the oxygen system had checked out satisfactorily during preflight.

"Immediately after we abort, A/C #9686, Lt. Outen's crew, also a spare, turns back at 1310 hours over Beachy Head at an altitude of 11,000 feet. In addition, A/C #3087, Lt. Kew's crew, yet another spare, aborts at 1310 hours over Beachy Head at an altitude of 11,000 feet. I do not know why the other two spares have turned back.

"We three spares now proceed on a course from Beachy Head to a point three miles north of the navigational fix at Brighton. There we follow the flight plan to base. Our B-17 lands at 1513 hours. The other two spares land shortly thereafter.

"This is our first and only individual abort, but we had no choice under the circumstances. Without oxygen we could not have flown above 10,000 feet.

"Since we had to abort we didn't get credit for the mission toward our 25, however, it did count as a sortie. It was a wasted trip for us but we are used to disappointments by this time.

"Dejected, we amble to the dressing room to shed flight suits and other gear. Later this afternoon, we join others in sweating out the

return of our group from the mission. All of the group's crews made it back to base. This was the best Christmas gift of all."

It is Christmas eve, the crew had done their best, now it is time for a little rest and relaxation at the Officers' and Zebra Clubs.

★ ★ ★

CHAPTER

23

Orginal Crew – Minus One

As though Mother Nature herself intended to see to it, the weather caused the warring nations to observe the Yuletide season. The Christmas holidays went by fast with parties at the base and trips to nearby towns to visit English friends.

It is on Thursday, December 30th, that the 384th is alerted to go back to war again. The group will send two full formations to attack the chemical and synthetic rubber plants at Ludwigshafen, Germany.

Wake up call by Private Hick is later than usual; about 0530 hours. Shorty is still in awe of their resident bard, so he spares him the usual rough time. On the way to a quick breakfast, the crew observes a beautiful day unfolding. The weather is rather cold but the skies are clear, bright, and cheerful. Sam revisits this raid:

> *"Breakfast complete, we proceed to the briefing room eager to start our 14th mission, again. The briefing officer informs us of today's target.*
> *"Our B-17s will join with the 2nd and 3rd Air Divisions' B-24s and B-17s to strike at the center of Germany's chemical and explosive industry. The target today is the GI Farben Industries' chemical and*

synthetic rubber plants in Ludwigshafen, Germany. Our huge armada of approximately 650 aircraft will cut south of the Ruhr Valley and proceed directly to the target. Expect heavy, intense, accurate flak and moderate enemy fighters. The 384th will be divided into two formations and will be led by Lt. Colonel William Buck. Colonel Buck will be riding in the Pathfinder craft piloted by 1st Lt. Robert Leoates (formerly of the 545th Squadron). A second Pathfinder will also accompany the group. The 384th will put up 23 B-17s including two Pathfinders. Expect a cloud density of 10/10 over the target so the group will salvo on the two Pathfinders. If there are no questions, you are dismissed."

Sam continues to relate the mission:

"Ludwigshaven is a new target for us. It will be a deep penetration of 600 miles flying over flak infested territory and at least moderate enemy fighters before and after the target.

"The good news this morning is that takeoff is not scheduled until 0800 hours so we won't have to worry about a predawn takeoff and forming up in the dark.

"After briefing we get dressed, grab our flight gear, and proceed via truck to the hardstand. The crew is gathered at the nose section of Doc for the normal preflight briefing from our aircraft commander. During the briefing I notice that our tail gunner, Gibby, is missing. Lt. Kaczaraba informs us that in order to complete his 25 missions, S/Sgt. Archie Retherfore, Jr. will be riding in the tail gunner's position today. We are our original crew, minus one.

"We will miss our crack shot but have faith in Sgt. Retherfore to protect our rear in view of the fact that he has been able to survive 24 combat missions.

"Seventeen aircraft, plus three spares, take off between 0807 to 0823 hours as the lead group in the combat wing. Seven aircraft take off from 0824 to 0828 hours as the high squadron, high group in the combat wing.

"Doc lifts off at 0828 hours to join the other 384th B-17s for local assembly. At 0844 hours we join our group leader, 2nd Lt. Henry Markow, flying in the number four position of the lead group at 7,500 feet.

"There is a problem; due to cloudy conditions the group has drifted too far south of the field. To rectify this situation the entire group must execute a 180-degree turn.

"*The group proceeds to the Molesworth navigational fix. Linkup is accomplished with other groups in the wings and divisions at 0910 hours at an altitude of 10,000 feet. Some difficulty is experienced during assembly because a number of aircraft from other groups are flying in our air space.*

"*The formation is approaching the Brighton navigational fix at 1015 hours at an altitude of 19,000 feet. From Brighton the formation turns right and heads out toward the enemy coast.*

"*I spot A/C #560, Lt. Morrison's crew, turning back at 1016 hours at an altitude of 21,000 feet. The copilot reports oxygen supply problems in the top turret.*

"*Then at 1020 hours, A/C #848, Lt. Stier's crew, turns back at an altitude of 18,900 feet. This copilot also reports an oxygen failure (the oxygen filler line broke on the ball turret and oxygen was leaking from the tail, left waist, ball turret, and radio positions). Four men are completely without normal oxygen supply. They must survive on portable oxygen bottles until the ship descends below 10,000 feet.*

"*Now, A/C#886, Lt. Lots' crew, is turning back at 1023 hours at an altitude of 11,500 feet. The copilot reports the pilot's oxygen system is out of service.*

"*A/C #274, Lt. Jacob's crew also leaves the formation at approximately 1100 hours. The copilot reports the propeller on the number one engine ran away (spinning out of control) and the cowling was hurled off with pieces of it puncturing the aircraft. In the distance I observe this B-17 ditching in the North Sea at 1125 hours. The 384th is now reduced from a 27 to a 23 aircraft formation.*

"*The formation enters enemy territory (France) at 1130 hours at an altitude of 21,000 feet. About this time the five remaining aircraft of the composite group tack on to the various groups in the combat wing.*

"*Lt. Morgan informs us that he sees, for the first time, P-38 escorts. On other missions, such as the last three raids, we had P-47s as our fighter support.*

"*So far no enemy flak or fighters have been encountered. Approaching the German target at 1153 hours, the flak begins and quickly intensifies.*

"*The bomb run starts at 1200 hours and it's bombs away on PFF at 1201 hours from an altitude of 22,000 feet on a magnetic heading of 180-degrees. There is a 10/10 cloud cover over the target so the bombing results are unobserved.*

"*The flak is still intense and Doc is being tossed to and fro by the shock waves from the bursting near misses, followed by the clatter of metallic hail against the aluminum fuselage. So far there are no reports of casualties among the crew.*

"*With a right-hand turn off the target the formation heads back to England on course along the briefed route. Looking back we observe large columns of smoke rising through the clouds from the bomb strikes far below. The flak continues, but now in moderation as we exit the area as fast as we can hoping to avoid encounters with enemy fighters. Lady Luck holds as we clear the target area some 15 miles behind. The Fatherland is now behind us as we cross into Nazi-occupied France.*

"*Suddenly seven fighters jump the formation as we enter French airspace. Two of them peel off and dive through the formation. Four others join these two.*

"*Gilly shouts, 'Two o'clock high, 109s.' They attack our group, centering their fire on the tail-end Charlies. Now they come at our crew, guns blazing from 200 to 300 yards out. We give them a volley of lead. They peel off and head for home. Not much fight in them today.*

"*The undercast has now cleared up and we have an unobstructed view of western France and the channel. It is 1412 hours. Meager flak is encountered about twelve miles southwest of Amiens, France.*

"*The formation crosses the enemy coast (France) at 1425 hours at an altitude of 22,000 feet. Let down begins at 1426 hours, altitude 10,000 feet. At 1500 hours, Doc plants his wheels on English soil. We're home again with mission 14 complete and with only slight damage to Doc. The entire crew is unscathed.*

"*In spite of our crew's good fortune, some of the other 384th B-17s did not make it back to Grafton-Underwood this day. A/C #888, Lt. Knapp's crew, lands at Auconbury due to a shortage of fuel. A/C #259, Lt. Cosentino's crew, lands at Gatwick with number four engine out. A/C #784, Lt. Larsen's crew, and A/C #703, Lt. West's crew, lands at Thurleigh due to gasoline shortage. We are most concerned about our friends in A/C#274, the Sea Hag, Lt. Jacob's crew, which ditched in the North Sea.*

"*Tired and thankful to have lived through another day in hell over Germany, we head for debriefing. Coffee and sandwiches are offered at the debriefing and we accept them as it had been a long, cold, and hungry trip.*"

Shorty speaks of that damn flak:

"Our bombs fell right in the center of as heavy a flak concentration as I have seen. I couldn't see the target due to the undercast but those antiaircraft guns weren't there to protect an area of grass and trees. The flak was heavy over the target, but we had good fighter support."

The substitute tail gunner, Sgt. Retherfore, who has now completed his operational tour of 25 missions, speaks of the bone-chilling cold:

"The worst part of the whole trip was that it was a little chilly — 20 degrees below zero. I saw only one plane over Germany that was an enemy fighter. It came out of the clouds and was immediately pounced on by one of our P-47s. It wasn't even a dog fight because the P-47 pilot sent the enemy fighter down in flames before it had a chance to fight back."

With the debriefing over, the crew trudges to their huts to rest their tired bodies. They still do not know the details regarding the *Sea Hag*, Lt. Jacob's ship, or the fate of the crew. They expect the worst, for life is brief in the North Sea in the dead of winter.

CHAPTER 24

Army versus Navy

The last day of 1943 brought with it the crew's last raid of the year and a very unusual one. As they lay sleeping on a cold, cloudy Friday morning, December 31, 1943, a jeep pulls up outside the hut to wake them up, as usual, on mission day.

Lt. Kaczaraba is our host for this unusual mission that will bring down the curtains for 1943:

> *"Glancing at the luminous dial on my watch, I mentally record the time as 0400 hours. The door to the hut opens and the operations clerk shines a flashlight into my eyes.*
>
> *"'Sir, y'all are flyin' today,' states Private Hick in his very best English. Sitting on the edge of my bunk I know the others, Morgan, Wirth, and Horsky have probably gone back to sleep for an extra 30 winks of shut-eye. I will let them sleep the extra winks but I can't, for I am the hut alarm clock. I must stay awake to get them up at the last possible minute. Wishfully, I hope the mission might be scrubbed due to weather or some other acceptable solution.*

"At 0430 hours, I wake the other officers and we dress quickly so as not to freeze. There is no fire in the hut and with the temperature outside around freezing, it is about the same inside.

"We discuss, as we walk briskly to the mess-hall, that the ground is frozen solid. Old-Man Winter has finally arrived in central England. The ground being frozen is good news because we will not pick up any wet mud on our boots. We are always careful not to enter Doc with wet boots. Water or wet mud on boots will immediately freeze at high altitudes with its colder temperatures and, therefore, increase the chances for frostbite.

"I have a feeling that this is going to be a long mission today so I eat a normal breakfast. We may not get back until late afternoon so breakfast must last all day."

At 0530 hours the flight crews assemble in the briefing room and wait for the target to be announced. Ship assignments are given and *Doc* is fit and ready for duty. The briefing begins by the S-2 Officer, Major "Pop" Dolan, a former World War I flying officer, hence the nickname Pop. Major Dolan clears his throat and speaks in his usual calm, steady voice:

"An unusual assignment has been given to the 384th for its last mission of the year. Our formation today will seek out and destroy the German blockade runner ship Orsone. Allied intelligence tells us this naval ship is located in the mouth of the River Garonne in southwestern France. Our group will take off at dawn, shortly after 0800 hours, and you can expect a long flight, about eight hours. Today the 384th will put up 22 aircraft, including three spares. The formation will be led by Captain Horace Frink in the We Dood It. *(This is Captain Frink's 27th mission.)"*

Captain Frink continues the briefing:

"I want a tight formation today, including the spares. Expect foul weather late this afternoon. A weather front is moving into our area so keep your eyes peeled for fighters, and most of all, for other B-17s to prevent midair collisions.

"By the way, it's been over three weeks since the Army and Navy game, which we lost. Today it's the U.S. Army vs. the German Navy. I plan to win this one. Let's score a touchdown by sinking this damn ship."

Lt. Kaczaraba continues to recall the raid:

"With mission briefing over, and after individual briefings, we dress out for the game. The crew discusses the upcoming raid in the back of the truck on the way to the hardstand and for the first time openly express their fears.

"My crew has completed 15 tough combat missions and are considered veterans, but seem to have lost some of the cocky confidence they had earlier. In the three months of flying combat missions they have been personally touched by the deaths of 32 friends. These losses are starting to show in the faces of my crew. I realize that fear and anguish has been hidden in each crew member during the last three months due to the constant pressure and fear of combat.

"In order to continue, each of us must accept the fact that next time some or all of us may die. The crew is also aware that we are approaching the end of three months, which is the average time before a crew is shot down. We have flown five more missions than the average number predicted by the Eighth Air Force before being shot down. My crew is starting to believe ... next time, we die.

"Again, as coach, I console the crew as best I can as we huddle in front of Doc. I advise the crew that if each man does his job, as he has been trained, we will survive this mission and our remaining ten. It is Sam's words, however, that seems to calm the crew, 'I have always believed in prayer when I need guidance and I believe the Psalm of David has helped me through many trials and tribulations.'

"And so it came to be that on this, our last mission of 1943, our spiritual coach, Sam, leads us in the Psalm of David, Verse 23. We all pray that the Lord will lead us 'Through the Valley of the Shadow of Death.' The prayer seems to relieve the crew's fears.

"Finally, at 0745 hours, we climb aboard with our flight gear. Four powerful engines cough, sputter, and then fire with a mighty roar. Lt. Morgan, Sam, and I run up the engines to full RPM. Doc vibrates as full brakes are applied with no energy outlet.

"At 0800 hours Doc rolls out to the perimeter track and maneuvers for our assigned takeoff position just behind the lead ship. It is 0810 hours and we take off as the low group of the 41st Combat Wing.

"We assemble over England and the 384th is slightly behind the wing. Our squadron is behind the 384th during assembly and most of the way to the English coast. In order to catch up, I climb the ship at

160 MPH, *which is ten miles faster than Standard Operating Procedure (SOP).*

"Cruising at 160 MPH, *we catch up with the group before reaching the first navigational fix at Molesworth. We proceed as briefed and the formation arrives on a line Molesworth to North Hampton at 0905 hours at an altitude of 4,000 feet. The formation departs the English coast at 1002 hours at an altitude of 9,300 feet.*

"We cross into enemy territory (the French coast) at 1024 hours at an altitude of 12,500 feet. The 384th does not encounter any flak or enemy fighters in route to the target area which is 60 miles north-northwest of Bordeaux, France.

"At approximately 1036 hours, Gibby, well rested from his day off yesterday, cracks over the interphone, 'Bad guys attacking another group at five o'clock low.' None attack us.

"The 384th's fighter escort is nowhere to be seen. Still the German fighters do not attack. They stay just outside the range of our guns. The enemy pilots observe the 384th's 22 B-17s rotating their ball turret guns anticipating an attack. They know that this means 44 guns are cocked and ready to kill if they make the attack.

"It is mystifying seeing the enemy so close, without our fighter protection, and still they do not attack. It is as if the hand of God is between our foes and us.

"We turn onto the target IP at 1207 hours, altitude of 13,400 feet. Due to a 10/10 cloud cover we cannot locate the primary target, the German Navy blockade-runner ship, Orsone.

"The formation heads for secondary targets, an airfield or other targets of opportunity. An airfield is soon located but due to an 8/10 cloud cover, the formation is still unable to release bombs. Fighters and flak are observed attacking other groups but we encounter neither. The lead aircraft does not give us the drop signal so we close Doc's bomb bay doors and start back to England.

"A 340-degree left turn is initiated after leaving the intended target. Still the fighters do not attack. After crossing the enemy coast (France) we head for home at 1428 hours at an altitude of 12,000 feet.

"An urgent weather report is received indicating London is socked in with fog and traveling north north-west toward Grafton-Underwood. The weather report indicates Grafton-Underwood will be at zero visibility within an hour. We are two hours away from our base. I request and receive permission from the lead aircraft to drop bombs in the channel on the way home.

"Over the channel bombs are released, some drop, others don't. Sam leaves his top turret position and heads for the bomb bay to determine what the problem is. He enters the bomb bay area with the bomb bay doors fully open and attempts to physically kick the bombs loose. With one foot on the narrow catwalk and the other kicking the stuck bombs, Sam hangs on for dear life while grasping the waist high rope lines that run fore and aft on both sides of the bomb bay. After several attempts, the stubborn bombs refuse to release. He is unable to continue the effort as his portable oxygen bottle supply is now empty. He must return to his top turret position."

Prior to leaving the bomb bay area, Sam informs the crew of a dangerous condition:

"'Lt. Wirth, we have three bombs aboard. The latch mechanism did not release. I recommend we leave them in place.'

"Lt. Wirth hears the loud rush of wind coming in through the bomb bay doors into his earphones as he answers, 'I agree. Lt. Kaczaraba, do you agree?'

"I decide to keep the three remaining bombs aboard and chance it to get home. I have confidence that we will make it even in this weather.

"As we approach England the group is given orders for each crew to scatter and find any base to land. It is too dangerous to fly formation in this pea soup.

"The first airfield we approach is the 306th Bomb Group at Thurleigh. It is congested with B-17s trying to land so I decide to head for our base, about 30 miles north. Lt. Morgan requests a heading for Grafton-Underwood from the radio center and we pray Doc will get us home safe and sound one more time.

"Upon arriving in the Grafton-Underwood area the visibility is about a quarter of a mile horizontal and maybe a 50-foot ceiling. I know that at one end of Grafton-Underwood there is a high church steeple so I plan to fly over the base, and if we get lucky, we may come close enough to the steeple and spot it.

"Breaking through the overcast the steeple is now faintly visible. From the steeple Lt. Morgan and I will try to line up with one of the runways."

Meanwhile below and on top of the control tower with mike and earphone tuned to the command frequency is Col. Smith, the Base Commander. The Colonel hears the drone of *What's Cookin', Doc?* engines somewhere in the overcast above. The *Doc* arrives over the field after homing on the radio beacon, which is called Splasher. By now the base personnel have set out sodium vapor landing flares at the upwind end of the active north/south runway and are lining the runway with more flares.

Col. Smith attempts to provide landing instructions to *Doc* from the roof of the control tower:

> "'Grafton, this is Dragoon D over the Splasher. Request landing instructions,' came the call from Lt. Morgan.
>
> "'Hello Dragoon D. This is Colonel Smith. The field is socked in, about a 100 feet and a quarter mile. Do you see the landing flares?'
>
> "'Negative.'
>
> "'What is your altitude?'
>
> "'One thousand.'
>
> "'Okay, home in on the Splasher and then turn south for two minutes. Then make a 180 and home in on the Splasher again. When you pass over the Splasher turn to 60 degrees for four minutes and let down to 500 feet. You'll be on the downwind leg. Then make a half-needle turn of 180 degrees to your left. Now you should be on the final approach at 240 degrees. Let down at 100 feet per minute to 100 feet. When you see the flares land toward them. Never mind hitting the runway. You get all that?'
>
> "'Roger.' The copilot's voice is confident but with a hint of panic. I decide to keep on talking.
>
> "'Just fly out a short distance from the Splasher south, and then make a 180 back to it. Okay?'
>
> "'Okay.'
>
> "'Then when you pass over the Splasher turn to 60 degrees immediately. I know you can do it!'
>
> "There was no answer. I could sense him concentrating on his instruments.
>
> "Now I can hear Dragoon D's engines over the Splasher and turning to 60 degrees. 'You're doing fine, Dragoon D. I hear you. Remember, turn to 60 degrees on the downwind and let down to 500 feet.'"

Lt. Kaczaraba is now fully concentrated on the task at hand:

> "The first pass is made and the control tower is shooting flares and turning the runway lights on. The flares are very faint as we pass over the field for the second landing attempt.
>
> "On the final turn, the ground suddenly comes into view. In shock, I realize that the left wing tip is only about three feet off the ground at

a 45-degree angle. Immediately I chop engines, the left wing lifts as I pull back on the wheel. Doc impacts the ground about three feet to the right of the runway. A big bounce, another, and one last bounce. The earth is frozen so Doc does not sink into the usual mud of Grafton-Undermud but rolls to a stop at the end of the field.

"All breathe a sigh of relief, however, we still have live bombs on board. The crew exits Doc immediately fearing an explosion or fire, but neither occurs. We truly believe that the Lord, on this day, has led us 'Through the Valley of the Shadow of Death.'"

It is 1725 hours and the crew had been flying for nine hours and fifteen minutes. Bone tired, they are thankful to be on the ground and safe.

Several 384th B-17s landed at various other air bases in England after the mission and one had to crash land. Information is provided at the debriefing for those crews that did not make it back to Grafton-Underwood:

A/C 444 Lt. Price's crew; A/C 688, Lt. Dasley's crew; A/C 211,Lt. MacPhail's crew; and A/C 525, Lt.Smith's crew, landed at Kimbolton and has returned to base.

A/C 888 Lt. Sprague's crew, landed at Little Stanton and has returned to base.

A/C 703 Lt. Robison's crew' landed at Molesworth and has not yet returned to base for interrogation.

A/C 848 Lt. Ulrey's crew, landed at Molesworth and has not yet returned to base for interrogation.

A/C 727 Lt. Harrison's crew, landed at Alcorbury and tonight returned to base.

A/C 560 Lt. Lotz's crew, landed at Farwell and has not yet returned to base for interrogation.

A/C 045 Lt. Jeter's crew, landed at Chelveston and has not yet returned to base for interrogation.

A/C 904 Lt. Stern's crew, and A/C 776, Lt. Wolf's crew, landed at Molesworth and has not yet returned to base for interrogation.

A/C 651 Lt. Herbert's crew, landed at Thorney Islands and has not yet returned to base for interrogation.

A/C 073 Lt. Stier's crew, crash landed at Whittlsey, seven (7) miles southwest of Peterborough. Eight (8) men bailed out, two (2) were slightly injured and taken to an undisclosed hospital. The pilot and co-pilot rode the ship down, crash landed and were back on base tonight.

A/C 725 Lt. Rich's crew, had nine (9) men bail out with the exception of the pilot in the vicinity of Ossham, Sussex. Only one (1) man, Lt. Webry, co-pilot, has phoned into the base but can give no further details as to whereabouts of the other eight (8) men and the pilot.

During debriefing crews are also informed of the status of the missing ship from the December 30th raid on Ludwigshafen, Germany, Lt. Jacob's *Sea Hag*. There is good news on this last day of 1943.

When Lt. Kaczaraba was circling over the field on the return from today's mission, another that hadn't made the trip joined him. It was Lt. Randolph Jacobs and the members of his crew who had survived a ditching at sea the day before.

They brought with them the story of an Italian kid who had given everything he had to preserve the American way of life. The kid was T/Sgt. Aldo J. Gregori (Greg) who had been riding as a gunner on the *Sea Hag*.

"We were over France, about 15 minutes from the coast, when the left outboard engine ran away," said Lt. Jacobs as he warmed himself over a cup of hot chocolate in the interrogation room. "The cowling flew off, parts of it being hurled through the fuselage, and the ship began vibrating violently. One wing shot upward and we went into a near vertical bank almost falling into a spin. The *Sea Hag* began losing altitude rapidly. She was at 7,000 feet as she recrossed the French coast. The engine was vibrating so badly that the fairing had started to tear loose from the wing."

"I'll never understand what kept that wing from coming off," put in Lt. David H. Davis, the bombardier. "It was under a terrific strain."

"We headed back," said Lt. Jacobs. "We thought we might make the coast of England, land just off-shore and sit it out. I didn't want to try a belly landing with those wings full of gas. The number one engine kept throwing off pieces all the way back and it was on fire. When I noticed how the port wing was heaving with the vibration and that even the metal was beginning to peel back, I decided it was high time we got down."

The *Sea Hag* was now down to 400 feet and one engine was afire when Lt. Jacobs phoned the radio room, "Here we go!"

At his radio table Technical Sergeant Doy Cloud punched out one more SOS. Then it happened, the *Sea Hag* hit the water. One wing and part of the tail were ripped off and the giant ship nosed down almost immediately.

"It threw us all around the radio room," said Lt. Davis, a veteran of the *Wearie Willie* ditching five months earlier. "The navigator and the engineer were swished right through the radio room door into the bomb bay, then the water coming in the open bomb bay swept one of them back into the radio room again."

"The crew begin plunging out of the sinking B-17, Greg standing by the hatch to help others out. He shoved us out, one by one," said Lt. Davis. "The plane was sinking fast as we swam away and she was just about under when the navigator came out. Right behind him and last was Greg. In the water I looked around and yelled at Greg. He was only about five feet away but I couldn't get to him. Loose control cables had twisted over his shoulder and when the ship plunged, it took him down with it."

The aircraft was afloat only 15 seconds. The nine survivors knew they were going to be picked up as they had received a confirmation on their SOS. They clung to their single raft for 28 minutes until an English coast patrol boat took them on. When they showed up at Grafton-Underwood today they were dressed in natty blue seaman's uniforms, (Image 24.1).

It was a day to remember for it was the last mission in 1943 and on the last day of the year. This was the only time the *Doc's* crew brought their bombs back and they almost didn't make it to 1944.

Tonight the crew will have a big New Year's Eve party at the Officers' and Zebra Clubs and will really bring in the New Year with a bang because they have something to celebrate. They lived through 1943 and are safe and sound at this moment, but don't want to think about 1944 and the dangers to be faced. Tonight they will celebrate the closing of 1943 and the coming of 1944. It is going to be a good year for the crew. They must believe that in order to survive.

Oh yes, in view of the fact that the U.S. Army lost two B-17s due to crash landings and did not sink the German Navy vessel, *Orsone*, the final score was:

German Navy = 2   U.S. Army = 0

Thus ended 1943

This near crash landing incident prompts a decision by *Doc's* crew to practice additional local landings in case they are forced to land in below minimum weather. The practice objective is to use the church steeple as a reference point, then to compute exactly the turning degrees and times necessary to align with the runways. So on Sunday, January 2, 1944 the crew practices for three and a half hours flying just over the church steeple on each approach. They did not attend church this Sunday but came close many, many times!

Image 24.1: Occasionally a missing crew would return, like these from the *Sea Hag*. Still wearing the sailors' pants provided by Air-Sea Rescue.

KO over Kiel

On Tuesday, January 4, 1944 the early morning weather in the Baltic Sea off the northern coast of Germany is very poor. The tail end of a gale is blowing northeasterly at Force Six, and increasing. The seas are quite high, it is extremely cold and there is a hint of snow in the air. A sea this cruel would ensure death within minutes for any unfortunate crew forced down into its icy grip.

Meanwhile back at Grafton-Underwood under their warm blankets, lie *Doc's* crew, fast asleep. Little did they know that on this day this same cold, icy Baltic Sea would challenge their very lives. Sam narrates today's upcoming mission over the dangerous skies of Germany:

> *"It is clear, but cold, as we leave our warm barracks and venture out into the predawn air. After a breakfast of coffee and toast is consumed, we head for the mission briefing.*
>
> *"At the briefing we are provided with all the necessary data to bomb the submarine pens at the Deutsch Werke Shipyard and Dock Company in Kiel, Germany. Kiel is located in northern Germany on the Baltic Sea so this will be the deepest penetration flown by our crew to date.*

"This mission will be different in two ways. First, our crew has been honored by being selected to fly the lead position for the 547th, which will be the low squadron. Second, our crew will be flying the B-17, Mad Money II, which is normally flown by the 384th commander. (Mad Money II, A/C #42-5838, is an original of the 384th Bomb Group and flew the group's first mission back on June 22, 1943 (Image 25.1). Doc is on sick leave for maintenance, therefore, not fit for duty.

"Takeoff is scheduled for 0600 hours. We wait a few minutes for Lt. Horsky to pick up new maps of Germany, then we are transported to the hardstand where Mad Money II is waiting.

"It is still dark as we start our preflight checks. This is our 17th mission so everything by now is more or less routine. Once on board some of our gunners begin to thread the belts of .50 caliber bullets through their guns. Others are putting on new or reconditioned barrels. This is done very carefully as these guns are our only defense and must be kept in good working order at all times. Lts. Kaczaraba, Morgan, and I are running the engines through their preflight procedures. Lts. Wirth and Horsky are making last minute checks of their instruments. We complete preflight checks and are ready to kick some Nazi butts with our first raid of 1944.

"It is now just past dawn and the sun is beginning its ritual across the heavens. Its warming rays strike our giant B-17 as it lays heavy and squat on the asphalt. The time is almost 0600 hours. Off in the still semi-darkness a lone engine coughs, sputters, and springs to life in a mighty roar. Engine after engine follows the first until the field is alive with roaring engines and whirling propellers.

"With engine warm ups complete, we taxi to the active runway. In the cold gray of dawn a green flare silently ascends into the glowing pale red sunrise.

"Mad Money II roars down the runway steadily increasing speed until its tires release their grip on Mother Earth. We are airborne for our first raid of 1944.

"The next two hours are spent forming up over England. We depart the English coast near London and proceed to fly our assigned course over the North Sea en route to the target area.

"Once over the channel our gunners test fire their weapons to determine if they are functioning properly. If there are problems with our guns, the mission must abort.

"Our flight eastward across the North Sea is peaceful as I scan the sky searching for bad guys. Looking ahead I am surprised to see land

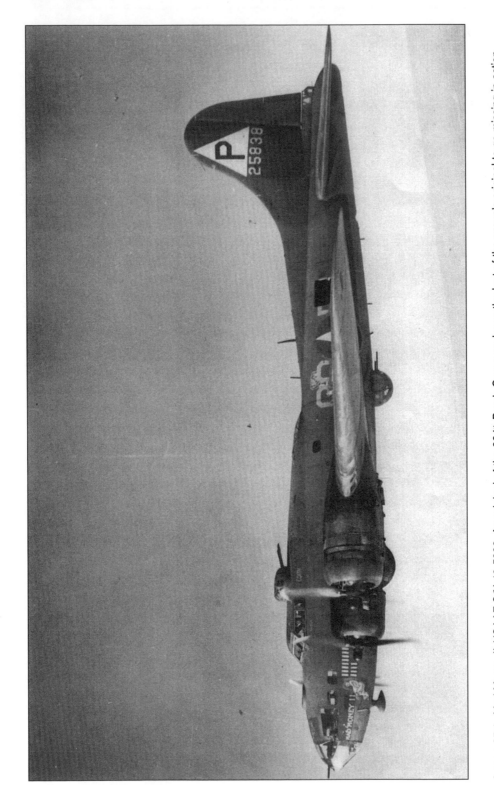

Image 25.1: *Mad Money II*, USAAF S/N 42-5838. An original of the 384th Bomb Group and was the last of the group's original to go missing in action, January 4, 1944.

— islands. This is our 17th mission and I know from experience that something isn't right. I check my watch. It is too soon to make landfall on Denmark. That shouldn't happen for almost an hour. I look ahead for the other wings in our formation. There are none. 'Lt. Kaczaraba, our wing appears to be off course.'

"'Gibby,' Lt. Kaczaraba calls, 'Do you see any wings behind us?'

"'No, sir.' replies Gibby.

"'Lt. Horsky, what are those islands ahead?' asks Lt. Kaczaraba.

"'Denmark, sir. East Frisian Islands.'

"'Lt. Horsky, check your charts, we're suppose to make the North Frisian Islands first based on our bombing approach.'

"'My charts are correct, sir. Those are the East Frisians off the coast of the Netherlands. Sir, I chart that our wing is on a heading 25 to 30 degrees to the right of our planned course.'

"The wing's lead navigator has now realized his mistake and plots a new course to intercept the main bomber stream. At this point our wing turns to a heading of due north.

"Shortly on our northerly heading, small specks materialize, growing steadily in size as we approach. They are B-24s of the 2nd Air Division.

"Our wing selects a space between two of the B-24 wings and slips into a line between them. I observe that we are in a tight formation compared to the B-24s.

"The Luftwaffe must have known where we are heading for we encounter hundreds of fighters at the base of the Danish peninsula. Now all hell breaks loose! Enemy fighters jump us from every direction and altitude, hitting us with every lethal weapon known to air warfare: guns, rockets, towed bombs. The Jerry planes overhead are even dropping bombs to explode among us.

"Our wing stays in a tight defensive formation and the Germans abandon us for easier prey. They concentrate on the loose knit formations of B-24s. These lumbering giants, scattered all over the sky, are not equipped with resealable fuel tanks as are B-17s. They are being shot up badly and are exploding into balls of fire and fall like autumn leaves. It is a sickening carnage.

"We pass over the Zuider Zee (an arm of the North Sea extending into the Netherlands) at our assigned bombing altitude of 28,000 feet. It is a clear day and the German cities below are visible as we pass over them. The Ruhr Valley is now coming into view. The Germans are igniting smoke pots around their cities in an effort to obscure our vision. Since they don't know our objective each over flown city reacts, in turn, with a profusion of smoke pots.

"German fighters are also spotted taking off from their air bases as we pass over them. Focke Wulfe Fw190s and Messerschmitt Me109s from several of the enemy airfields have their noses painted with bright colors consisting of red and yellow with black and white checker-board being the most predominant. We Eighth Air Force airmen know them as Goering's Flying Circus.

"About 15 minutes from the target, in the distance, Gibby spots our fighter support approaching. The fighters provide us with a few minutes of relief from the attacking German planes.

"We settle in for what we hope is a routine bomb run as we enjoy 15 minutes of peace while our little friends engage the enemy fighters in a swirling air battle on our periphery. Then suddenly we are on our own again; our fighters, with only limited fuel, must return to friendly soil.

"In the distance now, looms a wall of flak and we are heading straight for it. This wall of flak appears impenetrable; I pray that it will be gone by the time we get there.

"Suddenly all hell breaks loose again as enemy Fw190s and Me109s penetrate our group. They attack us head-on this time, raking the area with cannon and machine gun fire. The l09s are outfitted with 20mm cannons, which fire through their propeller hubs. Each deadly flash from its nose promises violent death.

"For the next 15 minutes I am in a state of absolute shock. Exploding flak shells, burning aircraft going down, crew members shouting over the interphones, and the concentrated, continuous fighter attacks stretch the 15 minutes into a lifetime of living hell. During the constant fighter attacks one of my .50 caliber machine guns jams but I continue to protect our topside with the remaining barrel.

"Making our turn onto the target the flak becomes even more intense as we open the bomb bay doors and begin the bomb run. Now all we can do is sit and wait for bombs away and hope to get out as fast as possible.

"Just before reaching the target a flak burst explodes immediately beneath us, jolting Mad Money II upward at least 50 feet. Gilly and Pete are tossed about like rag dolls within the fuselage. Our B-17 is now positioned almost directly over the target at 28,000 feet. The time is exactly 1130 hours.

"We are ready for bombs away … Maarumph. A tremendous explosion followed by a hail of shrapnel rips into our number two engine. It *begins losing oil pressure immediately. Lt. Morgan attempts to turn up the turbo-charger to see if the engine power can be increased but is unsuccessful. He is monitoring the instrument panels and notices the engine oil pressure is almost zero. He switches the engine prop feather button to prevent the prop from windmilling, which could cause a fire. After several attempts he realizes that the prop will not feather.*

"The damaged number two engine prop now starts to windmill. This is a very dangerous and undesirable condition as the vibration of the number two prop will be out of synchronization with the other engine props causing extreme vibration of the ship and a possible engine fire. I pray the engine will freeze up but it continues to windmill.

"Immediately following number two engine failure, we lose the supercharger on number four engine. We are now flying with only the number one and number three engines and in the confusion we have overshot the target. Under these circumstances we decide to jettison our live bombs. Lt. Wirth hits the bomb release switch and the bombs fall just beyond the submarine pens into the Baltic Sea.

"Due to the number two and number four engines being inoperative, we are forced to drop out of the 384th's formation. (See Missing Air Crew Report, Image 25.2.) Struggling to keep up with the formation on two engines, Mad Money II *is in trouble. Our buddies open up a path in the formation so we can slide back into our assigned flight position but we are unable to catch up.*

*"*Mad Money II *slips back about two miles. We are now sitting ducks for enemy fighters and flak.*

"From the top turret I watch our group fade away in the distance toward England. Now we wait for the enemy fighters to move in for the kill. I spot two German Me210s lining up in trail formation at the two o'clock position, 500 to 600 yards out. They head straight for us.

"My eyes are focused on the two Me210s as I line up my gun sights on the lead enemy aircraft. He banks smartly then hurtles headlong firing his cannons as he closes on us. My remaining .50 caliber machine gun barks back in response to the lead Me210s cannons. Firing in short bursts, he continues to bore in on me. I begin to silently recite the Lord's Prayer. My crew members are also probably praying for this may be the end of our lives.

"The Me210 quickly closes to within 200 yards before the German pilot abruptly banks left and roars back to join the other bad guy.

"The enemy fighters have made two passes and are lining up for a third. On this pass the lead aircraft makes the mistake of coming in

WAR DEPARTMENT
HEADQUARTERS ARMY AIR FORCES
WASHINGTON

MISSING AIR CREW REPORT

IMPORTANT: This report will be compiled in triplicate
Forces organization within 48 hours of
is officially reported missing

1. ORGANIZATION: Location **AAF Station 106**
   Group **384th** ; Squadron **547th** ; Air Force **VIII**
2. SPECIFY: POINT of Departure **AAF Station 106** ; Time **As Briefed**
   Intended Destination **Kiel, Germany** ; Type of Mission **Combat**
3. WEATHER CONDITIONS AND VISIBILITY AT TIME OF CRASH OR WHEN LAST REPORTED:
   9/10 to 10/10 overcast
4. GIVE: (a) Date **4 Jan 44** Time **1135** ; and Location **5 Minutes past Kiel,**
   of last known whereabouts of missing aircraft.   **Germany**
   (b) Specify whether (X) Last Sighted; ( ) Last contacted by Radio;
   ( ) Forces Down; ( ) Seen to Crash; or ( ) Information not available.
5. AIRCRAFT WAS LOST, OR IS BELIEVED TO HAVE BEEN LOST, AS A RESULT OF: (Check
   only one ( ) Enemy Aircraft; (X) Enemy Anti-Aircraft; ( ) Other circumstances
   as follows **Dropped blazing bomb-bay tank then dropped his wheels on the turn from**
   the target and left formation with 2 E/A attacking with unobserved results.
6. AIRCRAFT: Type, Model s **B-17F** ; A.A.F. Serial Number **42-58838**
7. ENGINES: Type, Model & Series ; A.A.F. Serial Number (a) **41-57485**
   (b) **41-58771** ; (c) **41-57499** ; (d) **41-57893**
8. INSTALLED WEAPONS (Furnish below Make, Type and Serial Number)
   (a)_____ ; (b)_____ ; (c)_____ ; (d)_____
   (e)_____ ; (f)_____ ; (g)_____ ; (h)_____
9. THE PERSONS LISTED BELOW WERE REPORTED AS: (a) Battle Casualty **X**
   or (b) Non-Battle Casualty_____
10. NUMBER OF PERSONS ABOARD AIRCRAFT: Crew **10** ; Passengers **0** ; Total **10**
    (Starting with pilot, furnish following particulars: If more than 10
    persons were aboard aircraft, list similar particulars on Separate sheet
    and attach original to this form).

Status	Crew Position	Name in Full (Last Name First)	Rank	Serial Number
MIA	1. Pilot	Kaczaraba, William (NMI)	1st Lt	O-798517 RTD
	2. Co-Pilot	Morgan, Myron Clinton	2nd Lt	O-678307 RTD
	3. Navigator	Horsky, Marvin Lewis	2nd Lt	O-43910 RTD
	4. Bombardier	Wirth, Theodore Matthew	2nd Lt	O-676902 RTD
	5. Radio Operator	Peifer, Wilbur Allen	T/Sgt.	6883954 RTD
	6. Top Turret	Honeycutt, John Samuel	T/Sgt.	33220825 RTD
	7. Ball Turret	Craden, Solomon (NMI)	S/Sgt.	36256490 RTD
	8. Tail Gunner	Polley, George Gibson, Jr.	S/Sgt.	31203817 RTD
	9. Right Flexible Gunner	Gilrane, Harry Alexander	S/Sgt.	12145636 RTD
	10. Left Flexible Gunner	Parker, Peter Franklin	S/Sgt.	15104380 RTD

11. IDENTIFY BELOW THOSE PERSONS WHO ARE BELIEVED TO HAVE LAST KNOWLEDGE OF AIR-
    CRAFT, AND CHECK APPROPRIATE COLUMN TO INDICATE BASIS FOR SAME.

Name in Full (Last Name First)	Rank	Serial Number	Contacted by Radio	Last Sighted	Saw Crash	Saw Forced Landing
1. Lovvorn, Hollie Ray	2nd Lt	O-748706		X		
2. Stearns, Clarence Grover	1st Lt	O-738045		X		
3. Booska, Maurice Arthur	2nd Lt	O-799714		X		

12. IF PERSONNEL ARE BELIEVED TO HAVE SURVIVED, ANSWER YES TO ONE OF THE FOLLOWING
    STATEMENTS: (a) Parachutes were used ; (b) Persons were seen walking away
    from scene of crash ; or (c) Any other reason (Specify) **Unknown**
13. ATTACH AERIAL PHOTOGRAPH, MAP, CHART, OR SKETCH, SHOWING APPROXIMATE LOCATION
    WHERE AIRCRAFT WAS LAST SEEN.
14. ATTACH EYEWITNESS DESCRIPTION OF CRASH, FORCED LANDING, OR OTHER CIRCUMSTANCES
    PERTAINING TO MISSING AIRCRAFT.
15. ATTACH A DESCRIPTION OF THE EXTENT OF SEARCH, IF ANY, AND GIVE NAME, RANK AND
    SERIAL NUMBER OF OFFICER IN CHARGE HERE.

Incl 1   Date of Report   **6 January 1944**

(Signature of Preparing Officer)
J. R. WYATT,
1st Lt., Air Corps,
Asst. Adjutant.

Image 25.2: Missing Aircraft Report #1483.

from a high rear approach to our B-17. This approach puts me in a good firing position. With my remaining barrel pouring a steady stream of .50 caliber slugs into the Me210 it explodes into a ball of fire. Down it falls leaving a trail of smoke and debris behind. Strangely, I feel no remorse for this enemy airman's death because on this day it's kill or be killed!

"During the melee with the German fighters, Lt. Kaczaraba was taking severe evasive action such as diving, climbing, and banking in order to throw the fighters fire off as much as possible and in doing so ... we are lost.

"Since Kiel is located on the northern coast of Germany, Lt. Horsky believes we are over the Baltic Sea somewhere between Germany and Sweden, but he is not sure. We must now make up our minds what we are going to do. Should we turn to a 270-degree heading, try to limp back to England or try to reach Sweden?

"Lt. Kaczaraba opens up the interphone to all on board positions to explain our situation and get feedback from the crew. 'Here's the situation. The number two engine is out and windmilling and the number four engine is not functioning. If we attempt to get back to England the windmilling prop might cause a fire over the North Sea. In that case we would have to ditch. The chances of surviving in the North Sea are very remote in this weather. If we try for Sweden, I will fly within sight of the Danish coast and we can probably crash land in Denmark if we are unable to make neutral Sweden. We must make a decision to try to get back to England or try for Sweden. How do each of you vote?'

"A New England accent from the tail battle station responds first, 'Sweden.' Gibby's vote is seconded in turn by each crew member to make Sweden the unanimous choice.

"Now Lt. Horsky must figure out where we are and plot a new course for Sweden. The best he can compute is that Sweden is about 120 miles northeast (Image 25.3).

"We leave the target area at exactly 1135 hours at 28,000 feet. Immediately two Ju88 German fighters approach us. The Ju88s are flying at the 3 o'clock position slightly out of range of our guns. This position places the enemy fighters directly across from Gilly's right waist battle station. He anticipates that the German fighters will make their attack any second but instead the lead fighter lowers its wheels. (This is the international signal to surrender. The surrendering aircraft would then be escorted to the nearest German airfield.)

"Gilly informs Lt. Kaczaraba of the signal to surrender. 'Surrender hell, stick some hot lead up his ass! We're going to Sweden!' Our bold

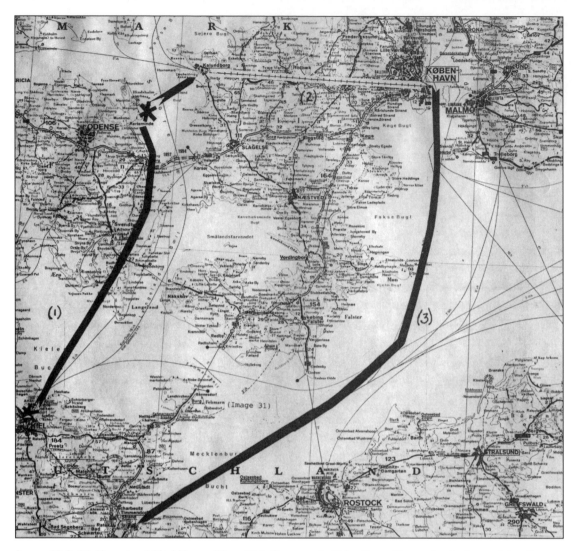

Image 25.3: (1) Air route of *Mad Money II* from Kiel, Germany to Kalundborg, Denmark prior to crash landing. (2) Train route taken by crew from Kalundborg to Kobenhavn, Denmark. (3) Boat route taken by crew from Kobenhavn to Travemude, Germany.

leader responds. Gilly answers the enemies surrender request with several bursts from his .50 caliber machine gun.

   "For some reason this infuriates the enemy pilots who quickly veer toward our limping bomber. They start their attack from 4 o'clock high, one trailing the other. During this pass the lead fighter powers up to the 11 o'clock position to allow his rear gunner a clear shot with his deadly 20mm cannon. Our crew, however, is well aware of this maneuver, having observed it many times before during previous encounters

with the Germans. Just as the leading fighter is at the top of its climb, I am in a perfect position to destroy him. The fighter is dead ahead, almost at a stall, and I hit it with my still functioning barrel. Smoke and fire erupt from the enemy fighter. Down it spirals, no chute is seen.

"The second fighter is making its pass. Gilly is tracking him. He makes the mistake of flying into Gilly's deadly, accurate fire. The fighter is hit several times but manages to limp away in hopes of getting down safely. The kill could not be verified but the fighter was smoking badly and going down uncontrolled. Lt. Kaczaraba shouts from the cockpit, 'Good shooting Sam and Gilly. I think the bastards got the message.'

"Looking for cover in case of more fighters, we drop down to 15,000 feet into dense clouds. Up in the nose of the aircraft Lt. Horsky is plotting a course on a heading of northeast to Sweden. He has no maps of this area, other than Germany, and is uncertain of our location.

"We continue to hop from cloud to cloud to provide cover from any additional fighters that may be in the area. Believing we are clear of fighters we drop on down and out of the clouds at 7,000 feet. Then to our surprise and delight we find we are flying roughly parallel to a sea-coast ... but whose?

"Flying along now at 4,500 feet our two remaining engines are maintaining a cruising speed of 140 to 145 MPH. The number two prop continues to windmill but does not pose a serious threat at this time. These small blessings bolster our confidence that we can stay airborne and make Sweden.

"Passing along the clearly visible sea coast, which we believe to be Denmark, we are impressed with its intricate waterways containing numerous ships and surfaced submarines. Cruising at 4,500 feet, I can clearly see a very large ship anchored near the shore and I suspect that it may be equipped with anti-aircraft guns. We discuss how out of place it looks among the smaller ships and boats.

"From my top turret position I spot two German fighters approaching. They veer off, staying out of machine gun range, and fly parallel to our B-17. Concerned that the German pilots are radioing data on speed, altitude, and direction of Mad Money II *to the anti-aircraft ship below, I report this to Lt. Morgan. Sure enough, a few seconds later, the sky is filled with tracer bullets and flak from below.*

"Lt. Morgan had barely received my warning when ... Maarumph. A blinding flash and deafening explosion erupts.

"Checking for damage to the aircraft my eyes are drawn to the right wing and I am shocked at what I observe. I warn our aircraft

commander, 'Lt. Kaczaraba, we have taken a direct hit on number three engine. The cowling is blown completely off. We are losing oil badly. There is also a large hole in the engine.'

"The direct flak hit had destroyed the number three engine. We are flying on our last engine, number one. The remaining engine, being located outboard on the left wing, causes our fort to slip in that direction. Lt. Kaczaraba now starts to turn Mad Money II eastward in an attempt to escape any additional anti-aircraft fire from the flak ship below (Image 25.3).

"Our altitude is now only 3,500 feet and dropping fast. Lt. Horsky believes our location to be near the northern tip of Denmark and Sweden to be only 45 miles away.

"At this time Lt. Kaczaraba orders the crew to throw everything out, all unnecessary equipment, helmets and ammunition in an effort to lighten Mad Money II. We do so in the hope to staying airborne a little longer in our attempt to make Sweden.

"Shorty now emerges from the ball turret. The ball turret, which is detachable, cannot be dropped because the special tool used to disengage the turret is mysteriously missing. This means that if we are forced to crash land with the aircraft wheels up, the Plexiglas ball turret will explode from the impact and possibly kill or injure crew members.

"Mad Money II continues to lose altitude at approximately 300 feet per minute. Air speed is 100 to 110 mph. The number one engine is straining to keep the plane airborne. We make a difficult right turn northeast and strike out over water. We believe we are between the main northern island of Denmark and Sweden.

"Mad Money II is trying hard to stay airborne. She shudders, the lone engine straining mightily to hold us aloft, but we are losing altitude every second. The realization hits us that we can't gain Sweden and if we keep on our present course we will have to ditch some 25 miles short of Sweden into the cold, icy waters of the Baltic Sea. With the real possibility of freezing to death in the Baltic Sea we decide to turn back and see if we can reach, what we believe to be, the most northern point on the main island of Denmark.

"At this time the decision must be made to bail out or possibly ditch into the sea. Lt. Morgan gets on the interphone to all positions, 'How'd you like to ride her down?' Each crew member responds, 'Roger.' This spontaneous reply from each of us sends a strong signal. We trained together, we fought together, we will go down together, and if necessary, we will die together.

"Lt. Morgan gives the order to ditch. The order sends each member of the crew to an assigned station to prepare for the impact of the impending crash landing. Also, each member in this situation has specified tasks to perform such as pulling the dinghies, getting emergency radios, flare guns, and emergency rations.

"We are trying to nurse Mad Money II back to dry land. With only 200 feet of altitude, Lt. Wirth shouts that he sees a strip of land, about a mile wide, jutting into the sea dead ahead. It is 25 to 30 feet above sea level and protrudes into the sea for three or four miles. Each crew member assumes his ditching position to absorb the impact of a crash landing. Down, down, down, down we drop to less than 100 feet.

"Both pilots are fighting the controls to land Mad Money II with only one engine operating and slipping to the left almost out of control. Engine power is continued until they are sure our giant bird will clear the sea, then power is abruptly cut.

"We barely clear the sea by ten feet. Praying, I wait for the impact. Lt. Kaczaraba gets the nose up slightly. We hit hard on a beach, tail first. Then, the nose pancakes down as our big bird impacts for a text book (wheels up) crash landing on the up slope of a small hill. The plane slides for a 100 yards or more to the top of the hill on the engine nacelles, ball turret and belly. The Plexiglas nose shatters, props are bent and the ball turret explodes into many pieces. The soil, being primarily sand, acts as a natural brake bringing our bird finally to rest. All electrical switches are cut immediately after the plane stops.

"Like a giant bird, mortally wounded, never to fly again, Mad Money II lies dead in the middle of a plowed field. We are ten eagles with broken wings; exhausted, dispirited, and dazed, but … we are alive! The time is exactly 1300 hours. (The actual crash location is 5km southwest of Kalundborg, Denmark, Image 25.4 and 25.5.)

"An eerie silence now prevails throughout the dead aircraft. Then, as if on cue, the crew comes to life and quickly scrambles out through the cockpit windows and the waist exit. Running from the ship, fearing an explosion or fire, we look around and discover that one of our crew is missing.

"Lt. Mike Morgan is sitting in the cockpit alone with dead silence surrounding him. He appears to be in a sort of dazed stupor, but is not unconscious. Outside we plead with him to get out before the plane explodes but he doesn't seem to hear us.

"It is my duty as engineer to destroy the aircraft, so I re-enter Mad Money II to do just that. But first I must get Lt. Morgan out. I go

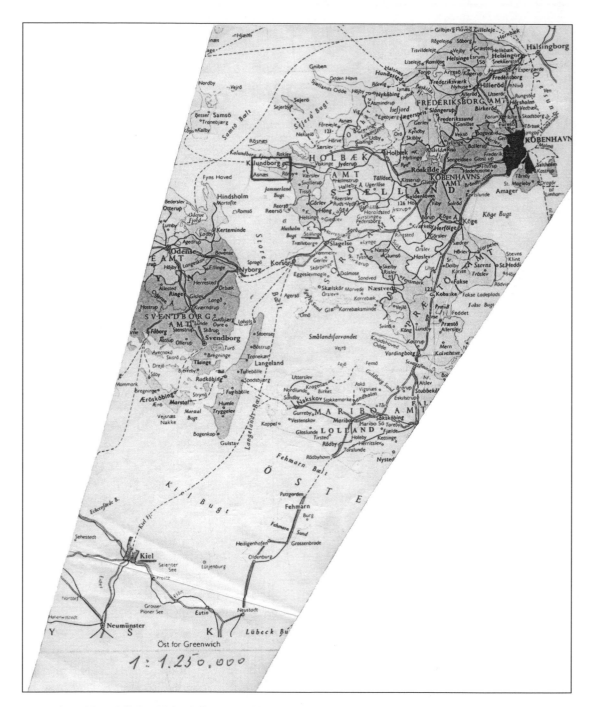

Image 25.4: Map of Sjelland Island, Denmark. *Mad Money II* crash area on Kalundborg Pennisula in brackets.

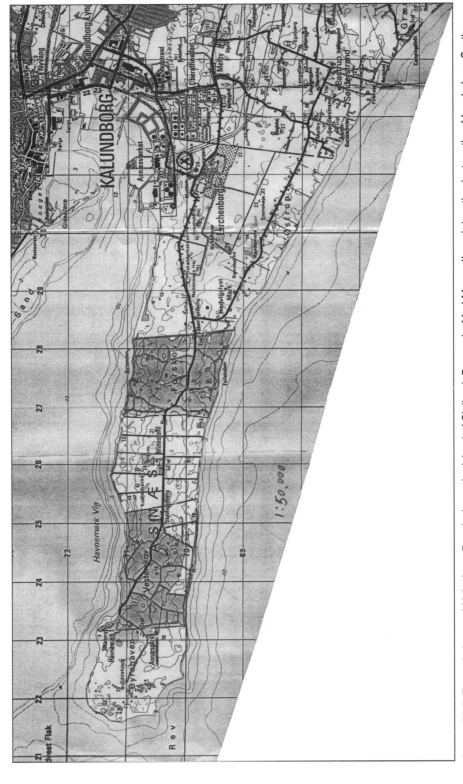

Image 25.5: Expanded map of Kalunborg Pennisula on the island of Sjelland, Denmark. *Mad Money II* crash location just north of Lercheborg Castle (see circle X).

forward into the cockpit to coax him out of the aircraft. He resists. Lifting him gently out of his seat, I drag him just aft of the cockpit. He now seems to be regaining his senses and direction. After further coaxing I persuade him to leave the plane.

"Lt. Morgan, now in control of his faculties, attempts to leave the aircraft. He tries to exit the nose hatch, (his normal escape route) but the hatch is jammed against the ground. He tries to force the hatch open but it will not budge.

"Next he climbs back up into the aircraft area behind the cockpit and into the bomb bay, walks past me, across the bomb bay cat-walk and out the rear waist door.

"As he passes through the bomb bay I am busy making preparation to flood it with gasoline from the wing tanks. The Army Air Corps Standard Operating Procedure (SOP) is to destroy the plane by flooding the bomb bay and setting it afire. The gasoline transfer valve is located above my head. I open it and the bomb bay starts to flood with very explosive 100 octane gasoline. By using a small hand pump over a period of about ten minutes, almost three inches of gasoline accumulates on the bomb bay floor.

"I now leave the bomb bay and climb a top Mad Money II. *Perched on the fuselage and looking through the radio compartment gun mount opening, my plan is to toss a British fire bomb into the bomb bay igniting the gasoline.*

"I toss several of these into the highly flammable gas, none work due to faulty detonators. Next I decide to try our B-17's emergency flare gun to set the fuel on fire. I shoot the flare through the open bomb bay compartment door into the gas, which is about six inches deep now. It still does not ignite and I have one flare left.

"I must succeed or the Germans will capture our bomber to use against us. (The enemy has, in the past, repaired B-17s and then joined the Eighth Air Force bombing formations. They have scored many kills using this strategy by communicating the formation's altitude and speed to fighters and ground AAA crews.)

"Trying one last time, but instead of shooting the flare into the gas, I plan to aim above it and hope to ignite the fumes. I fire the flare gun in a last attempt. The fumes ignite, creating a deafening explosion. The explosion lifts me off the ship and onto the ground some twelve feet below. Shocked, dazed, and confused, I am not injured except for singed eyebrows. Soon the plane is burning fiercely. Assured that it will burn completely, we flee the immediate area to survey our options.[1]

"Our next move is to try and get away from the beach. A farmer is nearby in the plowed field and we ask him if he has a boat we could use to escape to Sweden. He informs us that we are over 100 miles from Sweden. This shocks us, as we believed Sweden to be only 20 miles or so distant. He said it would be useless to try to escape. If we did get away from land in a boat the Germans would not hesitate to blow us right out of the water.

"We decide to hide as best we can in a clump of woods only a short distance from our still burning bird. In the woods we plan to come up with an escape plan. It is now 1330 hours, 30 minutes since our crash landing. In about 20 minutes we formulate an escape plan. We will hide in the woods until dark and then make our way east, which we believe will get us off this strip of land onto the large part of the island of Denmark.

"After an hour of hiding in the woods, we spot a German Army truck, about a quarter of a mile away, coming down a road. We are surprised that the Germans have located our bird so quickly.[2]

"The truck, loaded with German infantry, approaches the clump of trees where we are hiding. It stops near the still burning plane and the troopers jump out with submachine guns aimed in our direction. Spotting us they fire into the woods (Image 25.6). Bullets are ripping into the trees just over our heads. They shout in English for us to come out and surrender. We are only a stone's throw away from the Germans so we come out with our hands up.

"Fortunately Major Dolan, our Intelligence Officer back at Grafton-Underwood, had taught us how to handle this type of situation. In answer to the German's command to surrender, we line-up behind our aircraft commander and stand at attention. We were taught to remain still and not to walk towards our captors as this would give them an excuse to shoot us.

"The German infantry assembles us in an open field behind a farmer's barn. In a few minutes, from up the road, a black command car approaches with two German colonels. One is dressed in a green Wehmacht uniform (Infantry) and the other in a blue uniform (Air Force).

"Gilly jokes to us as he observes the German officers. 'They look like someone out of a Hollywood movie. Their uniforms are impeccable and their hats are curved down in a 50th mission crush. They really look sharp. They look like they came straight out of Hollywood casting.'

Image 25.6: The clump of woods where the crew hid is located approximately 100 yards north of the barn shown in upper right of image. Lerche Castle is left center. Image taken in 1952.

"Somehow, even under this sorry situation, we all laugh. The Germans seem to think we are just crazy Americans and look in amazement at our disheveled but mirthful band.

"After a short march under guard we arrive at a farmer's house. His wife provides us with bloodwurst and other excellent cold cuts. In addition we are given cheese, bread, and a pot of the most glorious tasting butter I have ever tasted. From here we are to be taken to a German Army camp.

"Our officers are put in the command car and we enlisted men in a truck. In transit one of the German soldiers, who spoke excellent English, informs us that they tracked our B-17 from the time we left the formation and that they knew where we were every minute of our flight from Kiel to the crash location. After about a half hour drive we arrive at the German Army camp. Here we are searched for contraband. All items of military value are taken and recorded on an official list of *Confiscated Military and Private Property* forms (Image 25.7). In addition, the Luftwaffe sent a telegram to German HQ Air District XI, Ic/Ass., Hamburg, Germany reporting the crash landing, (Image 25.8).

"Toward dark we are loaded back into the staff car and truck and taken to the outskirts of a nearby village and put into the local jail. The

List if confiscated military and private Property.

PETER F PARKER 15104380

1. Staff Sergeant PARKER:
    1 set (fork, knife, and spoon)
    1 pair of pliers
    1 screwdriver
    1 pocket knife
    1 file in cover
    1 small compass
    1 key
    1 book of matches
    1 rubber bag, empty
    1 dictionary (piece)
    1 bill (50 Bfres.)
    1 bill (25 Dutch Gulden)
    3 bills (@ 100 Bfrcs.)
    10 bills (@ 100 Ffrcs.)
    7 different coins
    1 identification tag

    EUS

2. Technical Sergeant PEIFER:
    1 rubber bag
    2 flies in cover
    1 book of matches
    1 lighter
    4 different paper slips
    1 purse
    11 bills @ 100 Ffrcs.
    3 bills @ 100 Bfrcs.
    3 bills @ 1 Engl. Pound.
    1 bill (50 Bfrcs.)
    1 bill (25 Dutch Gulden)
    18 different coins
    1 identification tag

    WILBUR A. PEIFER, 6853964

    EUS

3. Staff Sergeant POLLEY:
    1 immunization record
    1 razor
    1 rubber bag, empty
    1 cover with photographs
    1 compass
    2 small compasses
    2 packs of razor blades
    1 book of matches
    2 keys
    1 bolt
    1 safety pin
    1 coin
    2 identification tags

    EUS

    GEORGE C. POLLEY, 31203817

    117598

Image 25.7: Official German "List of Confiscated Military and Private Property" form.

4. First Lieutenant **KACZARABA**:
   1 cover with 2 photographs
   1 note pad
   3 pencils
   1 compass
   1 small compass
   1 file in cover
   1 rubber bag
   1 emergency first aid kit
   1 photograph
   1 pair of glasses with cover
   3 different silk maps
   10 bills @ 100 FFrcs.
   3 bills @ 100 BFrcs.
   1 bill (50 Bfrcs.)
   1 bill (25 Dutch Gulden)
   1 identification tag

WM. KACZARABA, 0798517

EUS

5. **Second Lieutenant WIRTH**
   2 screwdrivers
   1 pair of pliers
   1 bag with contents
   1 emergency XXX first aid kit
   1 signaling whistle
   1 rubber bag with contents
   1 compass
   1 pack of photographs
   1 fountain pen
   1 mechanic pencil and 1 pencil
   1 identification tag

THEODORE M. WIRTH, 0676902

EUS

6. **Technical Sergeant HONEYCUTT:**
   1 emergency first aid kit
   1 pair of gloves
   1 compass
   1 bag with contents
   10 bills @ 100 Ffrcs.
   3 bills @ 100 Bfrcs.
   1 bill (50 Bfrcs.)
   1 bill (25 Dutch Gulden)
   1 bullet
   1 identification tag

JOHN S. HONEYCUTT, 33220825

EUS

7. **Staff Sergeant GILRANE:**
   1 rubber bag
   1 book of matches
   1 signaling whistle
   1 small compass
   1 coin

10 bills @ 100 Ffrcs.
3 bills @ 100 Bfrcs.
1 bill (50 Bfrcs.)
1 bill (25 Dutch Gulden)

EUS

HARRY A. GILRANE, 12145636 / 117599

Image 25.7: (continued)

8.   Staff Sergeant CRADEN:
       2 Compasses
       1 Knife
       1 Lighter
       1 small compass
       2 books of matches
       2 tin cans with contents
       10 bills @ 100 French Francs
       3 bills @ 100 Belgian Francs
       1 bill (50 Belg. Francs)
       1 bill (25 Dutch Gulden)
       2 identification tags

SOLOMON CRADEN, 36256490

EUS

9.   2nd Lt. MORGAN:
       1 Emergency First Aid Kit
       1 Rubber bag with contents
       1 pair of glasses.
       1 signaling whistle
       2 dice
       2 books of matches
       1 pack of photographs
       1 dictionary (piece)
       7 different coins
       1 identification tag
Furthermore 12 different silk maps, 3 flash-lights, and 2 repair
kits have been found.

MYRON C. MORGAN, 0678307

EUS

10.   2nd lt. HORSKY:
       1 identification tag

EUS

MARVIN L. HORSKY, 0683910

O.U., 4 January 1944

S/ illegible
Captain and Commander
in charge.

117600

TELEGRAM FORM

DISTANCE – MESSAGE   –OBERURSEL–

NAME OF DISTANCE – MESSASE WRITER: 6-1 1

ACCEPTED: DELIVERED:

                                            DATE:

RECEIVED: TIME:

                                            TO:

DATE: – – –   THROUGH:

TIME: – – –   ROLL:

FROM: – – –

THROUGH: – – –

REMARKS:

S LFZV Nr. 42 1/4   2350 hrs.
To: Hq. Air District XI, Ic / ASS Hamburg – Plankenese.
General of the Air Force I Denmark, Section Ib Kopenhagen.
On Jan. 4, 1944 at 1300 hrs. emergency landing of probably Boeing near Asnaes,
About 5 kw. S.W. Kalundborg/Denmark. Crew of craft: 10 Americans. Capture of crew
Effected at 1415 hrs. – 1) KACZARABA, William, 1st. Lt., ASN 0-798517 T43, unhurt;
2) WIRTH, Theodor M. 2nd Lt. ASN 0-676902 T43, unhurt; 3) MORGAN, Myron C., 2nd
Lt., ASN 0-978307 T43, UNHURT; 4) HORSKY, Marvin L. 2nd Lt., ASN 0-683910 T43,
unhurt; 5) PEIFER, Wilber, T/Sgt., ASN 6853964 T41 43, unhurt;
6) HONEYCUTT, John T/Sgt., ASN 3320825 T42 43, unhurt; 7) CRADEN, Solomon, S/Sgt.,
ASN 36256490 T43, unhurt; 8) GILRANE, Harry, S/Sgt., no identification tag found, however ASN according to statement 12145636, unhurt: 9)PARKER, Peter F., S/Sgt., ASN
15104380 T42 43 , unhurt; 10) POLLEY, George G., S/Sgt., ASN 31203817 T43, unhurt.
Transfer of Nrs. 1-10 to Dulag (Luft) Oberursel will be Jan. 5, 1944.
Air Base Detachment A 54/XI, Vaehrloese (Branch Post 21).

all EUS   117585
                 117586
                              6-3224, AF (s).

Image 25.8: Telegram to German HQ Air District XI, Ic/Ass, Hamburg, Germany reporting crash landing and capture of crew.

Image 25.9: Close up image of Lerchenborg Castle. The crew's first night of captivity was spent in the cellar. Image taken in 1952.

jail turns out to be a medieval castle.[3] As we drive up I observe that it is constructed of stone with large wooden doors and many small windows covered with heavy iron bars (Image 25.9).

"We are taken to a cellar, which, I believe, was once a dungeon. It is dark and damp with small individual cells and dirt floors. The cells are closed in with a high, small window at the far end and a large heavy wood and iron door. There is a hanging platform on one side wall, which is the bed, one small stool, and a bucket. The rest of the room is bare.

"Today is a day that I know I will remember without fondness for the rest of my life. At the same time, however, I am grateful to my Lord to be alive. I say my bedtime prayers for I have promised my mother that I would do so each night. Extremely tired, I drift into deep slumber."

★★★

Book III

Grounded Eagles

★ ★ ★

CHAPTER

26

Destination: Dulag Luft

The crew is awakened before dawn to the shrill sounds of whistles on Wednesday, January 5, 1944. They didn't sleep much last night, not because of the cold, damp dungeon cell but because they were extremely dejected from being shot down and the bleak future they face as POWs. The full realization has settled into their minds that they are no longer free men, but prisoners of war.

Gilly relates the crew's first day as POWs and the trip to Dulag Luft:

"About 0530 hours, we are herded together and marched to a large room on the ground level of the castle. One-fourth loaf of black bread, one-fourth pound of cheese, and hot drinks are provided. The hot drink is supposed to be coffee, but it is far from coffee based on American taste. These provisions, which we believe to be for each individual's breakfast, instead turns out to be our food supply for the entire crew for the day. I didn't feel like eating so I only drank the hot something. Considering the meager rations for the day, I decide to save my bread and cheese.

"Herded together again, this time outside the castle, we are lined up in columns of twos to be marched by armed soldiers, with bayonets

prodding us, to the local train station. One of our guards instructs us to prepare for a long trip to the eastern part of Denmark. I am not quite sure what we are supposed to prepare as our sole possession is our uniforms. The crew's opinion is that we are going to Copenhagen but we are not sure.

"*The trip to the train station[1] is extremely cold as we march the three miles in the early predawn morning. Suddenly, we are ordered to halt just outside the depot. As we wait, one of the guards notices the local newspaper headlines. He buys one and reads it very quickly. He informs us that it is an article on our crash landing yesterday. Somehow, we weren't impressed with our celebrity status (Image 26.1).*

"*A German Officer is waiting at the train station and he assumes command of our little group. Standing in the icy wind, we wait and watch the civilians while the German Officer talks to two uniformed soldiers inside the depot. I observe that the scene at the depot is much like any back home as people are trying to get to work or some other destination. They are doing their best to lead a normal life in an occupied country. I am surprised; there seem to be more Germans in Denmark than Danes.*

"*Soon we are marched by the two uniformed soldiers to a civilian train. Next, we are marched into a passenger car. Civilians are sitting at the opposite end of the car.*

"*After a couple of hours into the trip, I eat a little of my cheese and bread. The trip has now lasted almost four hours. In the distance I see the silhouettes of high buildings. We are coming into a large city. I strain to see the sign above the station as we pull into it. I can now make it out, we had guessed right — KOBENHAVN (Copenhagen).*

"*We are told that it is a short distance from the train station down to the waterfront area of Copenhagen. We are not marched, but instead, are unceremoniously packed into the back of two small pickup trucks. A guard sits in the back of each truck to prevent any attempts at escape. Their attitude towards us seems to get better the further we travel from their base in western Denmark. This is probably because these are occupation troops and they do not have the brutal disposition of combat troops.*

"*While waiting on the waterfront to depart for a point still unknown, we have an unusual occurrence. Danes are giving us the V fingers sign for victory. They also ring their bicycle bells to signal victory. This is heart warming to us in contrast to our cold and dejected moods. Just before boarding the ferry, several Danes walk right past*

Image 26.1: Local newspaper headlines on Wednesday, January 5, 1944 reports the attack on Kiel, Germany and the crash landing of *Mad Money II* in Denmark.

the German guards, with their fixed bayonets, and speak to us in English. 'Give us your name and we will contact someone in England and tell them you are POWs.' The information is provided, hoping that somehow and someday it would get back to our families.

"This ferry, we believe, that will take us to Germany by way of the Baltic Sea is now boarded, (Image 25.3).

"One of our crew members, Shorty Craden, is Jewish. His dogtags[2] are stamped with a large H for Hebrew. This will not go over well with the Nazis. We decide to get rid of his dogtags to try and protect him. The crew decides to also remove their dogtags so Shorty will not stand out for punishment. We remove our dogtags and give them to a civilian sailor on the ferry. We hope he will turn them over to the Red Cross.

"The German guards, once on board the ferry, gives each of us a bottle of beer. Thank goodness Sam does not partake of this brew. He offers his to me and I gladly accept.

"The boat trip takes over five hours. Finally, we arrive at the port of the German city of Travemude. In Travemude we are turned over to Luftwaffe guards who herd us into an open boxcar. Later in the afternoon the train enters Hamburg, Germany.

"Our crew, along with other POWs, is marched to and herded together underneath the railroad station. Here we join other crews that had been shot down on recent raids. While we wait, several additional POWs are brought in. One is bandaged from his waist, up to, and including his head. This crew tells us they were also hit on the Kiel mission. Their B-17 caught fire and they barely escaped the burning aircraft. In less than an hour we are marched upstairs and out to the track siding to board a train.

"Now we experience an entirely different type of civilian population than in Denmark. A large group of Germans, mostly older men and women, are starting to encircle us. They have hate in their eyes and are waving clenched fists and cursing. They start to push and shove us. We are shocked, but not surprised, at their attacks. The Luftwaffe guards prevent them from further attacks. We know that these civilians would gladly string us up if not for the guards. Suddenly, in crystal clear English, an elderly woman looks directly into Lt. Kaczaraba's face and yells, 'Kill the sons of bitches.' On this occasion we are thankful to be under the protection of the Luftwaffe guards.

"Looking toward the city of Hamburg, I realize why the civilians are so hostile. Buildings are completely bombed-out and people are living *in them. None have escaped the daylight bombing of the American Eighth Air Force combined with the night bombing by the English Royal Air Force. The most visible destruction is the train terminal building itself that is almost totally destroyed, including the adjacent buildings.*

"*During the next hour, I observe hundreds of passengers as they fight for each available seat on the inbound/outbound trains. A monotone female voice announcing track numbers and city destinations such as, 'Hanover, Kassel, Frankfurt' is continuous.*

"*Still we wait in silence. At last we are marched aboard a train, led down a crowded aisle and told to sit down at the rear of a car. It is approximately 0630 hours. We have been up all night and are physically exhausted but too tense to sleep. It is the crew's opinion that we are going to Frankfurt, Germany where the Luftwaffe Central Interrogation Center is located. We are told the train trip will be an eight-hour journey.*

"*During the next few hours we are too keyed up to sleep as we pass through Hanover, Kassel, and many other towns and villages. I manage to doze off and on for a few minutes. As we enter the outskirts of a large city, the guards shout, 'Up, up, snell.' The train pulls into the station. It is Frankfurt-on-the-Main, Germany. It is 1600 hours Friday, January 7th, as the train screeches to a complete stop.*

"*Civilians in Frankfurt seem to have an indifferent attitude toward us as our tired, cold group of POWs stand on the station platform. This is probably because they witness hundreds of captured flyers passing through the station daily. The feeling in Frankfurt is exactly opposite from Hamburg, which is strange, even if the population is accustomed to large numbers of captured flyers. Here, as in Hamburg, the Frankfurt train station is heavily damaged. Its glass dome is shattered and its walls are almost completely destroyed. The entire city seems to have suffered major damage.*

"*We wait on the platform for about an hour in the extreme cold. Our uniforms consist of only a shirt (pullover), pants, and flight boots. These afford very little insulation from the sub-freezing weather.*

"*'MARCH,' shout the guards. We cross over several tracks to board a waiting train. Soon we are settled into a car. The train jerks and we start for a trip to an unknown destination.*"

The Central Interrogation Center located at Oberusel will be the destination for the crew. Oberusel is seven-and-a-half miles northwest of Frankfurt.

The interrogation complex at Oberusel is the collection point for all enemy airmen captured by the Germans. Orders from the highest Wehrmacht headquarters state that, once a captured enemy is determined to be an airman, he is to be transported to Oberusel immediately for interrogation by the Luftwaffe. All airmen captured are sent here for interrogation and then reassignment to a permanent POW camp. This center is called Dulag Luft, which means through going camp and is short for Durchgangelager. The permanent camps are called Stalag Luft (officers) and Stalag (NCOs). Stalag is short for Slammlarger and means permanent camp.[3]

Gilly continues to narrate the journey:

"The trip is short, about 30 minutes. We depart the train and are hustled into an electric trolley car. We are told this will be a seven-mile trip to the Central Interrogation Center. In a few minutes the train stops some six blocks from the center. We are marched the remaining distance in columns of two. The Central Interrogation Center appears large as we approach it."

The interrogation center consists of 14 buildings. The largest one, a U-shaped building, has approximately 150 solitary cells and is surrounded on three sides by a security fence. This building is known as The Cooler. Twelve other buildings serve as the headquarters, supply, Red Cross, interrogation catchall, officers quarters, ladies quarters, NCO, and enlisted quarters. The 14th building, located away from the others and surrounded by woods, is the Camp Kommandant's quarters of Lt. Col. Erick Killinger. The end of the journey is in sight. Gilly is surprised at the trip's end:

"It is almost 1900 hours, pitch dark, as we pass through the high barbed wire fenced gate into the interrogation complex. At this time, our Luftwaffe guards turn us over to the Dulag guards just inside the huge gate. As the Luftwaffe guards leave, we are surprised to hear one say, 'good luck.' Did he know something we didn't or was he just saying the only English words he knew? We would soon find out!"

CHAPTER 27

Mind Games

Inside their new home of high barbed wire and electric fences the crew stands huddled and shivering on this cold January 7, 1944 evening. They are lined up beside a long wooden building located behind two office buildings on the west side of the Dulag Luft. A German officer approaches. He instructs the crew to step forward.

Lt. Kaczaraba, being the senior officer, obeys as military courtesy dictates. The German officer then instructs the rest of the crew to fall in behind your senior officer. This is the first attempt by the Germans at Dulag Luft to break down the military chain of command.

The crew had been briefed back at Grafton-Underwood by Major Dolan to follow only orders given in accordance with their chain of command. The crew remains motionless and ignores the German's order. The real purpose of this little mind game is to determine which of the crew, being ingrained in military discipline, would not think and comply with the order, thereby give the Germans their first bit of military information. This individual, during interrogation, would be a good candidate to provide information on demand.

Lt. Kaczaraba simply said, "fall in behind me men." From the main gate we walk to a guard room, which turns out to be a heartbreak room.

Gilly sadly recalls the next German order:

> "'Officers will be interrogated separately from enlisted men.' This is the moment that we, as a crew, have dreaded since being shot down. This is the point in processing where crews are split up, officers into one group and noncommissioned officers into another.
>
> "Waiting for the guards to arrive, we huddle together for the last time, make small talk and promise to get together after the war. Such comments as 'take care of yourself,' 'this war can't last much longer,' or 'stick together and everything will turn out OK' are exchanged. We hug each other, shake hands and whisper a tearful goodbye.
>
> "After a few minutes we are taken individually to reception cells in the south end of this building for incoming processing. It is now almost 2000 hours. Due to our late arrival we will not be processed today, instead, each of us goes directly to one of the infamous Dulag Luft cells.
>
> "The German sentries lock the cells and boast, 'We are better to you than your own country. We provide you something you didn't have in England, your own private room.' I would soon learn why the guards thought this to be so humorous. They are correct, it is a private room — solitary confinement. That's about as private as you can get."

This building contains three wings used for solitary confinement and is called kuhler in German. The German word kuhler sounds like "cooler" in English so the POWs nicknamed any solitary confinement building, cooler. The cooler cells are very small and only large enough for a cot, small table, and a chair. The cell is eight feet long and five feet wide with a small window close to the ceiling and a solid door with a very small window at the top. Lt. Morgan recalls his first night in the Dulag Luft cell:

> "Late in the evening a German officer, posing as a Red Cross worker, comes into my cell with papers he wants to fill out. He says it is for the Red Cross. I give him my name, rank, and serial number. Then he asks me what bomb group I flew with in England. I reply, 'I don't remember.' This upsets him and he leaves. That night the temperature in my cell is normal and I enjoy a good night's rest."

That same night the rest of the crew also receives a fake Red Cross worker's visit. Gilly settles into his private room and relates his first night's experience:

"My cell is about eight feet by four feet. Eight feet up the wall is a window about 24 inches square. The first thing I notice is how hot the cell is, about 95 to 100 degrees.

"This lasts for a couple of hours and then the temperature drops to 40 degrees. The lower temperature is maintained for a couple hours and then increases back to around 100. This cycling continues all night."

Gilly didn't know at the time but this cycling of temperatures would go on for ten more days. Sam recalls his first day at Dulag Luft:

"Saturday, January 8th and I am awakened about 0700 hours to the sound of a metal tray sliding under my cell door. As part of the special treatment to go with the private room, I am given two slices of black bread, slightly covered with mold and with artificial margarine spread on it to hide the mold. The bread tasted like sawdust because it is mostly (20 percent) sawdust! The margarine tasted like axle grease, which was probably stolen from some German vehicle that is now stranded somewhere with a frozen axle. But worst of all was the Kraut's ersatz (artificial) coffee. Four letter words can't begin to describe how this concoction tasted! I am told that this coffee was made from grain such as rye, barley, and acorns.

"After my special breakfast I am marched back to the same building on the west side of the camp that we were to be processed in yesterday. I am taken to a reception cell in the south wing of the building for processing. Here I am photographed, fingerprinted, and instructed to strip down to shorts. Prior to stripping, any personal property is laid on a table. I am thankful that we got rid of Shorty's dogtags back in Denmark. If the Krauts discover Shorty's religion he would not leave this Dulag Luft with us. It is a practice of the Germans to retain Jews for later internment in concentration camps. As I stand shivering in my birthday suit the guards are going through each article of clothing in great detail. Every inch of clothing is examined for any and all types of contraband that might be used for escape. All items of government issued clothing are confiscated but I am allowed to keep my trousers, shirt, shoes, socks, and cap. This entire process lasts about three hours. I am then taken back to my cell of isolation.

"My second and last meal of the day consist of two more slices of black bread and Reich soup. This soup is mostly water containing dehydrated turnips. A rusty cup of water is also provided. If the service does not get better, I shall take my business elsewhere!"

Lt. Morgan tells of his first day of confinement:

"After my second and last meal of the day, which consisted of two slices of black bread with a rusty cup of water, I receive my second visitor. Again the so-called German Red Cross officer, comes to my cell with his list of questions. I refuse to answer any of them. This does not please him at all and he leaves in disgust.

"That night the heat in my cell is turned off and the temperature is extremely cold. I thought I would freeze to death. Even with all my clothes on, along with the merger bed cloths, I am barely able to keep warm.

"The next night, Sunday, January 9th the same thing happens. The phony German Red Cross officer comes by and gets the same results. That night they turn the heat up in my cell and I thought I was in a steam room!"

This up and down temperature treatment for Lt. Morgan would last for seven days. One of the main duties of the bogus Red Cross officer is to make a character analysis of each prisoner. The purpose of the analysis is to determine if he would be a good candidate for interrogation. This information is recorded on the back of the Red Cross form. It is then sent to Major Heinz Junge who is Chief of Interrogation and also Deputy Commander of Dulag Luft. During January, 1944 the Dulag Luft Commander is Oberstleutnant Erich Killinger. He started out with a small staff when he assumed command in 1941, however, due to the large increases of prisoners in succeeding years (from approximately 2,500 in 1942 to over 8,000 in 1943) his staff has increased from 50 to over 600 by 1944. After reviewing the Red Cross forms, Major Junge selects two members from each crew as the best candidates for interrogation. He usually selects one officer, for he knows, based on several years of experience, that information is more readily obtained from officers as a class than from sergeants. Past interrogation records indicate that they are more susceptible to flattery and respond more wholeheartedly to equal basis treatment. In addition, the officer prisoner attempts to fence verbally with his opponent, which leads to slips in security. Sergeants, on the other hand, are greater realists about interrogation and seem to sense that the Germans wouldn't be spending valuable time with them unless they wanted something. Sergeants are less easily flattered than officers and have fewer delusions about the real purpose of the interrogator's conversation.

Based on the Red Cross officer's evaluation and his own experience, Major Junge selects Lt. Morgan and Sgt. Gilrane as the best candidates for interrogation. After evaluation of Lt. Morgan's and Sgt. Gilrane's forms, Major Junge assigns their interrogation forms a number (The same number is always assigned to the form as the B-17 aircraft number that a crew was flying when shot down). The number stamped on Lt. Morgan's and Sgt. Gilrane's Red Cross form is 2-5838. He then assigns a proper Sonderfuhrer (Interrogator) to the prisoner. The Sonderfuhrer assigned to Lt. Morgan and Sgt. Gilrane is Major Waldschmidt, (Image 27.1). Major Waldschmidt is a well-trained and skilled interrogator. He is selected because of his knowledge of Americans and his fluent English. Major Waldschmidt, now assigned to Lt. Morgan and Sgt. Gilrane, proceeds to the Evaluation Department to secure the available information about his two charges. This information includes data gathered at the crash site, a study of the wrecked *Mad Money II* and other useful items either found at the crash site or taken from the crew.

Once the information is gathered at the Evaluation Department, Major Waldschmidt proceeds to the Intelligence Department to coordinate his information. Here he will spend the necessary time studying interrogation reports, evaluation reports, and other intelligence summaries.

His last stop is at the Squadron History Department. Major Waldschmidt's information indicates that his charges are

Image 27.1: Major Waldschmidt, the interrogator (Sonderfuhrer) assigned to interrogate Lt. Morgan and Sgt. Gilrane.

assigned to the 384th Bomb Group, 547th Bomb Squadron. He then reviews the file history of the 547th Bomb Squadron for relevant facts. The squadron history files contain comprehensive details pertaining to the squadron such as commanding officers, press clippings, photographs, and names of airmen shot down and other squadron data. It will take Major Waldschmidt almost a week to finish his research.

Sam reflects on his first week of confinement:

"During the week from Monday, January 10th, until Sunday, January 16th, I am pretty much left alone by my captors. This week of confinement and isolation provides plenty of time for me to think for there is no method to communicate with the other prisoners even though our cells are side-by-side. Communications are not possible because each cell wall contains four inches of insulation covered with

a three-quarter inch fiberboard for soundproofing. Each cell has a double casement type window located about ten feet from the floor. The window is either covered over with paint or frosted glass pane. Even if you could reach the window the handles have been removed. (The guards did have spare keys to open them, if necessary.) The entire cell is designed and constructed to be airtight and soundproof to provide total solitary confinement. Our captors have done an excellent job of total isolation for each of us.

"This isolation gives me time to daydream and I spend most of this week with memories of home and loved ones. I think of all the things I should have done or said before I left. More good-byes, more I love yous to my wife, more patience, more time spent with friends and all the other things I should have done during my leave home.

"Since this was the first time that I could think clearly after our crash landing, I think how lucky we are to have escaped the crash without injury. To be honest, it actually is somewhat of a relief to know that there will be no more jumping up at the sound of Private Hick on cold, black mornings. No more sweating out those long missions over Germany, fearing flak and fighters, and never knowing if your turn will come next. Of course, I would much rather be back at Grafton-Underwood if given a choice. So, during this week of total isolation and being ignored by my captors, I spend most of my time sleeping and daydreaming."

Beginning today, Monday, January 17th, Lt. Morgan and Sgt. Gilrane will be given special interrogations for one solid week to validate Major Heinz Junge's selection of them as best candidates to provide military information. Lt. Morgan nervously narrates his interrogation:

"I awake at 0700 hours to the sound of a rusty tray sliding under my cell door. The sentry informs me that after breakfast I am to be escorted to the Main Interrogation building. With those words, my stomach turns into knots. I decide to skip breakfast. I have been anticipating this interrogation with mixed feelings and some fear. This is the interrogation that Major Dolan had spoken about during classes back in England.

"The guard marches me down the corridor and out of the building. The Main Interrogation building is in another area of the Dulag Luft so I have a chance to get some fresh air as we march to this building. Once inside, I pass an office where women are working. Christmas music is in the background. It is Bing Crosby singing White Christmas.

I get homesick hearing this song. The guard escorts me to a door bearing the name, Major Waldschmidt. The guard stops, knocks, and waits for permission to enter.

"Inside I am impressed with the interrogation room for it is very large, almost 18 by 15 feet. In the center of the room is a large oak wooden desk facing the door. On each side of the desk is a large window. In between the windows, on the wall behind the desk, is a large map of Europe. I enter the room and the German officer behind the desk says in perfect English, 'Please come in and sit down. I am your interrogator.'

"He motions for me to sit in the chair at the end of his desk. He offers me a cigarette. I refuse it. 'You are Lt. Morgan?' 'Yes, and my serial number is 0678307.'

"The Major stands up and goes to the map. There is a red string extending from Grafton-Underwood, England to Kiel, Germany. The string then continues to the location in Denmark where we crash-landed.

"'Lt. Morgan, what was your target. Was it Kiel?' I reply, 'I don't remember.' Then he ask, 'How many bombs were you carrying?' I respond, 'I don't know. I just fly the plane.' He asks, 'Then you knew in advance what your target was for that day?' I reply, 'No, I just follow the plane in front of me.' He starts to yell, 'That is enough for today. Go back to your cell and see if you can remember more the next time.'"

Gilly relates his fears of interrogation:

"Tuesday morning, January 18th, I am called out for interrogation in the Main Interrogation building. I skip breakfast of black bread and imitation coffee. As I walk under guard from my cell, a light snow is falling. The five-minute walk to the Main Interrogation building is welcomed for it is the first time in over a week that I have experienced fresh air. As I enter the corridor inside the building, I hear screaming and cussing from one of the interrogation rooms. On the right side of the corridor a door quickly opens and an American officer is thrown out into the corridor and onto the floor where he is kicked and beaten. One arm is in a sling and a guard is hitting this arm with his rifle butt while a second is kicking him in the stomach with his boots. This goes on for 30 seconds and the American officer passes out. The two guards drag him down the corridor and out the door.

"This is very scary to me because I know that I am going into that same room next. I remember that Major Dolan had told us that this

type of treatment would probably happen so it was a frightening scene but not an intimidating one.

"*The guards lead me into an interrogation room and I am told to sit down. The interrogator introduces himself as Major Waldschmidt, then lays back in his chair and says in perfect English, 'Well, Harry, for you the war is over. We've got some pictures here of your neighborhood that I thought you would like to see.' He lays the pictures in front of me. In shock, I observe pictures of my street in Brooklyn, New York where I was raised and where my parents still live. I try to hide my amazement. The movie house just down the street from my boyhood home is quite clear. I am impressed with the details of the pictures. I can actually read what was playing at the theater on the day the picture was taken. I am amazed that my captors have this information.*

"*The interrogator continues, 'Harry, I know that on your last mission you were carrying the Norden Bombsight. Can you tell me about this device?' I reply, 'Sir, the Geneva Convention requires that I give you my name, rank, and serial number.' Just as I get the word number out of my mouth, the previously nice interrogator jumps up from his chair. He gets about three inches from my face and yells, 'You will go to the salt mines if you don't tell me the information on the Norden Bombsight.'*

"*I reply, 'Sir, I can only . . . ,' I am punched in the chest. This knocks me off my feet. After a few seconds I slowly get up, half dazed. Standing at attention I receive more of the same type questions.*

"*I reply, 'Sir, I can . . . ,' I am then struck with a cupped hand in my left ear. (The purpose of the cupped hand blow to the ear is to break the eardrum.) I go down, for the second time on the floor. The pain is terrible, but I slowly pull myself up and stand at attention, as before. I know that if I can maintain my military bearing the Germans will punish me less.*

"*Next, the interrogator pushes a set of papers to the edge of the desk in front of me. 'You will sign these papers or you will not leave this room no matter how long it takes,' he yells.*

"*I start to repeat my name, 'S/Sgt. Harry . . . ,' suddenly, the interrogator picks up the papers from his desk and flings them with all of his force into my face. A sheet of paper hits my eye and cuts my cornea. The pain is almost unbearable. I go to my knees for the third time. I slowly get back on my feet and snap back to attention. The interrogator has had enough. He orders the guard to take me back to my cell.*"

This same painful routine will be repeated on Gilly twice more on January 20th and 21st, 1944, each time with the same results. Gilly did not know it at the time but he had defeated Major Waldschmidt as surely as if he had shot him down in air combat. Major Heinz Junge had made a big mistake when he selected S/Sgt. Harry Gilrane as one of his best candidates for military information. Major Junge may be an expert on American habits and customs but he didn't know a damn thing about a tough Brooklyn street kid.

Lt. Morgan tells of his second interrogation:

"Early morning, Friday, January 22nd and my cell door swings open. Two guards grab me out of bed and rush me to the Main Interrogation building for another session. I am to be interrogated again by the same officer. This puts me somewhat at ease because I remember the last time I didn't have too much difficulty.

"The interrogation starts about the same as the first one. He starts by saying, 'Your bombardier, Lt. Wirth, and navigator, Lt. Horsky, have already told me everything I want to know but I want to ask you a couple of questions. What is your bomb group and who is your Commanding Officer?'

"I reply, 'I don't remember.' Then he says, 'Lt. Morgan, when do you think the war will be over?' I quickly reply, 'June.' He yells, 'June of what year?' I reply, 'June of this year, 1944.' He quickly replies loudly, 'Impossible! We are winning this war. I don't see why you Americans came into this war because we are going to win, regardless of your participation.'

"'Now, Lt. Morgan, since you refuse to answer my questions, I'll tell what I know about you.' He reaches down and pulls out the bottom drawer of his desk and picks out a black loose-leaf notebook. He leafs through the notebook and finally says, 'Oh, yes, here you are ... let me see ... Lt. Myron C. Morgan, born Morgantown, West Virginia, May 12, 1918. Parent's names are Marshal Blain and Anna Alice Morgan. Your mother's maiden name is Anna Alice Menefee. You graduated from Morgantown High School in 1936 and from West Virginia University, 1941. Enlisted in the Air Force in March, 1942. Received your wings April, 1943, Pampa, Texas. You and your crew left the United States by boat in late August 1943. Landed in England September 7th, and flew your first mission October 2nd. Your commanding officer of the 384th Bomb Group was Colonel Lacey who was replaced in November by Colonel Dale O. Smith. Your mission on January 4th was Kiel and you were leading your squadron, the 547th.'

"I am dumbfounded that he has these details of my life. He asks me a quick question seeing that I was wide-eyed with all of his information. 'The name of your new fighter is the P-51 Mustang. Isn't that correct?' I reply, 'I don't know. I never heard of that name.' He starts to yell and pounds the desk with his fist, 'That will be all for you. We'll send you to a Stalag Luft tomorrow.'"

In five days, Major Heing Junge's best candidates had beaten him and his Chief Interrogator, Major Waldschmidt to their knees. In Lt. Morgan's case, neither of the Krauts figured on the resolve of a mountain boy from West Virginia!

The remainder of the crew went through a similar, but less intense, interrogation process. The crew, during a total of eighteen days of severe, brutal and intensive interrogation provided only the information required by the Geneva Convention: name, rank, and serial number.

Sentimental Journey

It is Tuesday, January 25, 1944, about 0930 hours. Lts. Kaczaraba, Morgan, Wirth, and Horsky are being assembled for their departure from the Dulag Luft. They are bound for a transient camp located on the outskirts of Frankfurt. Here they will be processed to a permanent prisoner of war camp. The transient camp is located about seven miles southwest from the Dulag Luft where the crew has "enjoyed" their captor's "hospitality" for the last 18 days.

Lt. Morgan remembers the trip to the transient camp and to the permanent Stalag Luft:

> *"Once outside the Dulag Luft, after almost three weeks of individual isolation, with its stale, stuffy air, I breathe in the fresh, cold air. The change of scenery is also welcome as we wait for transportation to the transient camp.*
>
> *"Our two German guards soon flag down an electric trolley and crowd us into it. There are several civilians on board but leave as we enter the car. In less than 20 minutes we come to the end of the line and are ordered off the trolley. Next, we are assembled by the tracks and then marched a quarter of a mile to the transient camp.*

"*Inside this temporary wire enclosed camp, we are immediately processed into a large warehouse that is provisioned by the American Red Cross to supply American prisoners with clothes and other personal items needed during internment. Personal items are provided in the form of Red Cross POW kits, consisting of socks, soap, cigarettes, shirts, underclothes, toothbrush, etc. Again we are fingerprinted, pictures are taken, and some additional paperwork completed.*

"*From the warehouse we march to a smaller building that contains showers. This is to be the high point of my day, for here, we are allowed to take showers for the first time since January 3rd, over three weeks ago at Grafton-Underwood. The showers are hot, and we stay in until ordered out by the guards. It is amazing what a hot shower can do for the human spirit!*

"*Armed with our Red Cross kits and refreshed bodies, we are assigned to temporary quarters in one of several wooden barracks within the transient camp. The guards leave which frees us up to mingle with the other prisoners. A search for boys from the 384th is unsuccessful. It is late in the evening. I am tired and need sleep. Tonight sleep is sound for the first time since my last night at Grafton-Underwood.*

"*The next day, Wednesday, January 26th, we are herded out for roll call. At roll call we are told to be ready in 30 minutes for a trip to a permanent camp. Just prior to leaving this transient camp, the Luftwaffe guards march us into a large warehouse. Here a German officer addresses us. The purpose of his address is to warn us of civilian hostilities toward American and British flyers for the recent bombings of Frankfurt. Basically, we are told to keep our mouths shut, eyes straight ahead and not to make any contact or gestures toward the civilian population.*

"*In less than 30 minutes our preparations for the trip are complete. Our group of POWs, along with some 20 guards marches out of the transient camp into the streets of Frankfurt. The mile long march to the train station is accomplished with little attention from the local population. As we turn onto the street to the railroad station, it is obvious that the station has suffered additional and extensive bomb damage since we came through three weeks ago. The station is still intact but heavily damaged, including the adjacent buildings.*

"*Our 200 strong POW group is loaded into old confiscated WWI French box cars. These box cars are known as 40 Homme 08 chevaux, which means they were built to carry 40 men or eight horses. We are* loaded 44 men to a car. It is almost noon as the train jerks and we start our trip that we think will take us to northern Germany.

"The train moves very slowly. The coaches have wooden seats and there are no conveniences such as heat or light. There is a single bucket in our car for us to relieve ourselves. Soon the stench is overpowering. The Germans provide a ration of black bread and cheese to last us until we reach the permanent camp.

"The first night the train reaches Berlin. Here we are sidetracked for the night. About 2100 hours, air raid sirens go off and suddenly the sky is lit up with giant searchlights. RAF bombers are overhead and the flashing of German antiaircraft guns can be seen. In the distance the flashing lights from exploding bombs are visible. Seconds later thundering echoes of exploding bombs are loudly heard. The earth trembles under the tremendous impact of blockbusters as the English bombs are called.

"The RAF always bombs at night and we always bomb in the daytime. Many times in the pubs in England arguments would result with the RAF about how dangerous it is to bomb Germany at night. The British would rather sneak over to Germany at night, one by one, than fly over in daytime formation like we do. Oh well, to each his own.

"So here we are, sitting in a box car in the middle of Berlin, and hoping that the bombers overhead do not have the railroad marshaling yards as their target. Bombs are exploding within a couple of blocks of us but we are unharmed. At last, they finally finish their bombing and the air raid sirens sound the all clear. Another day will be granted us.

"In the morning, the next leg of our slow journey starts through the bombed out city of Berlin and finally into the open countryside. All day the train travels north-northeast and toward evening we come to a small village. The sign at the depot indicates it is the village of Barth. Lt. Horsky tells us Barth is located in northern Germany on the Baltic Sea (Image 28.1 and 28.2).

"The train moves slowly into the village and finally comes to an abrupt stop. The guards yell for us to get off the train. We file out and line up alongside the tracks. New guards are shouting orders and holding dogs on leashes.

"Finally, we are in formation. The guards count us and then prepare to march our group toward a fenced in area about half a mile in the distance. This will be our permanent POW camp, which I suspect will be my home for the duration of the war.

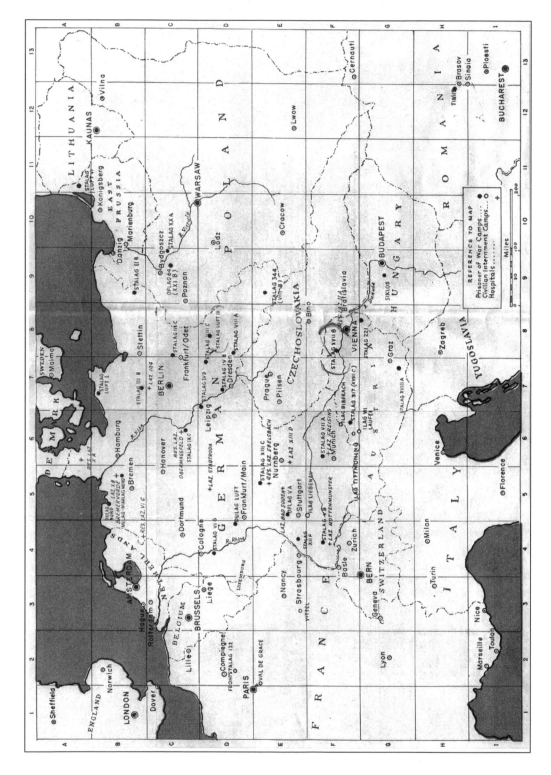

Image 28.1: Prisoner of war and civilian internee camps in Europe. Stalg Luft I is located at map grid B-7. Stalag XVIIB is located at map grid F-8.

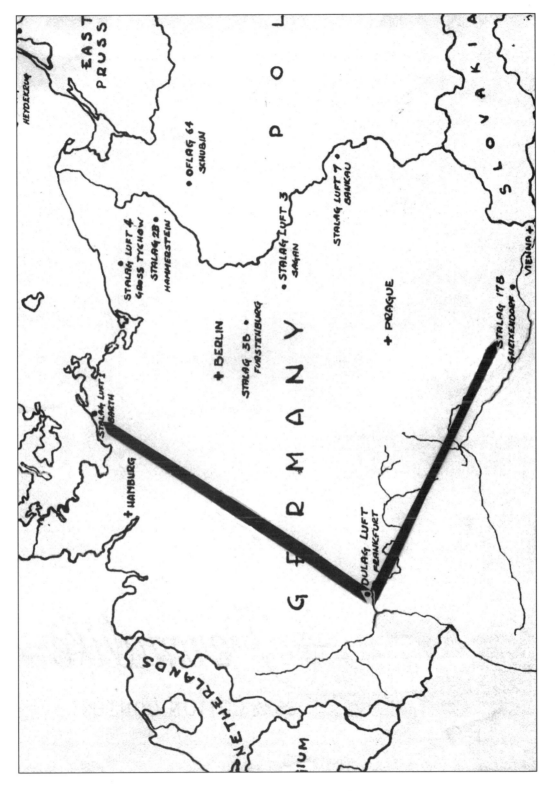

Image 28.2: Railway route from Dulag Luft (Frankfurt, Germany) to Stalag Luft I (Barth, Germany) and to Stalag 17B (Krems/Gneixendorf, Austria).

"It is Friday afternoon, January 28th, extremely cold and snowing as we wait alongside the tracks outside the town of Barth, Germany. Marching through the streets, I observe that stores, homes, and other buildings appear to be undamaged from the war. As we march the cobblestone streets echo the sounds from the guard's hobnailed boots. The shuffle of 200 pairs of GI boots further adds to the noise of marching soldiers.

"Our tired, dejected, hungry, and cold group of POWs silently approaches the camp with only the clump, clump of feet signaling our approach. The camp is in an open plain next to a wooded area of mostly small pines. The first thing I notice is the high fences and the higher guard towers located at each corner of the camp and one in between. Each guard tower has a mounted searchlight and a machine gun. In addition, each guard in the tower has a rifle. He is well armed to keep POWs in line.

"Approaching the camp we notice POWs coming close to the fence in order to gain a better view of us as we march by. They are looking for buddies and every once in a while you can hear a yell when someone is recognized. Their favorite yell to us is 'You'll be sorry' or 'Welcome to Hitler's Rest Home' and other remarks to make you feel right at home.

"As the POWs observe us and search for buddies, we do the same to them. Soon we recognize some boys from our bomb group. My God, how old they look! Most have long beards and their clothes are shabby with a mixture of GI and English uniforms. One POW is wearing an English jacket, a GI cap and air force pants.

"Entering the huge front barbed-wire gate, I look up and spot the large red Nazi flag blowing in the breeze over camp headquarters (Image 28.3). This foreign flag, with the hated swastika emblem, makes me shudder because I realize I am definitely in my enemy's hands.

"POWs follow along the fence and gather around us as we march in the front gate. It sounds like old home week with all the chattering going on between the old POWs and the new arrivals.

"Next, the guards march us to the German headquarters building and here I am officially entered into Stalag Luft I. Next, I am fingerprinted, photographed, issued POW dogtags, and bed clothing (Image 28.4). Then we are assigned a barracks and room number. Lts. Kaczaraba, Wirth, and myself are assigned to the South Compound. Lt. Horsky is assigned to the North Compound I.

Image 28.3: New arrivals entering the main gate of Stalag Luft I, Barth, Germany.

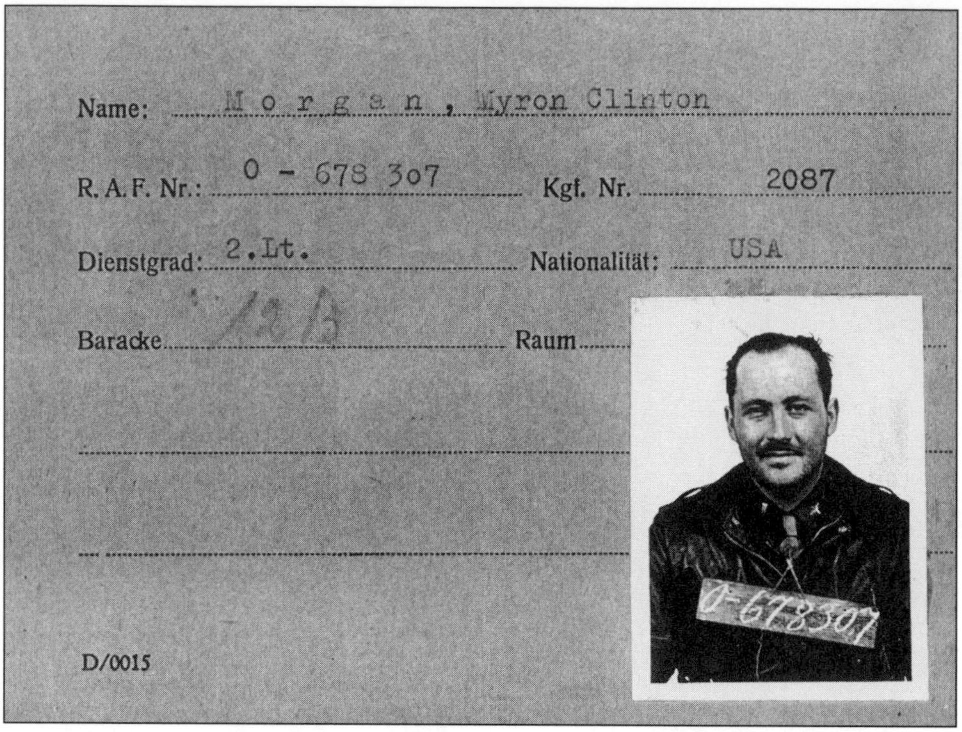
Name: Morgan, Myron Clinton

R. A. F. Nr.: 0 - 678 307 Kgf. Nr. 2087

Dienstgrad: 2.Lt. Nationalität: USA

Baracke 12 B Raum

D/0015

Image 28.4: Lt. Mike Morgan POW photograph upon entering Stalug Luft I, Barth, Germany on January 28, 1944.

"A single guard takes us to our assigned barracks. Here we are dismissed at the front entrance to find our room and pick out a bed. My first impressions inside the POW camp are very depressing (Image 28.5, 28.6, 28.7, 28.8). The inside of the camp gives me the absolute feeling of confinement as I observe the high barbed-wire fences, higher guard towers, and the many German officers and guards everywhere.

"The barracks are very depressing with their dim lights. The old POWs with beards and drab clothing make a very dejected atmosphere. It now dawns on me that my lifestyle will be very limited.

"The barracks are approximately 100 feet long and about 40 feet wide with a hallway down the center and rooms on both sides approximately 18 by 12 feet. The room doors have glass in the upper panel so the guards can check the rooms without coming in.

"It is almost dark when we enter the barrack. Inside it is gloomy and smells of strong tobacco, coal smoke, and human odors. The only light is a dimly lit 25-watt bulb at the end of the hallway, along with small bits of light filtering through the door glass.

Image 28.5: Guard tower, south of Mess Hall, North Compound, Stalag Luft I, Barth, Germany. This, the highest tower in camp, is the main one overlooking the entire camp. Two machine guns not visible in the picture were silent discouragement to many an ambitious kriegie's escape plan.

"My eyes become accustomed to the subdued light. I can now see my way to our assigned room, which is the second one on the right. We walk in, grab a bunk, which are triple decked, all wood with slats that are six inch wood boards. On top of the slats is a blue and white checkered mattress filled with straw. Lt. Wirth selects the top, Lt. Kaczaraba

Image 28.6: Stalag Luft I, Barth, Germany. One of the 25 guard towers. Note searchlights.

Image 28.7: Stalag Luft I, Barth, Germany. Outer perimeter fence.

Image 28.8: Stalag Luft I, Barth, Germany. Outer perimeter fence area.

the middle and I grab the bottom bunk. We make up our beds for we are tired from the long journey. It doesn't take long to settle in for the night."

Lt. Wirth lies awake thinking of home:

"In a short while my thoughts travel far away to Nebraska City, Nebraska. I fondly recall the embrace of my wife, Charlotte, whom I have not held in my arms in over five months. The worst part, however, is that I may never see her again.

"It is almost 2300 hours in Barth, Germany and 1500 hours in Nebraska City, Nebraska. Charlotte is probably at work. I will be with her in my dreams. I fall into deep sleep as I dream of her."

Back in Frankfurt, Gilly painfully remembers the trip to the NCO's permanent camp:

"It is almost 1300 hours Tuesday, January 25th and we are being packed into the 40 and 8 box cars. The German guards inform us that if one POW tries to escape we will all be shot. It is our duty to escape and each of us will try if the opportunity presents itself.

"Our crew, now reduced to six due to the separation of our officers, along with 42 other POWs, are packed into a single box car assigned to carry 40 men. The real problem is we get only half of the car. The German guards, which number four and their stove, occupy the other half. So we have 48 POWs in one-half of a boxcar meant to carry 20 men. The train starts off with a jerk and we head slowly east.

"We are stuffed into this box car to where it is impossible to lie down, bend over, or even get on our knees. The only possible position is to stand upright. When you must relieve yourself, you do, in that same position.

"We are told to expect to be in this box car for three days. Our captors provide a cup of water, thin soup, and one slice of bread to last all day. During the three-day trip we experience great hardships, in addition to the ordeal of standing constantly. The temperature inside the boxcar is well below freezing. I know this to be true because when I relieve myself my pants freeze almost immediately. In addition, the train makes many, many jolting stops and starts as it passes through numerous towns and cities. Each time the train makes an abrupt stop, bodies are thrown forward crashing into each other. The stench is breath taking and the over crowding is unbearable. After three days in this environment, we are sick, almost frozen, and dead tired.

"It is Friday, about 1300 hours, January 28th as the train pulls into Krems, Austria. Krems is located on the beautiful, blue Danube River. Our assigned prison camp is four miles northwest of Krems.

"The guards order us out of the box cars and form us into columns of fours. Each column extends 300 yards in length. Those that do not obey quickly are struck with gun butts, and several collapse. Some locals approach us with buckets. They offer water and show pity. The guards do not allow this. (These are German guards who have returned from the eastern front and are very strict.) Some locals secretly try to give us bread as we march toward the camp, about four miles distance.

"The camp is located on the top of a small mountain covered with pine trees. Entering the camp I am in awe of its size. It appears to cover about 30 acres (Image 28.9). The first order of business is to have our heads shaved. The next stop is a building, which I believe to be a gas chamber. The gas chambers of death in Nazi Germany are well known and I thought we might get gassed here. This is not the case as we are deloused and provided with cold showers. This is a good opportunity to wash the three days of stench from my clothes. Next, our captors provide blankets that are razor thin, and down we go into the camp.

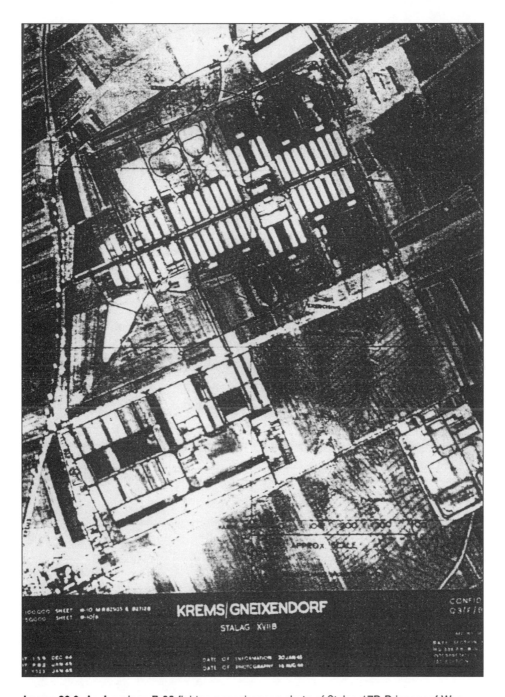

KREMS/GNEIXENDORF

STALAG XVIIB

Image 28.9: An American P-38 fighter reconaissance photo of Stalag 17B Prisoner of War camp taken on August 8, 1944.

"Some of the airmen we knew from combat flying or stateside duty greet us. It is a very strained meeting because we had been taught back in England not to confide in anyone until you are sure that he can be trusted. So, for the first couple of hours, our conversations are of small talk only, however, after a while we realize that they are all Americans and there are no German implants.

"Next, barrack assignments are given. Shorty, Pete, and myself to 19; Gibby to 39; Wilber to 37; and Sam to 38 (Image 28.10)."

It is almost 1700 hours and fully dark. Dead tired, but somewhat relieved under the circumstances, the NCOs begin their first night of many to come in confinement.

Each day they will be under the absolute control of their enemy, owing their lives to his humanity, and their daily bread to his compassion. They must obey his orders, go where he bids them, stay where they are told, await his pleasure, and possess their soul in patience.

The fortunes of war have dealt them a lousy hand. But now they do not give any thought to what their future might hold for that is in the hands of Oberst Kuhn, the German Kommandant of this POW camp known as Stalag 17B.

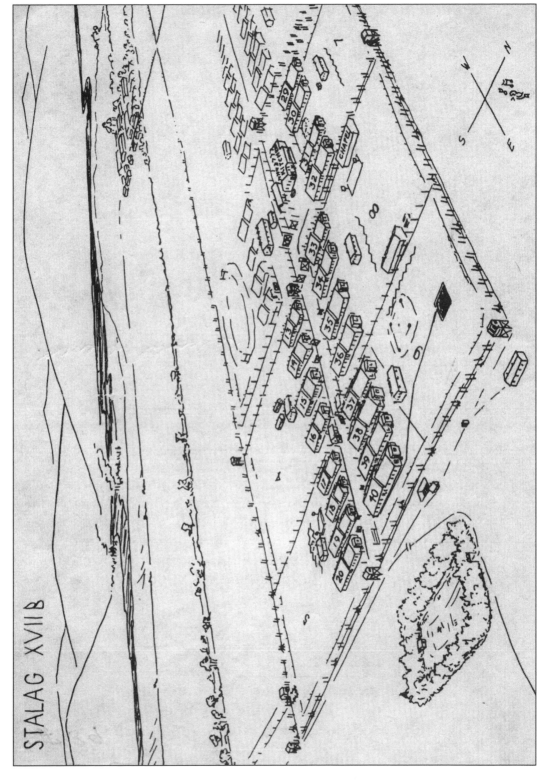

Image 28.10: Sketch of Stalag XVIIB. Barracks assignments are Shorty, Pete, and Gilly to 19; Wilbur to 37; Gibby to 39; and Sam to 38.

Stalag Luft I: No Country Club

In January when Lts. Kaczaraba, Morgan, Wirth, and Horsky arrived at Stalag Luft I[1], it consisted of two compounds. (A compound is an area with one or more barracks set aside within the confines of the camp to imprison a certain number of men.) The north compound (which is newer) and the south compound (the original compound), are separated by enemy headquarters and living quarters. This provides an excellent barrier to prevent any possible collusion for escape or uprising. The camp and each compound are separated from the surrounding area by a double row of barbed-wire fencing, ten feet high with each row spaced six feet apart, (Image 29.1). In case a POW gets over the first fence there is a mass of coiled barbed wire between the fences to greet him.

At each corner of the compound is a guard tower about 30 feet high (Image 29.2). From this high position the guard has a clear vision of two sides of the compound that extend from his tower. Each guard is equipped with a rifle and each tower with a machine gun. In addition, each tower is equipped with a high powered searchlight to provide excellent pinpoint illumination in an already well lighted area.

Image 29.1: Double barbed-wire fences enclose Stalag Luft I and separate the various compounds. Coiled wire between fences prevent kriegies from crawling through and under.

Lts. Kaczaraba, Morgan, and Wirth are in the South compound and Lt. Horsky in the North compound, however, with authorized documents, they can visit from time to time.[2] Lt. Morgan reflects on his first day as a POW:

"It is extremely cold as I roll out of my bunk for our first roll call on Saturday morning, January 29, 1944. Lts. Kaczaraba, Wirth, and I are discussing, as we dress, how lucky we are to be alive, generally unhurt, and capable of doing further harassment to the enemy.

"Wake up is at 0600 hours to fall out in formation for roll call at 0800 hours to be counted. Roll call will be twice a day, once in the morning and again in the evening just before our captors lock us up in the barracks for the night. This will be our first roll call or appell

Image 29.2: Stalag Luft I, Barth, Germany. Corner tower guard has a clear vision of sight for two sides of the compounds.

(German for official count). During roll call POWs are required to line up into regular army formation, about 20 men in a line and five lines deep. Each formation represents a barracks and is counted as a formation (Image 29.3).

"The guards count each formation one at a time. The method of counting is one guard counts from the front and one counts from the rear. At the conclusion of each formation the guards face each other and yell out the count together. If they both agree on the count then the number is reported to a German officer in front of the formation. If they don't agree on the count, the officer makes them recount until they both agree. When the count is correct the guards move to the next formation, and so on until all formations on the parade ground are counted. The total count is given to the Camp Kammadant in the center of the parade ground and if all counts add up correctly, then all formations are dismissed.

"There are certain POWs who are excused from roll call. Those kriegies (German for prisoner) who work in the mess hall, those who are ill or otherwise physically incapacitated, and the few who are on special details are allowed to be absent from formation. Special guards count these men who tour the barracks, mess hall, and other places during the outside roll call. Their count, added to the formation count, must tally with the official book count.

"Sometimes POWs attempt to disrupt or cause roll call count to be incorrect. When this occurs, armed guards come into the camp with their police dogs. The dogs are allowed to jump on their leashes and snap at us as they near each man. Usually this terminates the POWs' attempts to disrupt or cause an incorrect count."

Lt. Horsky recalls the fair share policy practiced in his north compound:

"The south compound is home for Lts. Kaczaraba, Wirth, and Morgan. It is the older section of Stalag Luft I. The south compound has a coal burning stove in each room, which is used for warmth and cooking.

"Once a week the Germans issue each man a loaf of black bread, a potato or turnip, and an issue of coal for each stove (about 54 pounds) in the barrack to cook and heat with. Sometimes, in addition to the regular issue, the Germans provide a cup of hot soup or cheese. On some servings the soup is good; other times it is hard to stomach. Either way it is consumed!

Image 29.3: Daily Roll Call. Twice a day this scene was enacted in all the compounds of Stalag Luft I; in this instance it's North Compound I. Five deep to facilitate Teutonic higher mathematics, each squadron stood at attention while being counted. Despite the common multiple the procedure was more often snafu than not — which necessitated frequent recounts. The latter were tolerable in the warm months, but with the advent of cold weather, bone-chilling gales would roar in from the Baltic in the background.

"In the south compound each man prepares his own food, thus he can ensure his own fair share. This is not the case in the north compound where meals are served in a communal mess hall (Image 29.4).

"The food in the central mess hall is distributed, usually to a group of eight to ten POWs, thus each POW must make sure he gets his fair share. The term fair share has a fatal meaning for it means the difference between life and death. If each POW does not share and share alike, then someone will go hungry.

"The food is always served in a single bowl for all eight to ten POWs at the table. The bowl is about eight inches in diameter and two inches deep, therefore, each POW's fair share is about three to four ounces of food per meal. On a daily basis this amounts to about six to eight ounces per day, which is equal to about one cup of food per day per POW.

"In order to ensure that each man gets his fair share, a practice of first at the table must serve policy is used. This policy requires the first at the table to fill each bowl with equal shares. He must be fastidious when serving to make sure that each bowl's content is equal for the server gets the last bowl. By requiring the first at the table to make this division and giving him the last choice of the bowls, a fair share for each is assured. Never again, in my life, will fair share mean more than it did during my imprisonment. For it is here, that life is served in small portions and we must share and share alike."

Lt. Morgan continues his recollection of camp routine:

"The daily camp routine soon becomes a way of life for us. Just like army life, certain routines have to be followed, however, beyond that the rest of the time is free. Roll call: twice a day, once in the morning and once in the afternoon before we are locked in our barracks for the night. Water call: once a day, in the morning, for instant coffee. Fuel call (coal briquettes): once a week, and bread and potatoes call: twice a week.

"The main method to pass time during our first few months is to tell war stories. These exchanges of battle exploits or other tear-jerking stories breaks the monotony during bleak evenings when the sun is below the horizon before 1600 hours, leaving the barracks dark and gloomy.

"One such war story involved an extraordinary incident during the 384th Bomb Group's mission to Kiel on January 4, 1944. The same mission we were shot down. T/Sgt. Fred Wagner, engineer and top turret gunner, fell from the bomb bay of his 384th B-17 at an altitude of

Image 29.4: The communal mess hall of North Compound I, Stalag Luft I, Barth, Germany, is the only one of its kind in American prisoner of war camps in Germany. Serving two meals a day, the Mess staff fed four sittings of 500 men each a total of 4,000 meals daily. Between meals the mess hall is on occasion a lecture auditorium, a play house, a school room, a church — all in all the most indispensable building in camp and, incidentally, the warmest.

28,000 feet as the plane was leaving Kiel. He had gone into the bomb bay to release several stuck bombs when his oxygen supply failed and he lost consciousness, and then slipped out the door. Reviving at a lower altitude of 10,000 feet, he was able to release his parachute in time. (T/Sgt. Fred Wagner was captured and spent the remainder of the war in Stalag 17B.)"

Lt. Kaczaraba reflects on the crash landing and how proud he is of his crew:

"All of the crew members were especially outstanding because they chose to ride Mad Money II *down. Mike did an excellent job of flying and checking the engines properly. His calmness and judgment are truly praiseworthy. He kept me from getting rattled.*

"Sam, immediately after the flak struck, called for an oxygen check. This kept the crew from getting excited and kept them from calling me on the interphone. All the way down he got oxygen checks. I noticed that he did this every time the crew seemed nervous. It gave them some-thing else to think about.

"Shorty stayed in the ball turret until the last minute in case of fight-ers. All crew members did a great job of getting into ditching positions and showed excellent teamwork and obedience.

"Sam's act of bravery in burning our B-17 after the crash landing, deserves the Distinguished Flying Cross (DFC). I intend to recommend him for this award if we survive this war."

Lt. Wirth tells of his wife's discovery of his POW status:

"I sent a letter home on January 1st. I wrote that 'while we have come back on various missions with numerous holes in our ship, so far our crew is as good as they ever were. I thought this a remarkable record, not an injury in 16 missions (Image 29.5).

"I think about how close our crew had come to a catastrophe. I thank God for being alive, even in a prison camp. All ten men of our crew are safe and I hope will survive this POW life. I also take comfort knowing that our loved ones will soon be advised of our health, safety, and POW status and camp locations.

"My wife, Charlotte, was notified in a somewhat unusual manner of my situation. When Mad Money II *was forced out of formation and we began our unsuccessful flight to Sweden, another crew in a nearby B-17 was watching* Mad Money II *as we headed north-northeast toward*

Mrs. Otto Wirth
Nebraska City, Neb.

Jan. 18, 1944.

Dear Barbara:

I suppose your mother has written you that Theodore is missing in action, since January 4. We just got the word Saturday the 15th. A letter from Theodore's best friend to his wife in New York City, which she sent on to Charlotte, came a few hours before the War Dept. telegram. Of course, we have known all along that he was in mortal danger every time he went out on a mission, but still it came as a terrible shock. We had had a letter written January 1, in which he said he had completed 16 missions, one more than the other members of his crew, as he went once with another crew when their bombardier was ill. He wrote – "while we have come back on various occasions with numerous holes in our ship, so far our entire crew is as good as they ever were" – He thought that a remarkable record – not an injury in so many missions made. So we were beginning to feel confident they would complete their 25 missions and be home before so very long. They had destroyed 7 German planes and damaged 6 –

I am enclosing a copy of a letter from Jimmy Wilson (his friend from New York) that came to Charlotte this morning. It gives us a considerable amount of hope but the waiting is going to be awfully hard, especially for Charlotte – she is bearing up as well as one could expect. This first letter of Jimmy's has helped us so much. She is sending copies of the part about Theodore's crew to as many of the parents of Theodore's crew as we know addresses – I sent a copy of it to Mary Durbin, and asked her to mail it to you – so you will probably get it before long. The letter I am enclosing is much the same, only more of it.

Barbara, we wondered if it would be too much trouble for your to look in the Milwaukee telephone directory and see if you could locate a family by the name of Craden. The ball turret gunner's name was Solomon Craden. He is a very small young fellow. Charlotte does not have his street address, only Milwaukee, we don't think his people would have any way of getting this information that Jimmy gave us, and it has been such a consolation to us that we would like to pass it on to them – (The official notice just said Theodore was missing since January 4) If they are not in the telephone directory, perhaps the Red Cross could locate them. We would be so grateful to you if you could find it possible to do this.

Written by Mrs. Otto Wirth, Mother of Theodore Wirth,
Bombardier on same plane as Solomon Craden, when it
went on raid January 4, 1944.

Image 29.5: Letter written by Mrs. Otto Wirth, mother of Lt. Ted Wirth.

January 6, 1944

"I can say, and I know that you will be glad to hear it, that his chances of being alive are excellent. Iím not going by what I was told. I saw the action. I could not tell you that he is in Sweden, but it is probable. When I last saw his ship, it was in trouble and going down, fully under control. As I see it, the worst that could happen to them is that they were forced down in Denmark and were subsequently taken prisoners. Contrary to what you might have read in the papers about treatment of German prisoners of war, they will receive the best possible treatment. Believe that. I do and I think I am in a better position to know the facts. I went back to Kiel the next day and got a great deal of satisfaction out of seeing the damage done on both days. More than that, I personally shot down a German fighter. When I came back I had a chance to read the Stars and Stripes, and I learned that two ships – one on each day – had landed in Sweden. We can both hope that one of those ships is his. I repeat, in any case I am confident that they are all safe.

"I need not tell you that Ted was held in high esteem by everyone in his Sq. I was talking to his sq. C.O. when I came back the second day, and if there had ever been any doubt about it, he removed it. We compared notes on the happenings of the day before and are both convinced that they are O.K."

Written by Jimmie Wilson, Bombardier, member of crew of accompanying plane which carried Solomon Graden in raid which took place January 4, 1944.

Image 29.6: Letter from Lt. Jimmy Wilson to his wife in New York City. Lt. Wilson, a close friend of Lt. Ted Wirth, flew the Kiel mission with the 384th Bomb Group.

Sweden. In the ship observing us was my best friend, Lt. Jimmy Wilson, the ship's bombardier. His observations were contained in a letter to his wife in New York City who forwarded it on to my wife in Nebraska City, Nebraska (Image 29.6). This letter to my wife was received only a few hours before the War Department's official telegram informing her of my status of missing in action (Image 29.7). This information was also communicated to other families of the crew. Charlotte made every effort to contact all families of the members of our crew, even contacting the Red Cross in each crew member's hometown."

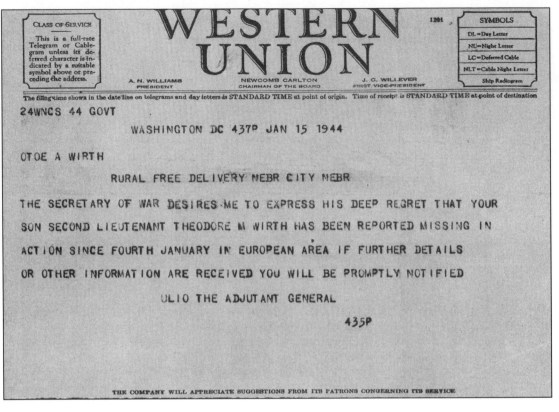

Image 29.7: War Department's official telegram informing Mrs. Otto Wirth of her son, Lt. Ted Wirth, missing in action status.

Lt. Morgan learns to understand and appreciate the other crew member's duties:

> *"During the next five weeks, and in some ways what seemed the longest period of my entire confinement, we officers re-flew every mission in detail from Emden to Kiel. These reflections gave each of us an introspective view of the mission from each other's point of view. Each of us saw events in a different light.*
>
> *"For example, some things that were of great importance to the pilot were not so to the bombardier. Throughout this exchange, we learned to appreciate the duties and actions each of us took during each mission. As we discussed our missions, where each time our lives were put in mortal danger, all of us could not help but feel some sense of security in this prison camp when compared to the chances of survival during our 16½ air combat missions."*

Lt. Wirth remembers the great expectations for his liberation from Stalag Luft I:

"It is almost the end of March 1944. The snows, during the months, have accumulated several inches. It covers the ground within our little grip of Germany. Due to severe weather, time is spent mostly in the barracks. Enjoyment is rarely experienced in this confinement as there isn't much to keep us occupied. Added to the boredom is the fact that cold dominates our bodies most of the time. The coal briquettes used for fuel last only four hours a day. This lack of heat forces us to stay in our bunks most of the day allowing each POW to at least retain his body heat. During these bleak cold March evenings, the sun is down by 1600 hours. Our barracks is dark and silent. There is little to give us hope. These are truly times that test our resolve to survive. It is a period of total adjustment from a carefree life style in England to one of complete confinement and lack of privacy with the resultant mental and physical degeneration.

"I, like all other POWs, spend most of my time dreaming of great expectations. Our great expectations are the allied invasion of the European continent and our subsequent liberation from this camp. It is on our minds constantly. Each little bit of news from newly arriving prisoners spur our hopes for invasion and liberation. Although this news is meager, it allows us to maintain a tiny ray of hope to cling to on each sunless day.

"Based on the news from incoming POWs, combined with our secret homemade radio, we know that Germany is taking a beating from the Eighth Air Force and the RAF. German cities, as well as the occupied territories, are being blasted unmercifully day and night. These air raids consist of 600 to 800 heavy bombers. We also know that across the natural barrier of the English Channel, there are thousands of men, ships, and all types of weapons ready to embark on a holy crusade to free Europe and us. These great expectations are burnt into our hearts, souls, and minds. But when will it happen?

"Our first three months as prisoners seems so terribly long as the first week in May rolls around. It feels like we have been here a lifetime, however, we are adjusting to a routine of doing nothing with a little less effort each day.

"The weather is starting to improve and the cold bleak days of the past winter are only a memory. Spring is in the air, spirits soar as we are able to get out and enjoy the sunny, crisp weather on the Baltic Coast of northern Germany."

Lt. Morgan tells of little victories over his German captors:

"During mid-May, the spirits of Stalag Luft I POWs soar as we witness hundreds of American bombers (B-17s and B-24s) heading east escorted by fighters. It is early afternoon and about 30 minutes later they come back over flying the opposite route. German targets have received the awesome power of the mighty Eighth Air Force this afternoon.

"Suddenly, the fighter escorts break formation and come barreling down looking for targets of opportunity to destroy. I can make them out now, P-51s. They sweep over the nearby airfield, shoot it up and move on to another target.

"Now one of the B-17s, with unused bombs, drops its bomb load on the nearby town of Strausland. The bombs can be heard exploding in our camp, which is located only a few miles away. The bombers and fighters now clear the area and it is silent. But not for long.

"A roar goes up from all over the camp. Each POW is excited with the knowledge that the Eighth Air Force bombers are actually this far into Germany. The celebration continues wild and unrestrained as the German guards look down in dismay.

"It is quiet again. I am left to my thoughts. We watch them disappear in the distance, heading west. Their roar is reduced to a whisper. Grounded eagles are proud and happy but also a little jealous.

"Oh, how I long to fly with them again, to land back at Grafton-Underwood, to go through debriefing, to have supper in the chow hall, to throw my tired body across my bunk and fall into peaceful slumber. But alas, these wishes will not be granted, but I will be content to relive my dreams for several nights.

"A couple of days later, we are privileged to have a visit from the RAF. It is early afternoon and most of the POWs are outside soaking up the sun following the long, cold and dreary winter. A group of us are watching a Fw190 making practice landings at the local Barth airfield when a formation of British Mosquitoes suddenly swarm down on the airfield. The Mosquitoes attack the airfield in pairs doing disastrous damage. The Fw190 falls in behind the first Mosquito hoping for a cheap kill. In his excitement, however, the German pilot overlooks the second British fighter. The Fw190 is now in position for the kill, sights are lined up and he is ready to blast the British fighter out of the sky. Bullets rip into aircraft metal but it is German metal, not British. The trailing British fighter came in behind the Fw190 and blasted it out of the sky. We are able to observe this dogfight as it unfolds less than a 1,000 yards away over the Baltic inlet (Image 29.8).

Image 29.8: When the Mcsquitoes shot up the flight line at Barth, a Luftwaffe pilot scrambled to get a crack at his enemy he forgot to watch his rear. Mosquito #2 caught him as he was try-ing to turn inside his intended victim. On-lookers from the Stalag saw the Kraut make a safe — but wet bailout from the flaming wreck.

"A few days later, we are again visited by the mighty Eighth Air Force. The Germans, however, decide that we will not be treated to any additional viewing of the destruction of their Fatherland or its Luftwaffe, so they force us to stay in the barracks. The official reason provided is that this is for our protection. Our bodies are inside the barracks but our eyes and hearts are outside as we sit in the windows and watch hundreds of B-17s on their way to destroy a Nazi target. These little victories serve to bolster our grounded eagle spirits to new heights.

"As the end of May draws near, we continue to get news from newly arriving American and British crews of an imminent invasion of the European continent. They tell of mass buildups of troops and equipment in England for the invasion. It soon becomes clear that without an invasion this war will remain static. We will also.

"There are three different news sources in Stalag Luft I. The first is the newly arriving POWs. This news is always at least two weeks old due to the time, after being shot down, for crew interrogation through Dulag Luft in Frankfurt-on-the-Main, Germany.

"The second source is newspapers given to us by the Germans. They are usually a week old and, of course, report only the nazi party line. These are usually crumpled-up and used for toilet paper.

"The third and main source of news is our secret homemade radio. This is an illegal radio, of course, and if discovered, severe punishment would follow. Parts necessary to assemble the radio were either smuggled into the camp or we used existing materials. For example, wiring inside the barracks is stripped of its strands and used to build the receiving band. (The many parts that are smuggled into the camp are by way of an elaborate distribution system. In England certain crew members, usually one officer and one enlisted man, have been secretly trained in this system to distribute, assemble, and interpret certain coded messages. Lt. Morgan is unaware that Lt. Wirth was selected and trained by MIS-X in these activities.) The radio plays a vital role to receive regular BBC news from London on the war effort. Once the news is received, it is typed on typewriters (which are provided by the Germans to be used for the numerous reports we must submit) and put into the camp's underground newspaper. Our newspaper is appropriately named POW WOW. (Prisoners of War Waiting on Winning.) Once the POW WOW is printed; our newspaper boys deliver a single copy to each compound in secret. The POW WOW is read only once at night, *under guarded conditions, and immediately destroyed, usually by burning.*

"It is almost the end of June, 1944 and our favorite pastime is just lying or sitting in the shade of the barracks. We are still excited about the invasion of France on June 6th and discuss it daily. Food has been cut again so we just try and conserve our energy.

"Mid-July, 1944 is here and the days seem to last forever. The sun rises at 0430 hours and it is usually daylight until 2300 hours. By now the thrill of the invasion has worn off and the war in France is at a stalemate. This knowledge tends to cause spirits to droop. I wonder if we will ever be liberated as the progress in France is so slow.

"During the latter part of July we are again visited by the mighty Eighth Air Force. Several hundred American bombers heading towards Peenemunde, Germany are observed. (Peenemunde is the secret site of the German V-rockets.) These formations are at a very high altitude and we can barely see the B-17s and B-24s. They appear like small dots or specks against a blue background. The formations take several minutes to pass over us. We feel content knowing that great destruction will be brought home to the German war machine today.

"In a short time we hear the formations winging their way westward and home. I feel certain that our 384th B-17s are a part of this destructive force and I am proud as a peacock.

"This time the formations are attacked by German fighters. We grounded eagles are only passive participants as the air battle unfolds. Our fighters try to protect the bombers as the Jerries try to shoot them down. I spot a twin engine P-38 American fighter with smoke and fire belching from its engine. It is swirling down to earth. I watch horrified, as the pilot fails to pull out of his death dive. He disappears from my view. I hear a crash. I know the pilot is dead. With heavy hearts we disperse and return to our hot, boring, and frustrating existence.

"The end of August rolls around and summer has just about played out its hand. At night the temperatures are starting to fall into the low 40s and a blanket is required. It is doubtful if my blanket or uniform will last another winter. The war news is somewhat in our favor but I know that it will take weeks, maybe months, to end or reach some type of agreement.

"The POWs take a vote in early September. The vote is unanimous. The war would be over before Christmas. If the vote results are correct, we have only four more months of confinement!

"Mid-September arrives and a hint of fall is in the air. Breezes off the Baltic Sea are becoming colder. The days are shorter and nights are getting longer.

"It is the first week of October and a grand and glorious event occurs. The camp receives a shipment of packages from homes across America. Each of our crew receives a package. For the first time in eight months we are blessed to have goodies from loved ones. We are careful to share with those that did not receive a package.

"October and November are now just a memory. We are confined to the barracks most of the time due to shorter and colder days. Most outside activities, such as sports, are curtailed.

"Mid-December, we witness a type of German fighter that our crew had discussed about whether it existed. The camp is buzzed by a German jet fighter. It has twin engines and travels at a very high speed when compared to the current propeller driven aircraft. It remains in the area just a couple of minutes and then disappears. Our engineer, Sam, had reported seeing one of these jets make a pass on Doc on one of our missions. This is the topic of conversation for the next few days. (This aircraft was the Me262 jet fighter, which was introduced too late in World War II to effect the outcome of the war.)

"When the invasion was under way and in our favor, we predicted an early end to the war. December 25, 1944 was voted by the camp as the date for the end of the war. Our entire plan for life in Stalag Luft I is geared to this day of liberation.

"The first of December rolls around and our prediction for the war's end and our liberation requires an adjustment. It is now mid-December so we decide to stay for the winter.

"December 23rd, just two days before Christmas. The strength of the camp has grown from approximately 2,000 in February 1944 to 6,000 by this time. Living conditions are extremely crowded and the food situation is very bad. The Germans have cut our food by two-thirds. We are, however, grateful for this much and all continue to share with others.

"December 25th, and my first Christmas in confinement. Homesick with memories of past holidays, I manage to get through this day and the remaining days of December 1944.

"It is the last day of 1944 and snow came last night to remind me that Stalag Luft I has been my home for almost a year. My brain is branded with the burning question of time. How much longer? At times, my country seems so far away that I wonder if I will ever get home.

"January 4, 1945 and I have been a POW for exactly one year. As the first year of German military imprisonment draws to a close, I look back on unhappy months and recall definite mental stages through which all American prisoners of war seem to struggle.

"When I first arrived at this fantastic place of barbed-wire and armed sentry towers, I was fresh from the enthusiasm of stupendous scientific combat. Though suddenly deprived of weapons and liberty, I retain my enthusiasm and am hopelessly optimistic. The war will end within three months!

"I lazily loaf, telling and listening to hair-raising 'there I wuz' stories. After a month, time begins to drag. I get the education bug and take a psychology class. Three months pass, and the war progresses slowly. Time really begins to creep. Still optimistic, home by Christmas, '45!

"Crowded quarters discourage scholastic concentration. Classes taught by inexperienced fellow prisoners fail to make time pass quickly. I turn to reading and entertainment with activities such as state clubs, debates, choirs, dramatic, and camp journalism. Time passes a little faster because these activities occupy both mind and energy.

"Christmas has come and gone. The war plods slowly onward. My mind shifts gears; instead of predicting victory, I begin to wonder when and if the war will end. An entire year has passed and barbed wire still pens me in. Now I expect nothing. I merely wait. Like a Chinese philosopher, I patiently wait. Some day, the war must end."

Lt. Wirth recalls the last months of imprisonment and the near starvation of the POW's:

"It is the first week in February 1945. Hunger dominates my very existence. Red Cross parcels that we were receiving once a month have stopped. This means that we will receive only the German starvation rations. The supply of our rations is in direct proportion to the area of Germany being overrun by the Allied forces. The more territory the Allied forces capture, the less food we receive. With each mile gained by the allies we receive less and less food from our captors.

"In addition to the lack of food, the water and lights are off most of the time. During the first week of March, lights are off continuously. By 1700 hours each day, the barracks are in total darkness throughout the long, cold, windy, winter nights. I am slowly starving within my dark isolated world of barbed wire.

"During the months of February and March, I lose over 45 pounds — typical with all of the POWs. I now know that thin men can and do

lose weight. It is so bad that our only concern is to ration our meager supply of food to keep us alive until the war ends. The war news is upbeat as the Russians are advancing from the east, the Americans from the south and the British from the west. Our only hope is for a quick end to this war.

"It is the middle of March and the camp is alerted by air raid sirens of American bombers overhead. The sirens signal us to get inside the barracks or stay inside. In my compound one of my barracks mates, Lt. E. F. Wyman, did not hear the sirens, or was too hungry to care and wandered out of his barracks. A nervous tower guard fires on him sending a bullet crashing into his head. He dies instantaneously. In another compound, at the same time, another POW is shot through the stomach. He dies a few minutes later. Our lives have deteriorated into a truly miserable state. Where are our liberators?"

Stalag 17B: More Than Just a Hollywood Movie

In late January, 1944, when T/Sgts. Honeycutt and Peifer, S/Sgts. Craden, Gilrane, Parker, and Polley arrive at Stalag 17B, the American Red Cross (ARC) had recently completed a visit to the camp on January 12, 1944. A report, based on the ARC visit, was prepared by the Army's Military Intelligence Service.[1] This report provides information on Stalag 17B such as location and strength, as well as information regarding treatment of the American prisoners of war.

**Military Intelligence Service Report
STALAG 17B
(Air Force Non-Commissioned Officers)**

Stalag 17B is situated 100 meters northwest of Gneixendorf, a village that is six kilometers northwest of Krems, Austria. Mostly peasants who raise cattle and truck farm populate the surrounding area. The camp itself was in use as a concentration camp from 1938 until 1940 when it began receiving French and Poles as the first POWs.

On October 13, 1943, 1,350 non-commissioned officers of the U.S. Air Force were transferred from Stalag 7A to Stalag 17B, which already contained POWs from France, Italy,

---

Russia, Yugoslavia, and various smaller nations. At the time of the first protecting power[2] (United States) visit on January 12, 1944, the American strength was 2,667. The Americans occupy five compounds (4,5,7,8, and 9), each of which measures 175 yards by 75 yards and contains four double barracks 100 by 240 feet. The barracks are built to accommodate approximately 240 men, but at least 400 men are crowded into them. Each double barrack contains a washroom with six basins in the center of the building. The beds in the barracks are triple-decked, and each tier has four compartments with one man to a compartment, making a total of 12 men in each group. Each single barrack has a stove to supply heat and cooking facilities for approximately 200 men. The fuel ration for a week is 54 pounds of coal. Because of the lack of heating and an insufficient number of blankets, the men sleep two to a bunk for added warmth. Lighting facilities are very poor, and many light bulbs are missing at times.

Aside from the nine double barracks used for housing purposes, one barrack is reserved for the infirmary and the medical personnel's quarters. Half of a barrack is used as a library, and the other half for the Man of Confidence[3] (MOC) and his staff. A half of another barrack is used as a theater and the other half for Red Cross food distribution. Another barrack is used for a meeting room. In addition, one barrack is used as a repair shop for shoes and clothing. Two barracks are not used because they are considered by the Germans to be too close to the fence, thus making it possible for POWs to build short tunnels for escape. One of these buildings is used as a gymnasium, and the other as a chapel. Latrines are open pit type and are situated away from the barracks.

Two separate wire fences charged with electricity surround the area, and four watch towers equipped with machine guns are placed at strategic points. At night street lights are used in addition to the searchlights from the guard towers to illuminate the area.

The U.S. Senior NCO is Staff Sergeant Kenneth J. Kurtenbach who is the MOC. Major Fred H. Beaumont is the Senior American Officer (SAO) and the medical officer, but takes no active part in the camp administration. Captain Stephen Kane is the sole chaplain and acts in an advisory capacity whenever called upon. There also exists a security committee.

The following German officers are in control in the positions indicated.

Oberst Kuhn	Commandant
Major Wenglorz	Security Officer
Major Eigl (Luftwaffe)	Lager Officer
Oberstabarzt Dr. Pilger	Doctor

The blame for the bad conditions that exist at Stalag 17B is placed on Oberst Kuhn, the camp Commander, who is both unreasonable and uncooperative. Four months have elapsed since the opening of the compound before the MOC is granted an interview with the commandant to register protests. Weeks pass before written requests are acknowledged. Frequently, orders are issued to the MOC verbally and are never confirmed in writing. Some cooperation is obtained from Major Eigl, but since there is friction between him (Luftwaffe) and the other German officers (Wehrmacht), his authority is extremely limited. Treatment by guards is harsh and restrictions are oppressive. Relations between POWs and Germans are poor. Three POWs in this camp have been shot in violation of the Geneva Convention and others have been beaten. Treatment in this camp is worse than any other German camp with the exception of Stalag 2B.

The treatment at Stalag 17B is not considered good, and is at times even brutal. An example of extreme brutality occurred in December 1943. Two men, Sgts. Ralph Lavoie and Jim Proakis, attempting to escape, were discovered in an out-of-bounds area adjoining the compound. As soon as they were discovered, they threw up their hands indicating their surrender. They were shot while their hands were raised. One of the men died immediately, but the other was only injured in the leg. After he fell a guard ran to within 20 feet of him and fired again. The guard then turned toward the barracks and fired shots in that direction. One shot entered a barracks and seriously wounded S/Sgt. Binnebose who was lying in his bunk. Permission was denied the Americans by the Germans to bring the body of the dead man into the compound for burial, and medical treatment for the injured man in the outer zone was delayed several hours. The following is the Official War Crimes Office Report relating to this escape attempt's tragic ending.

OFFICIAL WAR CRIMES OFFICE REPORT

TO: War Crimes Office: concerning shooting on December 2, 1943, at Stalag XVIIB in Krems, Austria, re-attempted escape of Sergeant James Proakis and Sergeant Ralph Lavoie. Prisoners were crawling from their barracks toward a fence when their presence was discovered and German camp guards fired on them. Sergeant Proakis stood up and ran toward a slit trench (in mid-compound) but was cut down by machine gun or rifle fire. Two guards approached and fired bullets into his body. Sergeant Lavoie, although wounded, stood up when the guards approached. One of the guards showed intent to shoot him and Lavoie lunged forward to protect himself and was shot through the right shoulder. Then he was shot again through the neck and he lost consciousness. Inside a barracks, Sergeant Binnebose, while sleeping in his bunk, was seriously wounded by bullets fired by the indiscriminate shooting of the German prison guards. The two men outside had surrendered when shot, according to an eyewitness and one of the victims. Evidence was given that firing continued after surrender, well within the fence, but even after incapacitation. This was "unlawful wounding," violating the Law of War, Geneva Prisoner of War Convention of 1929.[4]

In another case, a mentally sick POW was taken to the hospital where no provisions were made to handle cases of this type. In a moment of insanity the POW jumped from a window and ran to the fence, followed by a French doctor and orderlies who shouted to the guard not to shoot him. He was dressed in hospital pajamas, which should have indicated to the guard that he was mentally unbalanced even if the doctor had not called the warning. As the patient climbed over the fence the guard shot him in the heart.

There are 30 recorded cases of guards striking POWs with bayonets, pistols, and rifle butts. Protests to the commandant are useless. In fact, on one occasion the commandant is reported to have stated that the man was lucky to get off so lightly.

Food is poor in quantity and quality. In January, a one-day ration issue for five POWs consists of three potatoes, one cup of soup, 22 grams of bread, half a cup of ersatz coffee, and three grams of margarine.

When supplies of Red Cross parcels are received in the camp, the German authorities reduce their ration issue. Even though the MOC and the Protecting Power make protests to the Commandant, this practice continues. As soon as the Red Cross supplies are exhausted, the Germans again issue the normal ration.

For the first three months of confinement absolutely no eating utensils are supplied to POWs. At the end of that time, one bowl and one spoon are given to each third man. POWs are able to make bowls and spoons from Klim (milk spelled backwards) cans, which also serve as drinking mugs.

The health situation is bad. Twenty-five wounded men are arriving weekly. Many wear field dressings two and three weeks old. The Chief American Medical Officer declares that the Germans delay badly needed medical supplies shipped from Geneva. Three American medical officers and a dentist are here.

In general, the health of the POWs is not good. Approximately 150 attend sick call each day with skin diseases, upper-respiratory infections, and stomach ailments. About 30 percent of all cases at sick call are for skin diseases attributed to the conditions they live in. The acute shortage of water (available four hours each day), lack of hot water, lack of laundry facilities, and over-crowded sleeping conditions create many health problems.

The clothing condition in the camp is not satisfactory because most of the men had received inadequate issues when they passed through Dalag Luft.

There are insufficient blankets. Two thin cotton blankets are supposed to be issued by the Germans. Many POWs describe these as tablecloths. Only two-thirds of the men are fortunate enough to be issued one.

As in other camps, the leather flying jackets most of the men wore at the time of their capture were taken away, but after repeated protests, some of these were returned. Shoes are a problem but the repair shop operated by POWs alleviates the condition to some extent. The Serbian shoes issued when GI shoes are not available from the stock Red Cross supplies prove to be inadequate in quality to withstand the cold and mud.

Incoming mail delivery is very irregular and considered unsatisfactory by POWs. Since all of their mail has to be processed through Stalag Luft 3, censorship often delays it four and five weeks. Surface letters require an average of four months for delivery compared to three months for airmail. Surprisingly enough, personal parcels often arrive in two months, but the average time in transit is three to five months.

When parcels are delivered to the camp, a list of the recipients is posted in the barrack. These men are required to lineup outside the delivery room. Before the POW can take possession of his parcel, the German guard opens the parcel, takes everything out, and punches holes in any tinned foods. POWs are permitted to keep the containers. No items are ever confiscated from these parcels as far as can be ascertained.

Representatives of the International Red Cross Committee and the Protecting Power (United States) visit the camp approximately every three months, and always transmit the complaints of the MOC to the German authorities in a strong manner. On many occasions, the representatives report unsatisfactory conditions at the camp to the State Department, and make every attempt to correct such conditions at the time of the visit.

Captain Stephen Kane is the sole chaplain for Americans. Among many other activities, he serves 300 communions daily. Kane, hard working and inspirational, is a pillar of morale. Germans do not directly interfere with his activities but guard him more closely than other chaplains.

Even though repeated requests for additional chaplains are made to the German authorities, Captain Stephen W. Kane carries the full ecclesiastical burden for the camp. The POWs cooperated with Father Kane in converting a barrack into a chapel for religious services. Father Kane holds daily services for the Catholics of the camp, and offers additional services for the Protestant POWs. His untiring efforts on behalf of the men contribute a great deal to the morale and discipline of the camp.

End of report.

As a result of the harsh treatment by the Germans to Stalag 17B POWs, the United States Department of State sent a telegram to the German government on May 2, 1944 protesting this treatment (Image 30.1).

Sam remembers and relates his first full day in Stalag 17B, which includes his introduction to the camp's Man of Confidence, Sergeant Kenneth Kurtenbach:

"As a precaution to guard against internal camp security, we newly arriving POWs are brought before the camp Commander, who lectures us on camp administration and security. After this brief orientation, I request to speak with Sgt. Kurtenbach in private. At this meeting I confide to Kurtenback that I know the secret letter codes, having been trained as a Code User (CU) by MIS-X back in England. Kurtenbach is jubilant.

TELEGRAM SENT

DEPARTMENT OF STATE   PLAIN

Washington,
May 2, 1944

Charge Department

From the Special War Problems Division
DEPARTMENT OF STATE TO:
W... Col. Brown
Date: 5/2/44

AMLEGATION,
Bern.

1522, Second

Legationis 2511, April 20.

Please request the Swiss Legation, Berlin, to deliver the following textually to the German Government:

The Government of the United States has received three reports by neutral observers who have visited Stalag XVIIB during the last five months. These reports indicate that the standards of treatment experienced by American prisoners of war at Stalag XVIIB are far below the standards of the Geneva Prisoners of War Convention.

The action of the German authorities in decreasing the food rations of American prisoners of war since January 24, 1944 from the ration of troops at base camps is clearly contrary to Article II of the Geneva Prisoners of War Convention. There is no provision in that Convention which relieves the detaining Power of the responsibility of providing a food ration for prisoners of war which shall be equal in quantity and quality to that of troops

-2-

troops at base camps. As the Commandant at Stalag XVIIB has explained that the reduction in rations was ordered by the German High Command, the German Government is clearly responsible for this infraction of the standards of the Convention. Moreover, the German authorities have not provided adequate facilities in order that the prisoners may themselves prepare additional food which they might have. This, too, is a violation of Article II of the Treaty and of a clear obligation upon the German Government. A detaining Power which does not provide at least a bowl and a spoon for each prisoner to use while eating can not be considered to be providing properly for the maintenance of its prisoners.

Neutral observers have consistently reported that Stalag XVIIB is extremely overcrowded and that this situation is partially responsible for some of the deficiencies which are set forth below. The German Government is reminded in this connection that it is obligated under Article 10 of the Geneva Prisoners of War Convention to lodge prisoners in buildings or barracks affording all possible guarantees of hygiene and healthfulness and to provide dormitories which shall afford to the prisoners the same standards of space, air, arrangement and bedding as for troops at base camps.

Although

Image 30.1: Protest letter on conditions at Stalag 17B from United States Department of State (Hull) to German government.

-3-

Although the German Government is bound by Article 13 of the Geneva Prisoners of War Convention to furnish prisoners a sufficient quantity of water for the care of their own bodily cleanliness, it is reported that in March but one-third of the American prisoner in Stalag XVIIB had had one bath in five months.

The care of American sick and wounded at Stalag XVIIB has been a matter of concern to the American Government for it is known that the infirmary is unsuited for the purpose to which it is being put. There are no kitchen facilities for the preparation of special diets. There is no hot water for bathing, the quarters of the sick are inadequately heated, blankets and bed linen are not available in sufficient quantities, and no pajamas have been furnished by the German authorities.

Such clothing as has been furnished to American prisoners of war at Stalag XVIIB has been furnished through Red Cross channels and has not been furnished by the detaining Power. Moreover, in spite of the view of the German Foreign Office that the obligation to provide prisoners of war with clothing is not modified by the availability of Red Cross supplies and in spite of the obligation upon the German Government under Article 12 of the Geneva Convention to provide clothing, linen and footwear for the prisoners, that German Government has not even furnished

material

-4-

material so that clothing and shoes of the prisoners could be repaired and for which there is a great need in the camp.

The American Government reminds the German Government that German prisoners of war in the United States have consistently been provided with shelter, food, clothing and medical care which is equivalent to the very high level enjoyed by members of the American armed forces. In view of this situation and in view of the obligation which the German Government has under the Geneva Prisoners of War Convention, the Government of the United States protests vigorously concerning the conditions which now exist at Stalag XVIIB and requests the German Government immediately to take the steps necessary to grant to Americans held at that camp the standards of treatment which are prescribed by the Geneva Prisoners of War Convention and to assure the American Government that such steps are being taken without delay.

HULL

(BG)

711.62114 I.R./133

SWP:ETB:DP   CE   Le

Image 30.1: (continued)

"'I was hoping to receive more CUs to broaden my code network. Each POW only gets to write two letters a month, therefore, I can use more CUs.'

"After leaving the meeting with Sgt. Kurtenbach, I am accompanied by two other POWs, who never let me out of their sight for two days. The purpose of their company is to make a positive identification to verify my identity. Casually, the two POWs question me about my group and squadron. They also question other POWs from my group and/or squadron to verify my background.

"All of the informal security checks must have passed for after two days my escorts disappear. Their departure is a relief for there are two options for failure to pass the security checks. Return me to the Germans claiming I am not a U.S. airman, or drown me in the camp latrine because of suspicions that I am a German impostor.

"Sgt. Kurtenbach had already set-up a subcommittee to handle CU correspondence. Sergeants Al Hadden and John Susan were in charge of the CUs in the correspondence section. Sgt. Susan was assigned the task of organizing the CUs in the camp. I am to report to him for future instructions."

Gilly remembers the *Doc* crew's foray for freedom:

"We had been in confinement only a few days when Shorty and I decided to form a tunnel digging team. Shorty, Pete, and I are assigned to Barrack 19A while Gibby is assigned to Barrack 39A. I ask my other crew members if they would like to become tunnel diggers and all agree, except Pete and Wilber. They feel that their best chance to survive the war is to just sit it out. Sam replies that he would participate in the tunnel digging but did not want to be an escapee. (Due to his MIS-X code user training and potential for aiding others to escape by corresponding with MIS-X, Sam believes his duty is to stay in Stalag 17B until liberated.) Their replies surprise me. We are determined, however, and a few days later, with the support of many other POWs, the tunnel work begins in earnest.

"It is obvious to me that some of the POWs look upon tunnel digging as a means to pass the time and are not really serious about escaping. This is not our case as we have full intention of escaping from this place.

"Digging a tunnel is not a simple task and serious planning is required prior to actually digging. There are many problems to consider.

"Number one is location. Not just any location will do. It must be from under one of the barracks. Barrack 39A (Gibby's barrack) is *selected because it is relatively close to the fence, being about 150 yards in a direct line.*

"Number two is detection. The work must be completely hidden from view. This is a constant problem as patrol guards walk through the camp during the day and the tower guards are always looking for any unusual activity. Having lookouts posted at certain locations to signal approaching roving guards will solve this. Compound #9 has been divided into two sections, with the portion nearest the gate designated as the S, or safety zone, and the portion nearest to Barrack 39A being the D, or danger zone. If a roving guard enters D zone, a watchman will tail him and warnings will be relayed to the Barrack 39A security POW. If a German gets too near Barrack 39A, he will be delayed in order to give the POWs time to cover the tunnel entrance. Other POWs will keep the tower guards distracted as much as possible. There will be about 100 watchmen used as lookouts, none of which will know exactly what they are guarding.

"Number three is obstructions. The routing of the tunnel must be carefully calculated to prevent interference with barracks pillar foundations, telephone poles extending underground, or other underground obstacles. The route must be direct as possible to prevent unnecessary work.

"Number four is accessibility. The tunnel entrance must be accessible from a room in the barrack. This room should be one that the Germans rarely inspect. Gibby, in Barrack 39A, is the barracksfuehrer. He selects the cleaning room where mops and brooms are stored. The room has a strange smell and the Germans avoid it like the plague.

"Number five is time constraints. The tunnel must be completed within a certain time frame. The total time to complete the work must not be greater than two months. Every two months the Germans inspect under each barrack and the tunnel must be complete and ready for the escape prior to this inspection. This inspection is done by guards, (called ferrets by the POWs), usually accompanied by a German police dog. This inspection is always done at night using powerful searchlights. The dog's job is to locate freshly dug dirt and to start scratching at it. This notifies the ferret and he then pushes a pointed steel rod into the fresh dirt, going down four to five feet. This method allows the ferret to determine if there is a tunnel beneath the fresh dirt. Stalag 17B has experienced ferrets and the chance of their missing a tunnel is very rare.

"Number six is tools. The tools to dig the tunnel must be made from existing materials. Digging tools must be fashioned from cups, cans, or spoons. The best tools are made from the Red Cross powdered milk (KLIM) cans, which measure about four inches in diameter and depth. This method is slow and backbreaking as the digging must go on 24-hours-a-day until complete.

"Number seven is disposal. The problem of disposing of the dirt without the Germans discovering it is very important and critical to the success of our tunnel. We consider two methods of dirt disposal. The first method is to store the excavated dirt in the walls of the barracks. This was determined not to be a viable method as the walls are constructed with thin boards on the inside and tarpaper on the outside. The boards will bow with very little weight from the dirt. In addition, POWs remove the wallboards from time to time for firewood. The method that we will use is that of spreading the dirt around camp. POWs will fill their pockets with dirt, drift around camp slowly and discharge the contents of their pockets at any location that they would not be noticed.

"Number eight is Escape Committee approval. After finding solutions to the first seven problems, approval is required from the Escape Committee. Escape plans are not rubber-stamped. Each must pass the review of the Escape Committee. Such factors as support for the escape must be considered. This support includes passports, civilian clothes, and routes. I am confident that the first seven problems are solved and the eighth, Escape Committee approval, will be requested in a few days.

"With these problems to face, our band of diggers embark on our tunnel to freedom in early February. Shorty, Gibby, six others, and myself will work on the tunnel in three-man shifts, twelve hours a day, seven days a week. In addition, many other POWs have volunteered as watchmen or to spread the dirt about the camp.

"A collection of digging cans and cardboard boxes are assembled in the 'odorous' cleaning room. The plan is for the tunnel to be dug due north for 30 yards to avoid going under Barrack #40, which is under special observation by the guards because of its closeness to the fence. This means that this section of the tunnel would run parallel with the fence (Image 30.2). The tunnel will then be dug due east towards the fence for about 230 yards. It must clear the fence and the tunnel exit must be a few yards into the wooded area of the camp cemetery. This means digging for 260 yards in less than 60 days, over four yards a day.

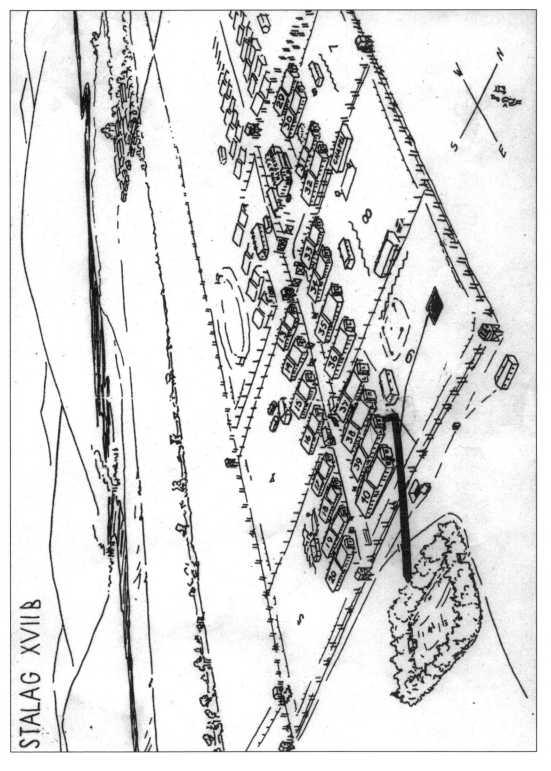

Image 30.2: Sketch of Stalag 17B, Krems, Austria indicating escape tunnel routing from Barracks 39 into wooded area of camp cemetery.

This will be a difficult task with our crude tools but we are confident of our success.

"The tunnel is started the next morning after the guards normal bi-monthly inspection. The shift starts with one man in the tunnel and the other two passing the dirt back in cardboard boxes to the dirt disposers. Only one man can be in the tunnel actually digging due to its small diameter. On the first day a few feet are excavated in the downward direction, then black topsoil gives way to mostly clay. This is the type of soil we had hoped for as it will provide strong walls to support the surrounding earth. This will prevent us having to shore up the tunnel walls against possible cave-ins. As the tunnel progresses it takes more men to pass the cardboard boxes out of the tunnel to the disposal men for distribution of the dirt.

"Each shift has a designated man to actually do the digging. At first the digger can dig for his total shift but as we get further into the tunnel the air gets staler and less of it, thus, the amount of time a digger can stay in the tunnel is reduced proportionately. The digger has the worst job and the dirt passers, the second worst.

"The best job is the POWs acting as watchmen. Their task is to warn the men inside the tunnel when a German enters Compound #9 gate, which is less than a 100 yards away. If the guard enters the gate, the watchmen must alert the tunnel diggers and if the guard continues in the direction of Barrack #39, they must give the order to get out of the tunnel. It is important to be out of the tunnel if discovered by the guards, for then you are protected by the agreement. (The agreement with the Germans is that only those caught in the tunnel or caught in the actual act of escaping will be shot.)

"As we start our third day of this labor intensive effort, I am ordered to report to the MOC, S/Sgt. Kenneth Kurtenbach. I report, as ordered, and am given a severe tongue lashing for not clearing the escape plan with the Escape Committee. S/Sgt. Kurtenbach informs me, 'You can proceed with your tunnel and you can dig as many tunnels as you please, but any escape plans must be coordinated and cleared with the Escape Committee. Do you understand?' I submitted the escape plan to the Escape Committee that day.

"The escape plan covers two areas that will require Escape Committee support. The first is clothing. Clothing for the escape will be made from bed sheets, blankets, uniforms, towels, and pieces of Red Cross kits. Dye for the clothing will be made from indelible leads, permanganate of potash, gentian violet borrowed from the hospital, cof-

fee or tea, and boiled bookbindings. Dyeing will be done in the barrack at night. Each article of clothing must be dry before the morning roll call.

"At this time I am not sure how many POWs will actually make the escape, however, the escape plan indicates we will make 20 civilian suits. Belts will be made from black tar paper removed from barrack walls or made from cutting strips from leather boots. Removing the pockets and belts from our uniform tunics and rounding off the sharp corners of the collars turns the uniforms into coats. Pants will be made from dyed uniforms or from scraping our wool blankets with a razor to resemble serge material.

"The second support required from the escape committee is documentation. Travel permits, work permits, ration coupons, personal IDs, and even passports will be counterfeited. All will be hand-drawn and forged with colored stamps that will be hand-carved from rubber shoe heels.

"I am granted preliminary approval to continue the tunnel. Final approval will take another week.

"The next morning, our fourth, the tunnel is started again. After six days the tunnel section running north and parallel with the fence is complete. In six working days we have dug 30 yards. We are on schedule.

"Digging operations continue for 40 more days and we are slightly ahead of schedule. We have completed 46 days of digging, and if our calculations are correct, the tunnel exit should be in the wooded area next to the camp cemetery (Image 30.2). Tomorrow night we will go out. Pictures for fake passports (Image 30.3), papers and civilian clothes are hidden in Barrack #39A in preparation for the escape. As I lay in my bunk daydreaming on this eve of our foray for freedom a soft snow is falling over the camp.

"Normally, when the guards come into the barracks in the morning, they yell 'Rous, rous, drop your cocks, and pick up your socks!'(The POWs, during their basic training, were awakened by this greeting and had taught it to the Germans). They then rap the foot of our wooden bunks with the sticks they carry.

"This morning is quite different. Guards armed with machine pistols and dogs come into Barrack 39A suddenly and literally chase the POWs out. Some jump out windows into the two or three inches of snow that had fallen the night before. Guards line up the POWs and hold their weapons on them. A German camp officer enters Barracks

Image 30.3: Escape pictures of Sgt. Harry Alexander (Gilly) Gilrane taken during March, 1944.

39A, along with Gestapo men in their leather overcoats. Gibby, being the barrack fuehrer, is ordered to report to the German officer. The guards start a search and soon open a wall. Inside they discover faithful copies of civilian suits and other escape material. Next, they go directly to the tunnel entry hidden in the wash room under a concrete basin. The German officer yells down into the tunnel to demand anyone there to come out or else. Immediately the guards fire down into the tunnel with their machine pistols. There are two POWs in the tunnel at the cemetery exit point making final preparation for our escape tonight. I know the two POWs are not hit for the tunnel makes a 90-degree turn after about 30 yards. The guards refuse to go down into the tunnel for fear of booby-traps.

"How was our tunnel discovered? Do we have a German plant in our barracks? Did one of our POWs rat in exchange for favors? Did the Germans know all along? No, none of these had divulged our secret. It was Mother Nature. What had tipped the Germans off is the snow that had fallen last night. The dirt under the camp is fine and compact so the tunnel was dug only a few feet down without fear of cave-ins. The heat from the barrack had vented down into the tunnel and had warmed the snow above melting a line stretching from the barrack all the way out of the camp to the nearest clump of trees in the cemetery.

"After the Germans finish searching the barrack, they bring a fully loaded honey wagon (a tanker used to pump out the latrines), down to

the barrack. The German officer and Gestapo leave the barrack and the Sergeant of the Guard is left in charge to supervise running a hose into the tunnel entry. It is his intention to literally drown anyone in the tunnel with sewage from the tanker. Gibby realizes what is happening and protests. The sergeant ignores Gibby and gives the signal to start the pump. Gibby, in desperation, turns to the sergeant, whom he had gotten to know, and asks him, 'What would your mother say?' It was as if the sergeant had been slapped, and he stops the pump. The two POWs in the tunnel are allowed to exit and are thrown into isolation to await trial. We are then ordered, under German supervision, to refill the tunnel.

"Ironically, and lucky for us, we knew that German guards walked out to the clump of trees at the cemetery in the morning, so we assumed the guards who came back in the evening were the same ones. They weren't. The tunnel was going to surface only a short distance directly in front of a machine gun that was manned 24-hours-a-day!"

During the entire life of Stalag 17B (over five years), not one POW made a successful escape. This record can be credited to the detailed methods used by the Germans in guarding POWs confined in Stalag 17B.

★ ★ ★

CHAPTER

31

Code Warriors

During his 16 months of confinement at Stalag 17B T/Sgt. Sam Honeycutt would write several coded messages hidden within letters home to his wife and family. A letter written in early March, 1944 gave him the satisfaction that he could still carry out the war behind barbed wire. Sam describes the events that allowed him to provide pertinent intelligence to MIS-X:

"Though mostly confined within the perimeters of Stalag 17B, on occasions some POWs are taken on errands into Krems to off-load trains or some other tasks. These POWs are an invaluable source of information concerning military operations that could be signaled back to the states by secret letter code. The camp's intelligence unit is responsible for identifying and questioning any POW who had access to the outside.

"It is during the first week of March, 1944, that I am ordered to report to Sgt. Susan to receive information that had been obtained by a POW on an errand to Krems. Provided with a sealed envelope and ordered to prepare a coded letter, I proceed to a designated barrack and a cubicle within the barrack where all the camp CUs are assigned for security reasons.

"The sealed envelope contained a message detailing a large German Army force of men and equipment concentrating on the north side of the Danube River, east of Krems.

"I request help from another CU as the codes are difficult to write. You must use certain words that will properly fit the general tone of the letter as well as the secret message. The other CU and I need to help each other to find the right words. It is meticulous work. While I work on the letter, the other CU also stands security lookout. We also have a security guard outside in case a ferret or guard shows up. If a guard shows up the security CU will detain him with a question or some other distraction. The CU on security at the cubicle door will alert me to give me a minute to button up.

"I decide to use the weather as the main subject matter of the letter as the camp and area are blanketed with about eight inches of snow. The Germans had been using the POWs to clear the camp and local roads of snow so I thought this to be a proper subject to fit the local conditions. The coded letter is completed on March 3, 1944 and placed in the regular camp mail on that day."

In early May 1944, one of the 24 women sorting mail at the New York Censor's office stopped sorting when she spotted a return address of Stalag 17B, Krems, Austria. It was her job to examine incoming mail and pull all letters and packages with a return address of a POW camp in Europe. She put Sam's letter in an overhead routing box, which a messenger emptied every hour. She knew the letter was important but did not know why.

Sam's letter was placed into a security envelope that afternoon and flown by courier plane to Washington, DC. Alerted that a letter was en route, MIS-X dispatched an officer to meet the courier plane at Bolling Field Air Force Base, five miles south of DC on the Maryland side of the Potomac River. Thirty minutes after the letter arrived at 1142, the decoding section had deciphered Sam's message. The deciphered message read:

Heavy German concentration four miles east of camp and north of Danube.

It was signed "Runt" and the return address was Stalag 17B, a NCOs' camp in Krems, Austria. "Runt" was the code name that MIS-X had assigned to Sam (see Appendix D).

A study of the Red Cross list of POWs by MIS-X revealed the sender to be T/Sgt. John Samuel Honeycutt, an engineer and top turret gunner, in the 384th Bomb Group operating out of Grafton-Underwood, England.

Apparently, from his message, the Germans were building up their forces around Krems in anticipation of a possible Russian offensive in this area. This coded letter from Sam clearly required immediate action. Following a discussion with the Pentagon, MIS-X decides to act on the message at once.

Sam remembers a BBC broadcast message that he would never forget for it confirmed that he was not a passive POW victim, grounded and inoperative, but an active resister capable of carrying on the war behind barbed-wire:

> *"About midnight during the third week in May, 1944, we are gathered around a radio listening to a BBC broadcast. We regularly monitor the BBC at a specific time of night when signals are forthcoming. The majority of signals are intended for ears other than ours.*
>
> *"Using the BBC is one of the cleverest ways of communication — the cryptology is simple, yet foolproof.*
>
> *"We had been alerted previously for a special signal to come through on this night. We have no clue as to what it concerns. Our speculations run wild.*
>
> *"Several times the guards wander through the barracks on their rounds. We are trying to monitor the radio broadcast for our signal. The radio was quickly in and out of its hiding place several times — each time requiring setting up the antenna and taking it down again. We are certain we will miss the broadcast and end up stationing a watchman about the area to detour the guards.*
>
> *"Finally, the time arrives and we are ready. The BBC comes in loud and free of static. It is short but sweet, 'RAF bombed an area of German concentration around Krems, Austria last night with destructive results.'"*

T/Sgt. John Samuel Honeycutt never knew who received his coded messages he addressed to his relatives or wife, but his efforts provided the War Department with valuable intelligence relayed through MIS-X. Had the enemy discovered his or other CUs' actions, they could have been executed as spies. In recognition of the contributions made by the CUs, Colonel Russell H. Sweet, Chief, Captured Personnel and Material Branch (Image 31.1) awarded them each the Bronze Star and a letter of appreciation.

WAR DEPARTMENT
MILITARY INTELLIGENCE SERVICE
WASHINGTON

22 August 1945

2nd Lt. Theodore M. Wirth
RFD #2
Nebraska City, Nebraska

Dear Lieutenant Wirth:

The particular service which you performed for the War Department while a prisoner of war in Germany merits the highest praise, and is greatly appreciated. Your name will be entered on the permanent official records of this Branch, along with all those who were connected with this exceedingly valuable activity.

Sincerely yours,

RUSSELL H. SWEET
Colonel, GSC
Chief, Captured Personnel
and Material Branch

Image 31.1

★ ★ ★

CHAPTER

32

Small Victories

After the shutdown of the tunnel spirits were low for a few weeks. In order to survive and to keep their morale up, small victories over the Germans are necessary. The POWs first small victory occurred in early April, 1944.

Shorty, the Brown Bomber, tells of the first victory called The Dysentery Pit:

> *"Stalag 17B is now surrounded by five German Army emplacements, a tank corps, and four other German emplacements composed of regular infantry. As a result, we are bombed quite regularly by allied Air Forces. (Stalag 17B area was bombed 297 times over a four-year period.)*
>
> *"During bombing, we are ordered into slit trenches for protection (a slit trench is dug into the ground about five feet deep and two feet wide). In the trenches, sometimes all night or all day, there are opportunities to dig fake tunnels to play jokes on our captors. We start a couple of fake tunnels, and one in particular, is fairly sophisticated with a couple of turns. About half way into this fake tunnel, we decided to dig a pit about three feet deep by two feet wide. You could not crawl through this tunnel without crawling over it.*

"After completing the pit, we invite everyone in Compound #5 with dysentery (almost all had it) to visit the pit. These visits go on for about a week. After the pit is full, we place a cardboard cover with a layer of dirt on top of it.

"Next, we let it be known via rumors to the guards that a great escape is planned and it is to be from this slit trench on a certain date. Sure enough, on this date, we are herded out of the barracks and into the open compound area. The senior guard, in all his glory, comes into the compound with his pistol drawn and into the slit trench he went.

"He located the suspect tunnel opening and went inside. In a few minutes we heard his highly excited voice cursing. He then made a hasty exit from the trench. Our German hero had indeed discovered our pit and bathed in the after results of the lousy German rations provided us. His uniform was OD (olive drab) and it smells to high heaven. His smelly exit from Compound #5 is proceeded by tremendous applause and the joyous laughter of several hundred POWs. Morale skyrockets and this small victory lasts us several weeks."

Gibby tells the story of his War with Vermin:

"Delousing. For me it means a shower to clean off two months of dirt and foul body odor. I will soon learn, however, that it also means hours of discomfort. I look forward to the shower but soon discover that delousing is an ordeal that must be tolerated with it.

"The first delousing for me is during the last week of April, 1944. My body has not made contact with soap and water since arriving at Stalag 17B in late January. Barrack #39 mates warn me in advance of the despised procedure, but I doubt their sincerity. I will soon discover, however, that delousing is the worst process imaginable.

"The delousing routine is conducted about every three months or whenever we have too many fleas and lice on our bodies or in the barracks. On the day of delousing, Barrack #40 is used as a spare bunkhouse for the POWs while Barrack #39 is being fumigated. It is extremely cold today and the compound is covered with about three inches of snow as we are herded outside of Barrack #39 with our blankets. We march under heavy guard up the hill, out the main gate, along the lane, and up the hill to the delouser.

"The delouser is located on the crest of a hill above the camp where every cold wind tries its gale force first before it sweeps down the hill into our barracks. We wait outside a small shed used for undressing for *an hour or more on this cold April morning while the wind is testing its force.*

"There is now available space inside the shed and the guards start shoving as many POWs as possible into it. We resist being crammed into this small shed with its dirt floor; however, the resistance ends when our captors stick bayonets into our backs and force us in. The shed is now overcrowded and the doors will not close. Five or six guards solve this by throwing themselves against the door and forcing it to close and lock. Inside we wait another half-hour in the cold, semi-dark surroundings.

"Finally we are ordered to undress. We strip down naked and stand with our clothes and blankets. Next, we are lined up single file and as we are leaving we hand our belongings to a Frenchman who puts them in the delousing oven where they are gassed to kill the vermin. On tap next is the shaving of heads. Several POWs do not like having their heads shaved. I feel trouble and possible conflict brewing. To prevent cutting their hair so close, a group of POWs has rubbed ersatz butter (made from coal oil) and sand in their hair, which, of course, plays havoc with the electric shears that the Frenchmen wield with great zeal. This causes extreme repercussions in the form of a special contingent of guards being sent down from the garrison. The officer in command is an older-looking lieutenant whose face is badly scarred. This special contingent lines our naked bodies up in the snow and their officer inspects our heads for evidence of sabotage. After singling out the offenders, he drives them out of line with the butt of his revolver amid his terrible epithets of Verdamdt Americanisch. *Solitary confinement will be the reward for those POWs who wanted to keep their hair.*

"Standing outside naked in the snow we wait our turn for the showers. Finally, after 30 minutes, our group of about 30 is ordered into the showers. The duration will be exactly one minute. If you do not soap up and wash it off quickly in less than 60 seconds ... you are shit out of luck.

"After the shower, we proceed, still naked, to another cold room. Mere body heat is the only deterrent from the cold. In this room we wait our turn to be inspected for lice. If you have lice Jerry makes you rub a blue colored jelly in your hair and private areas that gets rid of them. In fact, it not only takes the lice off, but also takes all the skin and hair off.

"From there we proceed into a fairly large, colder room. The fumes from the POWs' clothes, who have already left, are bad. It isn't long

before my head aches. I feel sick, dizzy, and can almost taste the horrible stuff. Some POWs pass out. For another hour we stand, first on one foot, and then another. We talk to pass away the time about how long this war is going to last or listen politely to some new Kriegie tell war stories. With everyone naked you can see that most POWs have flak scars and/or bullet wounds.

"Half frozen, finally we receive our uniforms. The smell is so foul from the strong chemical gases used on them that many POWs pass out or throw up before they can put them on to reach the fresh air in the outer courtyard. I experience the trapped feeling of resentment that overwhelms me after the shower and the putting on of these putrid smelling garments. I am torn between suffocating from the fumes or freezing to death from removing my clothing.

"Now we wait outside for our guards to march us back to Barrack #39. We must wait until the guards arrive with the next group to be run through this terrible process. As the next group arrives we yell, 'You'll be sorry.' They answer with a 'blow it out your barracks bag,' but they are not sure that our warning is not true. The guards, when they finish cramming that batch in, start us off. We are marched back to the main gate and counted two-by-two through it.

"Soon I am back in my barracks lying on the sack, hungry, tired, and half sick from the fumes still coming from my clothes. After this experience, I plan to shy away from the hair-shaves and one-minute showers administered at the delouser. In short, I now despise the damn delouser too."

Gibby also discovers that it's a small world in the following account:

"It is during the spring and early summer of 1944 that I notice one of the German guards walking with a limp and carrying a cane.

"My outgoing personality is such that it forces me to have conversations with all, friend or foe. In the coming weeks I slowly get to know this particular guard quite well. I discover that this German unter officer (equivalent to our noncommissioned officer), was a sparring partner of Max Schmeling before the war. Thus, the POWs gave him the nickname Maxie.

"During one conversation (he spoke excellent English), Maxie revealed that he had been a fighter pilot and was shot down and badly wounded during an attack on a bomber formation. He would have to walk with a cane for the rest of his life, which effectively ended his

fighter pilot career. Thus, he was reassigned to lesser duty as a POW guard.

"As I got more familiar with Maxie, the details of his last mission became the topic of conversation. Maxie recalls, 'My fighter group was alerted to attack a formation of B-17s that had bombed Bremen and was on their way back to England. We scrambled and intercepted the formation while still over Germany. When I arrived in the area of the American formation, my squadron commander ordered our 30 fighters to attack two B-17s that could not keep up with the formation. We formed up in combat positions and had made many attacks on the two B-17 stragglers. Just as we were closing in for the kill, another B-17 broke formation to come to the aid of the two stragglers.

"Our commander then ordered us to concentrate on the B-17 that had broken formation. We would finish off the two cripples after we destroyed the newcomer. During my second pass on the tail of this B-17, I received several hits in my engine and fuselage. The hits in my fuselage also struck my left leg as I was banking away to my right.'

"'Do you think the tail gunner hit you or another position, I ask?'

"He replies, 'Without a doubt, it was the tail gunner because of the angle of my fighter's right bank.'

"I am almost afraid to ask. 'Do you remember what date you were shot down?'

"'October 8, 1943, I shall never forget that day,' replies Maxie.

"It became crystal clear to me that I was responsible for Maxie's injury. I realize that it is really a small, small world, after all. My secret was never revealed to Maxie or to anyone else until after the war."

Gilly relates the second small victory over their captors called, The Rocket that Farted:

"It is during March, 1945 that this small victory occurred. The black bread and turnips the Germans give us creates a great deal of body gasses. As a result, we have the best farters in German captivity. Some of the boys can actually carry a tune for a short period of time. We decide to stage a fake escape rocket by igniting the gases as a propellant. We gather our five best farters and practice for several days.

"Barrack #29B is selected as our launch pad for it is in line with a guard tower and the officers' quarters up the hill. We are sure that our rocket blast will be observed.

"Practice is complete and we are ready for initial firings. The Gaseous Group is assembled with a match ready under each performer's butt,

which are protruding out the barracks' windows. At a given signal, our farters expend a mighty effort. In the inky blackness, after the large searchlights have swept the area, a four-to-six inch brilliant blue flash, in staccato fashion, is quite visible to our captors. Each ignition is performed in series to give the appearance of several rockets trying to start. Of course, our captors watch the firings and each night we are honored with a visit by them to the barracks. Three times we are called out of the compound, lectured about escapes and punishments (death), and made to stand for hours. While we are standing outside in the compound, our visitors go through the barrack with a fine toothed comb but find no evidence of our escape rocket.

"Again our morale sky-rockets. This small victory is the topic of conversion for at least a couple of weeks."

The Russians Are Coming!
The Russians Are Coming!

The month of March, 1945 proves to be the darkest days of Lt. Morgan's imprisonment. He struggles with his confinement at Stalag Luft I:

> "In early March the Germans stop providing water and electricity. Food is almost out with only starvation amounts being provided. We complain to our captors about the water stoppage. Their response is to provide shovels and concrete culverts. We are told to dig our own well if we want water. This will be a difficult task due to our weak condition.
>
> "We are a few feet above sea level so the well will only need to be about 15 feet deep. The only location available to dig the well is in the middle of the parade ground. The problem with this is that over 9,000 prisoners have used the straddle trenches next to the parade field as latrines for several years.
>
> "After digging for a few days, we hit water about 20 feet down. The water will require sterilization but there is no fuel for fire to boil it. We have to choose, we must drink unsterilized water or die of thirst. The well provides only about a cup of water per day per prisoner. Even under these pitiful conditions, I sense the end of the war and our liberation.

"*Rumors spread throughout the camp on a daily basis concerning the closeness of the Russians and our liberation. During the third week of March, Colonel J. R. Byerly, our Commanding Officer, issues orders for all POWs to be prepared to leave on short notice. This is more than adequate for I have nothing to prepare. There is no food and the clothes I wear day and night are all that is left of my uniform. I fear that if the move involves a ground march some of us will surely die because snow and ice still cover the ground and temperatures at night are well below freezing.*

"*The big event on the last day of March is when a few Red Cross parcels arrive in camp. The quantity of the parcels is meager, however, it is an improvement over what we have had for the last three months. Also, on the last day of March we learn of a major offensive westward by the Russian Army. Our spirits begin to soar like the eagles we once were.*

"*It is Easter and my second in captivity. I reflect back on the spiritual side of my life during my military career. An Air Force adaptation of an old military adage states, there are no atheists in a B-17 going down. I believe this to be true as I remember how interest in church attendance progressed during my training and combat periods.*

"*During training in the Flying Training Command, Sunday worship was attended by less than ten percent of the cadets. After commissioning and during combat readiness, training chapel attendance increased to about 50 percent. Following the first rough combat mission, when several 384th Bomb Group crews were lost, just about everybody found the time to get to the base chapel. As POWs we hold church services in a mess hall and everyone attends. I often wonder how many promises made to God during our POW ordeal will be honored when and if we survive this confinement.*

"*I worship on this Easter morning with a true belief in my heart. The service is uplifting and I shed a tear as we sing the words from that wonderful old spiritual hymn,* Softly and Tenderly: *'Come home, come home, ye who are weary come home.'*

"*Early one morning in late April I am awakened by someone yelling in the barrack doorway, 'the mess hall is on fire.' We bounce out of our bunks and rush to the scene of the fire. As we arrive it is obvious that the wooden building cannot be saved. In a few minutes, despite the combined efforts of the Germans and POWs, the mess hall is a pile of ashes (Image 33.1).*

"*From this day on the POWs in the north compound, where Lt. Horsky is imprisoned, must cook on a stove in their room. It will be*

Image 33.1: Panoramic view of Barth Compound I. Foreground right are remains of the mess hall after the fire. Late April, 1945 and snow is still on the ground.

difficult due to fuel shortage, but at least, each will get a fair share of our meager food supply.

"The last week in April we learn that the Russian Army is inside Germany on several fronts. The local civilians are moving out and leaving their worldly goods behind to the Russians. In the distance the sounds of the German army blowing up military installations can be heard. They are destroying anything of military value within the immediate area to prevent use by the Russians.

"In anticipation of a Russian artillery barrage on the city of Barth and our area, POWs are busy digging private foxholes. A feeling of despair prevails within each of us. We can't fight or leave. We can only dig a hole, crawl into it, and hope for the best.

"As we dig I hear the German Army blowing up the nearby anti-aircraft school buildings and its equipment. The ground shakes as each explosion echoes throughout Stalag Luft I. The concussions knock me around in my hole. The earth literally shakes above my head and below my feet. My private foxhole is now my home as I wait for death or deliverance.

"Late in the day on April 30, an advance party of the Russian Army arrives on the outskirts of Barth. The mayor of Barth has hung a white bed sheet from the steeple of the Lutheran Church. This is a sign to the Russians that Barth is an open city and will surrender.

"The advance party of the Russian Army is now entering Barth. It is a rag-tag army and is destroying everything in its path. As the army

enters Barth, the mayor and his wife realize their fate and commit suicide, along with several mothers and their babies. Young girls and women are being raped in broad daylight. The men are being shot or pistol-whipped. Tonight the Russians will be occupying Barth enjoying their spoils of war.

"The next morning, May 1st, we awake to find Stalag Luft I deserted by our German captors. This is the long-awaited day of freedom! The Germans have completely abandoned the camp. This allows us to wander about as we please. At first we are disoriented as it is difficult to absorb this new-found freedom after 16 months of constant confinement.

"This disorientation last only a few hours. Now there is just one thing on our minds and that is to get to the British or American lines as soon as possible. We have confidence that the Eighth Air Force will soon send in B-17s to get us out. With this in mind, our Commanding Officer, Colonel J.R. Byerly, orders a group of us to secure the local airfield for American aircraft use and our long-awaited evacuation. Most of this day is consumed making the airfield useable. Several destroyed German planes are on the field. These are removed by sheer manpower. In addition, land mines planted along the runways are removed. The end of the day finds the airfield ready to receive our flights to freedom.

"We have not eaten since breakfast, which consisted of a single slice of black German bread. Extreme hunger due to the day long labor has weakened us considerably. We are not used to laboring so physically after 16 months of confinement. Scavenging for any kind of food, we stumble upon a small herd of cows. Several are driven into the thick pine woods and we butcher them with axes. Our first meat in 16 months! Each of us receives more than his fair share this night.

"Early on the morning of May 2nd several hundred Russian enlisted soldiers enter our camp. Most are drunk even at this early hour of the morning. They are a mixed bunch, some are Mongolians, most are white Russians, and all are drunk. The soldiers are drinking a combination of vodka and benzine. First a shot of benzine chased by a shot of vodka. For the most part these Russians simply ignore us and do not care if we leave the camp or stay. They have food but do not offer us any.

"Later in the morning Russian officers enter the camp and immediately take control of everything. No respect is extended to our senior American or British officers. There is no recourse by our senior officers for we are technically under their control. The Russian officers give

orders to destroy the camp. We ignore the orders until ordered to do so by our senior officers. Then joyfully, post-by-post, wire-by-wire, we tear down the hated fences; next the guard towers; and then the gates. This destruction is by physical strength of arms and sheer body weight.

"*It is early afternoon and orders are received from our senior officers to be ready to march out of camp by 1900 hours today. Assembly is to be on the baseball field with a minimum of personal items ready to travel by foot. By 1800 hours our group is assembled and ready to journey westward to some unknown destination. As we wait, the word is received that the Russians have changed their minds. We are to remain in the camp. Instead, General Ike will send in American planes to evacuate us. This is a big disappointment to us as we are mentally, if not physically, ready to leave this place.*

"*In order to relieve the frustration Lts. Kaczaraba, Wirth, Horsky, and I decide to take a hike into Barth. For 16 months we have viewed this town from our distant isolation. Now we are going to see it up close. The hike is about a mile, and as we enter the town, we see a large force of the Russian Army entering also. This bunch is mostly drunk and none walk. Every kind of civilian transportation is in use by these hardened and vengeful troops. Wagons, horses, oxen, buggies, bicycles, and trucks are in use. The fear on the German civilians' faces is evident. This band of drunken soldiers, bent on revenge, rambles into Barth where every house or building seems to have a white flag hanging out of every window. Every flagpole is also decked out with a white flag indicating the Germans' surrender and obedience to the conquering heroes.*

"*The destruction inflicted on the stores, shops, and other businesses by the earlier advance party of the Russian Army is appalling. Looting is now being done on a wide scale basis. Inside some of the buildings civilian men are lying on the floor in pain and moaning as a result of pistol beatings or bayonets being stuck into their stomachs. Dead civilians are stacked in the streets. They probably did not move fast enough when spoken to by a drunken soldier. This is all observed within an hour after leaving camp.*

"*Darkness is now approaching and our feet move briskly as we walk back to the security of the camp and fellow Americans. Back in camp this is all very confusing. While we have no great love for the Germans the atrocities committed by the Russians should not be inflicted on any man, woman, or child, regardless of the sins of their government. In my bunk this night I hear the continuing sounds of gun shots and screams echoing from the town.*

"The next day, May 3rd, martial law is declared for the entire area. This means that we cannot leave camp. The next two weeks are total confusion, not only among the lower ranks, but also among our senior officers. Neither the Russians, nor our senior officers, seem to have a firm course of action for our evacuation or even what the next day may bring. The only instructions we receive are to stay put and wait for the B-17s from General Ike.

"This type of forced confinement by the Russians, when freedom is only a walk away, is difficult to swallow. It starts to strain my nerves. Many of our fellow POWs have already walked out to find freedom somewhere west of Stalag Luft I. Many are talking about it and so is our crew. Then we decide to do what we had always done in a time of crisis. We will vote as a crew, minus our NCOs. The vote is unanimous, we will stay and continue to follow orders given to us by our commanding officer and those orders are to stay put.

"For two weeks we wait impatiently for the arrival of General Ike's birds to fly us to freedom. We wait without electricity, and with little food and water. We wait silently for in the last 16 months of confinement we have already talked about anything of importance and many things that were not. The days of waiting pass slowly as we search the sky for incoming B-17s.

"Then on Mother's Day, May 13th, B-17s are spotted inbound to the local Barth airfield. They come in just over the treetops. I rush to be among the chosen few for freedom. They land on the only cleared runway, roll up to a hangar and stop in front of my group. The door swings open and a crewman shouts, 'Thirty-five of you, jump aboard!' With those sweet words ringing in my ears I scramble on board.

"The B-17 is immediately airborne and flying at treetop level to avoid any possible enemy anti-aircraft fire. Even at this late date, which is seven days after Germany has signed surrender terms, there are still German armed forces that either do not know the war is over or have decided to fight on in spite of the surrender.

"Flying at a very low altitude I get a bird's eye view of the tremendous destruction that the mighty Eighth Air Force and the Royal Air Force have unleashed upon Germany. Cities are in complete ruins, bridges are laying in the rivers, power plants are in shambles, airfields are junk yards, railway centers look like twisted, mangled steel toothpicks, and buildings seem to have been cut off about waist high. Only the extreme rural areas appear to be untouched by our bombs. The Eighth Air Force suffered 44,000 combat deaths in order to inflict this *awesome devastation. Our dead paid a high price for the destruction of the Fatherland.*

"*In a little over two hours our B-17 touches down in Leon, France. From here my group of 35 and others are loaded into large cattle trucks and transported to the Leon train station. Our rail destination is Reims, France where we debark from the train and load into Army trucks. The next, and last, destination is a large tent city known as Camp Lucky Strike. Large is an understatement. This tent city is home for almost 40,000 ex-POWs. Some 26,000 of these are from the Eighth Air Force. I feel extremely lucky to have survived and to be at Camp Lucky Strike.*

"*The incoming processing here is similar to the previous processing of incoming POWs at Stalag Luft I. First, we are stripped and deloused. Meager and worn out uniforms are piled into a large container and soaked with DDT. Next, a warm shower by the side of a stream. I even have my own bar of soap. This is the first warm shower I have had in 16 months. I stand naked and let the warm water soak into all my body pores. It feels too good to describe. Lastly, we pick through a bin of fatigue uniforms, underwear, and socks. None fit, I don't care, they are clean and new.*

"*When it is time to eat we are told to eat in small amounts as our stomachs may not accept this new diet plus the larger amount would cause stomachs to swell up. Some POWs do not listen to these instructions, and they die. In this case too much can kill you quicker than too little.*

"*Our time is spent living in tents at Camp Lucky Strike. Cots are used for sleeping. When it rains I crawl inside my sleeping bag to stay dry as the tents leak badly. Toilets are slit trenches screened off by Army olive drab canvas hung on poles.*

"*After a week here, I am shocked when I accidentally run into S/Sgt. Pete Parker, our left waist gunner. It is quite a happy surprise to see him because I had no idea he was here. Pete informs me that he did not know if the rest of the crew was here or where they may be located. I did not recognize him at first. He had shrunken and his eyes seem to be farther back in his head. He appeared to have aged ten years. He told me about his march from Stalag 17B. The march was a distance of 280 miles over a period of 18 days. (This march is covered in detail in Chapter 34, 'Eagles Can Walk Too.') I spend a couple of hours with Pete catching up on the status of the rest of the crew. The next day he left for the United States.*

"During my stay here, tragedy struck. One day a soldier went off the deep end and opened fire with his rifle killing 13 ex-POWs. The Germans couldn't kill them but friendly fire did! What a hell of a way to die!

"I have been detained at Camp Lucky Strike for over two months and want to go home to my family very badly. At long last, on July 31 my group of POWs are loaded into trucks and driven to LaHarve, France. This seaside harbor city is almost totally destroyed. The town is in shambles from bombing. Only German concrete pillboxes remain intact. At the harbor we walk out on to a temporary metal floating pier since the harbor facilities are destroyed. We board a ship and with a slight detour by way of England, we head for our country and home.

"In England we are transferred to a Landing Ship Tank (LST) for the final leg home. It is very crowded and we must sleep in shifts. The LST rolls back and forth for 16 days in the Atlantic and at long last we arrive in Newport News, Virginia. It is August 16, 1945, exactly two years since we left the United States as a crew for England and combat. An Army band greets us. I walk down the gangplank and kiss the ground of my beloved country. God bless America."

★ ★ ★

CHAPTER

34

Eagles Can Walk Too

The POW life of hunger, boredom, and extreme cold at Stalag 17B continues for the *Doc's* NCOs into late March, 1945 but somehow, each member senses that the end is near.

Sam remembers the last days as a POW and, at last, his march to freedom:

"Based on our secret radio broadcasts from the BBC, we are aware of the Russian Army's advance west towards Vienna, Austria in late March, 1945. Vienna is only 50 miles east of Stalag 17B. There is now a sense of fear and anxiety on the faces of our captors for they realize the war may be lost for them.

"By April 6th, the Russians are within 15 or 20 miles of us. I can hear their big guns rumbling to the east. Rumors have run rampart for the last week that the Germans will be moving Stalag 17B POWs west to protect us from the Russian Army. The truth is the Germans are concerned about protecting their own butts. These rumors of evacuation are confirmed on April 5th when a new German captain appears in camp. He is giving speeches about Russian soldiers shooting American POWs. These speeches are intended to convince us not to cooperate or aid the Russians.

"The next morning, after roll-call, we are informed of the real purpose of this new German captain's visit to the camp. He has orders from the German High Command to evacuate all POWs from Stalag 17B. We are to be prepared to evacuate the camp the next morning, Saturday, April 7th.

"The entire camp is like a mad house. A fever of excitement sweeps through the camp like wildfire. Any material that we can get our hands on is used for bonfires. These bonfires rage all day and most of the night. Final trading is fierce over the fences as our guards now turn their heads and look the other way.

"I have noticed a major improvement the last few days in the guard's attitude toward us. It is a situation where they fear their officers but fear the Russians more. They must appear to do their duty when observed by their officers but want to win favor with the Americans for possible protection from the Russians. Russian troops are reported to be 30 kilometers from Krems and heading on to St. Polten. My best guess is that the Russians are about three days from capturing Stalag 17B. Tonight I observe their big guns flashing and know they are close.

"I am up early this Saturday, April 7th to start packing. The rain is pelting on the barracks tin roof as I joyfully pack my few meager possessions.

"We are issued our remaining Red Cross parcels. They must last each man for seven days. Our captors inform us that we will be marching west. Based on this information, I surmise that the march will be back into Germany for a last stand against the allies.

"My belongings are packed and I hope they will keep me alive to get me to God only knows where. My survival kit consists of one Red Cross parcel, which is good for a few days if eaten in small amounts, two blankets, both German issued and referred to by POWs as tablecloths; three pairs of socks, which are razor thin; and one-half loaf of black German bread. In addition I have a pair of GI boxer-type shorts, two bars of soap for trading with civilians or guards, and one GI-issued overcoat.

"I complete packing by mid-morning and impatiently wait for the rest of the day. About 1500 hours we get the word to be up by 0600 hours and be ready to leave at 0700 hours the next morning. We are also told that American POWs will be in eight groups of 500 men each. Two hundred POWs will stay behind because of sickness or wounds.

"Sunday, April 8th, dawns clear and cold. I am up and ready to move out at 0400 hours. My last meal at Stalag 17B is consumed and consists of a handful of dry barley and raisins.

"I fall out of Barrack 38B and assemble with the first group of 500 men. It is 0800 hours. My group passes through the main gate of Stalag 17B at exactly 0815 hours, 75 minutes late. Thousands of times over the last 15 months I had dreamed of walking through this same gate to freedom.

"A mixed combination of guards marches us out the main gate. They consist of the German Army (Wehrmacht), Air Force (Luftwaffe), Schutzstaffel (SS) and Austrian Militia (Volkstrum) and total about 40 for my group. The seven groups behind mine are scheduled to leave at about 30-minute intervals.

"I am overjoyed to be out of this hell hole but am uncertain as to our destination or if I will live to get there. Long columns of prisoners now stretch behind me from the camp down the mountain road to the edge of the Danube River. My group is leading the way as we move slowly along rural roads through the Austrian countryside. We have no conception of where we are going other than west to another camp.

"It is tough going for our pitiful, ragged band of POWs weak from lack of nourishment. We move through winding mountain trails and past many German fortified positions waiting for the advancing Russian Army.

"Mid-afternoon and my morale is high as I walk west with the sun in my face. After passing through the towns of Gneixendorf, Rehberg, and Senftenberg we have covered about 14 miles. The countryside has a terrain that reminds me of the rolling hills of North Carolina where I spent many days hunting and fishing during my youth.

"Late afternoon and just on the outside of the town of Lugendorf we approach a large apple orchard. The order is given to halt. We will spend the night here. Our bed will be Mother Earth.

"It is almost dark and we have not received any food from the Germans. My slice of black bread now beckons me to consume it. It is difficult to shallow with no water available. I am in fair condition considering the little food and exercise during the last year and a half.

"It is still cold at night in the mountains so we start a fire to ward off the damp night air. The guards immediately order the fire to be extinguished due to Russian planes in the area. We don't want to be bombed this late in the war so we comply. Two other POWs and I will sleep together tonight as we did on many nights in Stalag 17B in order to keep warm.

"Down in the Danube Valley I watch German flares and gun flashes as they light up the valley. They reflect a rainbow of colors off the blue

Danube River. Later tonight I hear planes to the east and bombs exploding somewhere near Krems. I pray the bombs don't fall on Stalag 17B as 200 American POWs are still there and helpless.

"Monday morning, April 9th, I awake to find the ground covered with a light frost. A heavy fog blankets the entire area. Roll call is next and 30 men of my group of 500 are missing. I speculate that they sneaked out during the night and probably went back to their former home to await the Russian liberation. Personally, I'd rather take my chances in the open country as most of my youth was spent hunting and fishing in the wilds. I feel safe in the country. (Those that did return to Stalag 17B, would spend most of April in the air raid trenches to avoid the Russian artillery barrages.)

"We form up for the day's march and get underway at 0900 hours. By now the morning sun has burned the fog away and the light frost has melted. It is a warm, sunny morning as we pass through the town of Lugendorf. We are not provided any breakfast so I eat my last piece of black bread. I am beginning to believe the Germans plan to starve us to death on this march.

"The marching this morning is better than yesterday as most of the terrain is downhill. We pass through the towns of Himberg and Muhldorf still heading generally west along the Danube River. Each hour a ten-minute break is allowed and by noon we have completed about seven miles. It is lunch time but we get no food from the Germans. I must eat my Red Cross parcel food of crackers and jam.

"The clusters of tired POWs continue the march this afternoon and cover another seven miles before reaching the village of Raxendorf. We assemble in a large open field and prepare to spend the night here. Four thousand POWs are dead on their feet because of the 14 uphill miles walked the previous day. Fourteen miles may not be a long journey in one day for a normal, healthy, well-fed man, but to a POW living on a near starvation diet and no exercise for 16 months, it is pure hell. We do not expect to get any food from the Germans. We are not disappointed. For supper I eat the last of my Red Cross parcel crackers.

"Tonight I will sleep on the cold, damp ground again. No fires are allowed, as before. This stop, we are informed, will be a 24-hour rest, which is a welcome relief. Tonight is again cold and I am able only to doze before the shivering of my body awakens me.

"Fortunately, Tuesday, April 10th starts with a fairly warm day. The 24-hours of rest will allow me to dry the overnight dew from my blankets and clothes. It will also allow my feet to heal as they are in bad shape.

"Today, for the first time we receive a breakfast of dry barley from the Germans. It is delicious but after almost three days without any real food anything would taste good. In addition, for supper we are given a loaf of bread for every 18 men, about one slice per man. Today I get a chance to wash my face and shave in a mountain stream. It is cold but refreshing (Image 34.1)[1].

"About mid-afternoon we are buzzed by two American P-51 Mustang fighters. The fighters make a wide turn to position for a ground attack. The German guards drop flat on the ground or into ditches for protection. A POW has a hidden American flag and very quickly spreads it out to let the fighters know that we are Americans. Both fighters spot the flag, salute, and pass over us at no more than a 100 feet. With the guards on the ground in a prone position,

Image 34.1: T/Sgt. John Samuel (Sam) Honeycutt, on the third day of marching, washes up during a 30-minute break.

several POWs attempt to flee for freedom. On seeing this, the guards fire several shots at the POWs and yell at them to halt. All obey. No one wants to die at this late stage of the war.

"Today we learn that two of our guards have died of fatigue and exhaustion just outside the town of Poggstall. No pity from me, may they RIP (Rot In Poggstall). None of us have fallen out of formation ... yet!

"Toward evening we start preparing for another cold night. We scurry around for scrap wood to build a fire to provide some warmth throughout the night. Again the guards order the fires extinguished and again we sleep on the cold ground.

"Wednesday, April 11th, up at 0600 hours. The early morning temperature is warm and I pray for another sunny, warm day. Our guards give us a breakfast of dried lima beans, about a half handful per man. I check the contents of my Red Cross parcel and realize that I am out of this supply of food. From now on I will be at the mercy of the Germans for my food supply and survival.

"*After our abundant breakfast, we form up and move out, west/southwest. The weather is warm and we cover nine miles by noon. We stop for a 30-minute lunch break.*

"*Resting on the side of a bare hill, without any trees at all, I notice a steady steam of high ranking German officers in all manner of transportation speeding past us heading west. This is a sure sign that the Russians are sweeping through the German defenses east of us. The effect of the fleeing officers on the common German soldier is demoralizing. I detect a loss of discipline within the ranks of our guards. This gives me confidence that the war is drawing to a close.*

"*For lunch today we get a rare treat, a bowl of hot soup, almost four ounces. I devour the soup and soon we are ordered to form up to continue our march westward.*

"*As I look ahead the terrain is changing from rolling to more level ground. This should make the marching somewhat easier.*

"*On this, our fourth day out, most of us are sunburned and have dry, chapped lips due to the last two days of marching west into the sunshine. Our tired band of travelers covers an additional eleven miles and at dusk we find ourselves just east of the small town of Laimbach. This evening for supper the Germans provide bread and nothing else.*

"*This night Lady Luck smiles on me for I get to sleep in one of the nearby barns. As I settle into my bed of straw, I remember playing as a youth in my Uncle Walt's barn filled with hay. Soon I am fast asleep dreaming of the day when I will hold my wife, Pauline, once more in my arms.*

"*I awake fresh this morning, Thursday, April 12th and am up at 0530 hours ready to resume our westward journey. No food is provided for breakfast.*

"*We stand in an open field in a steady downpour for almost six hours waiting for marching orders. The German explanation for not starting the march until noon is that they are waiting on food supplies. At noon we receive no food but continue our westward march in a steady downpour of rain. In order to keep warm I walk as fast as I am physically able. At the end of the day we have covered another 14 miles. My clothes are soaked down to my cold, wrinkled skin.*

"*Tonight I will sleep in wet clothes and hope my body heat will dry them out. Again tonight, I am lucky for I get to sleep inside. Inside, in this case, in an abandoned paper mill factory outside the town of Isperdorf. My bed will not be a bed of warm straw but a bed of cold concrete. The paper mill will serve, at least, to protect me from the steady rain throughout the long and cold night.*

"*Tonight we receive no food from the Germans. In the last 25 hours I have eaten one thin slice of bread. My body is young and resilient but I cannot continue on one slice of bread per day. Sleep does not come easily this night due to hunger and the cold hard concrete of the paper mill floor.*

"*On unlucky Friday, April 13th I pray for good luck in the form of dry weather. My prayer is not to be granted for it continues a steady downpour of rain. We leave the factory at about 0800 hours and line up for breakfast from our captors. None is provided.*

"*Again, we stand in formation for about three hours in a steady downpour of rain. Same excuse from our guards; waiting for food to arrive. My clothes are still very wet as we head west on today's march. It is about 1500 hours in the afternoon and the rain finally stops. We continue to plod along. The German officers detour us to secondary roads and in some cases, pathways. We are no longer marching on busy routes and highways. This is probably to prevent our guards from observing half of the German Army fleeing west away from the oncoming Russians.*

"*During the last rest stop of the day we are told that our beloved and long time President has died. The news of President Roosevelt's death seems to zap the remaining energy from my tired, wet body. Most of us average 20 years of age, thus, he has been our President since we were seven years old. This is as long as most of us can remember. He was a good peacetime President and a great wartime Commander-in-Chief. I whisper a silent prayer for our President and for the future of our country.*

"*Today we have covered about 14 miles and are just outside the town of Klam. For supper a hard biscuit is provided, no water. Tonight I get to sleep inside a barn. Thank God for these barns for they allow me to sleep soundly and dry out my ragged, wet clothes.*

"*The rain continues the next day, Saturday, April 14th. The Germans decide to keep us in Klam for another day. We need this rest for most of us are experiencing dysentery badly and discomfort from sunburned faces, lips, and hands.*

"*I am damn hungry. Today will be a good day for it will be a day of feasting. The Germans kill a cow and agree to share it with my group. The guards, who number 39, get half, and our group, which numbers about 500, gets the other half. So much for share and share alike. We appoint a detail to gather some firewood to cook our cow. They do a good job and soon we have a roaring fire. Our meat is just starting to cook and suddenly a squad of Schutzstaffel (SS) troopers arrives and orders us to put the fire out. We protest and the SS black uniformed thugs pull their Luger pistols from their holsters. Reluctantly we put out the fire. Fortunately, the SS thugs do no shooting today. We eat our steaks raw. Tonight I sleep soundly in my dry bed of straw.*

"Sunday, April 15th dawns clear and warm. The Germans had no food for breakfast. The march gets underway at 1100 hours. Jerry waiting on food supplies, again! We are heading almost due south. From time to time I catch a glimpse of the Danube River. The mountains are beautiful in this area. The forests are well kept and the mountain streams sparkle in the bright sunshine. We are still traveling on back roads as we pass through Saxen, Baumgantenberg, and Mitterkirchen. Today we have covered 18 miles. Up ahead is the fairly large town of Naarn and as we pass through it the people view us with disgust, but there is no violence. We leave the town and halt for the night in a large open field. Again tonight, we receive no food from the Germans. I harvest and eat leaves from a nearby tree for my only meal of the day. The guards allow me to build a small fire and boil the leaves to tenderize them. The leaves appear to be oak and have no taste. Again tonight I get lucky for I have a barn to sleep in for a few hours."

Gilly relates his near death experience on this day, Monday, April 16th:

"I am up at 0630 hours hoping for some scraps of food, any food, however, none is provided by our captors. The march gets underway at about 1000 hours and shortly we are through the town of Au. The terrain is flat and walking is fairly easy.

"As we approach the town of Mauthausen, I observe sights that I shall never forget. As we march, up ahead is the infamous Nazi Concentration camp of Mauthausen.[2] A group of Jews, guarded by SS troops, are filing past our columns heading east. They are in a deplorable condition. Ragged clothes hang on human beings that resemble skeletons. Skin clings to their bones. Their eyes appear over-large and are sunk deep into their heads. Head hair is cut close with a stripe shaved through the center. They are in a pitiful state, well beyond the limits of human endurance from starvation and total maltreatment. They are the walking dead.

"My group continues the march westward for a quarter mile and something is along the side of the road that resembles stacked logs. As

I come closer I realize that these logs are Jews. They have been shot, killed, and left sprawled by the wayside like so much human garbage. These human logs number around 20. I now know that there was truth in the lectures I had received in England about the German's anti-semitic hatred. My mind has a difficult time accepting this treatment of fellow human beings.

"We Kriegies from Krems are now halted in front of a concentration camp. A group of Jewish prisoners approaches us. Tall, black uni-formed SS troopers guard them. The officer in charge is walking along side the column of Jews. He pulls his gun out of its holster, and, at ran-dom, blows a Jew's brains out. I am about five feet away. The blood and brains explode from the victim's head and land at my feet. Then the SS officer struts a few feet further and repeats this deadly game. Next, he slowly turns around and stares at me. He locks his eyes into mine and says, 'you, come forward.' I thought I had bought the farm but step forward as ordered. Now he orders several other POWs to step forward. We are marched, at gunpoint, up to the concentration camp and through the large iron gate.

"Inside a grotesque scene reveals many dead bodies. They are stacked like large piles of trash. Inmates are being gassed faster than their bodies can be disposed of. They lay rotting in the sun. The stench is unbelievable. An SS trooper walks up to a woman with a yoke around her neck pulling a wagon. He strikes her in the head with the butt of his rifle several times. She does not moan or make a sound as her skull cracks open. The SS killer chuckles as he walks away.

"Up ahead are several barracks with human beings that look like skeletons hanging out the windows. I cannot describe the inhuman acts and atrocities that take place in this camp of death for the next two hours as we await our fate. Next, we are marched into a cold, concrete bunker and told to undress down to our shorts. We are left in this bunker almost naked all night with no heat. Tonight we sleep on con-crete cots not knowing what tomorrow will bring.

"The next morning at 0700 hours, along with several slave laborers confined to the camp, we are forced out of the bunker. Our clothes are returned, next we dress and then stand formation for a roll call. After the roll count the camp's Jewish work gang is moved out leaving us standing in formation. The same SS officer that had forced us out of formation yesterday is approaching. He is a sadistic son-of-a-bitch and again he stops directly in front of me. With an arrogant grin on his face

he places his pistol to my head and tells me that I have been selected to die. He then laughs and struts off.

"In a few minutes another SS trooper arrives, whom I believe, to be my executioner. Instead, he orders us to follow him, and to my amazement, he leads us back through the death camps large iron gate where we rejoin our fellow POWs. My feet are much lighter now and will be for the next couple of days. I believe the little guy on my shoulder spared my life again on this day."

Sam continues his account of the ordeal of this march:

"We are told that we will be staying another day at Mauthausen. It is Tuesday, April 17th. I am desperately hungry. About 0900 hours, we are given a loaf of bread for nine men, which is the only food for the last two days.

"This 24-hour rest is welcomed as my stomach is in constant pain. Air raid sirens have been going off all day but I see no aircraft. It is now 1830 hours and dark when the air raid sirens start again. They continue until 0300 hours the next morning. Still no aircraft.

"Wednesday, April 18 up at 0500 hours. No sleep last night because of air raid sirens. Received a cup of very thin soup for breakfast and a dog biscuit. I save the dog biscuit in case we are not granted any more food today.

"Our group forms up and we leave the death camp area at 0600 hours. We are about four miles down the road from the concentration camp when we stop for a ten-minute rest.

"As I lay beside the road a large column of slave laborers passes us heading west. This group is different as it consists of both men and women. They wear all manner of clothing and most have the Star of David on their backs. They look like the walking dead. Prodded by SS guards, carrying rifles with fixed bayonets, they trudge slowly down the road to a day of labor, if they survive.

"As they pass me, the walking dead hold out their hands and with begging eyes plead for food. When the SS troopers aren't looking I toss the only food I have, my dog biscuit, to a starving Jewish slave. Maybe he will live another day.

"Then I observe a scene that will forever be locked in my memory. An SS trooper is standing on the running board of a truck as it approaches a group of Jews from behind. The truck is moving very slowly down the road and is now alongside the Jewish slave laborers.

The SS trooper has his rifle barrel in his hands as if to use it as a club. As the truck moves alongside the slave laborer's column, he rains blow upon blow on top of the laborer's heads. Skulls crack like eggs and the yolk of blood and brains pour out.

"*The blows are struck at random. He is not selective as to gender. The Jews fall like fodder in a field ready for harvesting by the grim reaper. Their bodies are left lying on the side of the road where they fall. The other slave laborers step over and around their fellow Jews as they continue their march. They show no shock, no remorse, no anger, and no revenge. Death has lived with them for so long, it is commonplace.*

"*We are ordered up and start our westward march again. In a few minutes we come across another deadly scene of bodies lying along the shoulders of the road and in the ditches. These laborers have bullet holes in their heads. The murdering SS bastards have earned their pay this day.*

"*We continue our march southwest toward the Danube River through St. Georgen, Luftenberg, Pasching, and Wilhering. By my count this is the eleventh day of this painful journey. Today, by noon, we have marched ten miles and there are still several hours of daylight left. Traveling almost due south I spot the blue Danube River again. Have not received any food for lunch. All my thoughts are on food, food, and food.*

"*We cross the Danube, turn back west and walk another four miles. The old provincial city of Linz is up ahead. We enter Linz through the ancient arch gateway. Passing through Linz, the locals are very hostile. Some are throwing stones and others insults. We do not react to stones as they strike us. It is pouring rain as we continue to be paraded through the city streets. To add to the cold rain, stones, and insults, air raid sirens are sounding. The air raid sirens serve to drive the locals into houses and office buildings. The streets now belong to us.*

"*We leave Linz and walk another four miles to the farm village of Wilhecing. We will stop here for the night. Today we have marched 20 miles in twelve hours.*

"*It is almost 1800 hours. We line up for roll count. The Germans tell us that there will be no food now, but maybe later on ... perhaps. Need food badly, very tired, my will to continue is doubtful. In the mountains at least there was water, here we have none.*

"*We drop where we halt and lay down on the wet, cold ground for the night. It is 2200 hours and pitch dark in the open field where we lay exhausted.*

"In about 30 minutes I spot lights coming toward us. The Germans are approaching with small buckets. We receive some very thin soup, less than four ounces per man and a loaf of bread for eight men. I will live another day!

"After our meal the air raid sirens sound again. This time the uneven sounds of British bombers are heard. (The RAF aircraft fly at different altitudes and the engine sounds appear to be unsynchronized.) The bombers pass over us heading toward the city of Linz, only four miles distance. Tonight I will not be impressed with the RAF bombing accuracy. Their bombs are exploding, not in Linz, but all around us. Will this be the end of my deplorable life after all I have been through? God, I don't want to die this way, not at the hands of our allies. The earth is shaking and trembling from the impact of the British bombs known as Block Busters. The bombing goes on for about 20 minutes. Now all is quiet. It is pitch dark. I am shaken, but unhurt. Believe me, it is a hell of a difference between delivering bombs and receiving them.

"The next morning there are several bomb craters less than 100 yards from my group. Some of the craters have unexploded bombs stuck in the mud. Doubts continue to haunt my mind if I will survive this war.

"The rain stops this morning, Thursday, April 19th. We rise about 0800 hours. It is cloudy and cool. I'm still soaked from the rain yesterday and the wet ground from last night. We leave our overnight area at 0830 hours. Many of the POWs are ill, almost all have dysentery. Some of those with dysentery are unable to keep up with the strenuous march due to attacks. They become stragglers and fall behind the formation. Rumors are that the German guards, behind the marchers, are shooting POWs that fall back. The Germans label them as attempting to escape. After a few days the POWs with dysentery learn to do the dysentery dash. This requires a POW, when he feels an attack coming on to dash to the front of the column and do his thing while the column is marching by. In this way he does not fall behind the column and denies the guards the opportunity to shoot a POW.

"Today we have covered 15 miles. We are halted at 1200 hours to allow the American Red Cross (ARC) representing the Protecting Power (United States) to check on our condition. Where have they been for the last twelve days? In order to impress the ARC, the Germans give us a small loaf of bread and a can of meat to be divided among seven men. We are informed, in the presence of the ARC man, that we will get a hot meal tonight. It did not happen. The ARC promises us that we will receive parcels in a few days. I hope their word is better than the Jerries!

"Some of us manage to find barns to sleep in tonight. I am fortunate for my barn contains bins of wheat. I cook it for several hours until it is somewhat palatable and I eat until full. I will live another day.

"Friday, April 20th the sky is clear. It continues to be cool. Up at 0600 hours, no breakfast. We form up and start westward again at 0700 hours. Today the marching is very hard as I am extremely weak from hunger and don't know how much further I can go with a cup of watery soup every two days. It is becoming very difficult to go 20 to 25 miles a day. My body has very little energy left and my youth is being snuffed out like a candle in the wind. The end of this war is now in sight. I must go on!

"We are traveling over dirt trails. It is slow going as the terrain is rising in elevation. We are passing through the village of Neumarkt and the locals appear friendly. There are tears in some of the old women's eyes. Do we look that pitiful? The day is almost over as we pass through the village of Kallham. We have covered 16 miles. A miracle considering our condition.

"I am again fortunate tonight for I will get to sleep in another barn. About 2300 hours the Germans give us some warm soup, very weak and very little. No bread. It tastes so poor, but I must eat. I sleep dry and sound this night.

"Up at 0600 hours on this Saturday, April 21st. Advised that we will bivouac outside Kallham for 24 hours. Good news! We need rest.

"Rumor has it that we will receive Red Cross parcels today. I pray that this rumor is true. It will be the first Red Cross food since leaving Stalag 17B, over twelve days ago.

"Late this morning U.S.-made trucks with Red Cross emblems on the doors arrive. There are supposed to be two parcels for five men. We have not received ours yet, maybe this afternoon. The Red Cross parcels never came.

"Today my total intake consists of one small turnip, which I found in a field and boiled. Things are bad, POWs are stealing food from local farms, from the guards, and from each other. We are at our lowest ebb of humanity. Our situation has got to improve or we will become animals. It starts to rain early in the evening. I lay in my bed of straw listening to the raindrops on the barns' tin roof. Tired and hungry, I thank the good Lord for getting me through another day.

"It rains all through the night and at dawn on Sunday, April 22nd it is cold and cloudy. We leave the barn at 0500 hours. No food is *provided for breakfast. Off again at 0700 hours, still heading west. Just as we start our march, the weather turns to ice, snow, sleet, and hail as this higher elevation brings extremely cold temperatures.*

"In a few hours we are at the timberline of heavy pine forests. In the distance I see the Swiss Alps. Our elevation is several thousand feet and temperatures are steadily dropping. I am completely soaked, my clothes are frozen and I am chilled to the bone.

"Throughout the day's march we have been climbing uphill covering 14 hard miles. Towns passed through include Evglach, Riedau, and Taiskirchen. People are much friendlier, probably because they are so far removed from the war. Rumors have it that we will reach our new camp in three days. I pray so for I am very tired and weak.

"We stop in Aurolzmunster for the night. About dark, our captors give each of us a bowl of soup and a loaf of bread for every five men. It is decent. Some will sleep in local barns tonight, but I will not. Tonight, I will use my GI overcoat as a barrier against the cold, frozen ground. I am very tired but I won't allow myself to sleep tonight. I am afraid that my frozen clothes will drive my body temperature down and death will be my companion in the morning.

"Extreme cold greets me as I rise from a sleepless night on Monday, April 23rd. It continues to rain and snow this morning as it has all night.

"Up at 0500 hours, no food provided. We are on the road at 0700 hours heading west into the rain and snow. Today we cover 15 hard, cold miles. We pass through the towns of Eitzing, Mairing, Ranzing, Surten, Freiling, Seinberg, and Durtcham. As we approach the town of Altheim we halt for the night. Rumor is we will lie over here 24 hours. Altheim is only a few miles from the Austrian-German border. This is our 16th day of marching.

"The guards allow us to move about somewhat. I manage to get back and visit my best friend, Shorty Craden. He still has his good humor but has lost weight. He wisecracks, 'If I had wanted to march, I would have joined the damn Army.' For supper Shorty and I enjoy each other's company and a piece of half-cooked meat provided by the Germans. Shorty and I manage to sleep in a barn tonight. There seem to be no horses in the barn or area. I wonder if there is a connection between this lack of horses and our meal? I am very tired. Tonight I sleep soundly.

"Tuesday, April 24th the rain and cold continue to be our constant companions. Word is received that we will lie over here for another 24

hours. I need to shave and wash but don't have the energy to do even this simple task. I just want to rest and stay warm. I stay in the barn most of the day to regain some of my strength. Later in the day, I am able to slip out and trade two packs of cigarettes for a small potato with a local farmer. I usually have cigarettes to trade as I don't have the habit. This gives me an advantage over the other POWs when barter-ing with locals. In addition, the Germans give us very thin barley soup. I save the potato from my trade for a rainy day. I went to my straw bed early and slept soundly all night.

"Wednesday, April 25th our 18th on this God-forsaken journey to our new POW camp. I step outside my home of the past two nights and find the rain has stopped. The ground is hard and covered with a heavy frost. It is still extremely cold. Rumor is we will reach our destination today. The guards tell us we are going to a Russian prisoner of war camp outside the small city of Braunau-am-Inn located on the Austrian-German border.

"Four thousand POWs move out at 0700 hours, again with no food. I slowly consume my small raw potato during the morning march. The day is cold, but fair. We cover eleven miles and are halted. It is almost 1400 hours.

"We walk through the ancient gate into the city of Braunau-am-Inn. This city has no meaning until the guards point out the Pommer Inn. It was here, on the second floor, that the head Nazi, Adolphus Hitler, was born.

"We pass through the town and proceed toward the Russian POW camp located three miles north. News is received that the Russian camp is full. The guards detour our column and we march a couple of miles south. We stop a few miles outside the small village of Rossbach in a recently cleared pine forest overlooking a small, but beautiful, swift-flowing mountain river. The river is the Inn River and it flows past Braunau-am-Inn. Four thousand tired, cold, and hungry former eagles are grounded in the middle of a cleared pine forest.

"'This is it,' our guards shout. I look around and see no barracks, tents, or shelter of any kind. There are only tree stumps and piles of branches left over from the clearing. After 18 days, 13 of them march-ing, under miserable conditions covering over 280 miles, this is it!

"There is nothing here. I am shocked and dismayed at the camp. We have received no food today from the Germans, however, our first con-cern is shelter. It is 1500 hours. Shorty, three other POWs, and myself start to gather branches to build a lean-to for five of us who have joined

together. In about three hours we have constructed a rough lean-to. It should provide some shelter from the cold and rain.

"We now hear reports that the Red Cross has arrived with 3,200 French food parcels. I receive no parcel tonight. I have eaten only a small potato today. It is now almost 2100 hours. We five will sleep as one tonight to keep warm. Tomorrow has got to be a better day!

"It is extremely cold as I awake on Thursday, April 26th. For once my body craves water more than food. Lack of water is a serious problem. I have not had any in two days. The only way to get water here is to climb down very steep inclines in the surrounding forest and trap the water as it slowly trickles from small springs in the rocks. I must lay with my face forced into the ground and try to lick up as much water as possible. It is a difficult and time-consuming task for I am in a weary, malnourished condition. I am exhausted after the trip down the mountain for water.

As I lay on the ground trying to regain my strength, I can hear heavy bombing, strafing, and artillery fire to the southwest of our camp. I hope this destruction is by Americans. I believe they are getting closer to our location. Around 1000 hours, we receive the French food parcels; three to four men. The French parcels have more sweets than the American ones but the bulk food has to be cooked.

"Today is pleasant and we will use this opportunity to refurbish our lean-to home. Most of the day is spent in adding space for the five of us. The finished dwelling is 10 feet by 16 feet. Two-thirds of the dwelling has a roof of pine branches mixed with mud and pine needles. It should give us some shelter from the rain, snow, and cold. We are exhausted after working all day, however, there is some pride in our labor.

"A few minutes of daylight remain. I sneak in the twilight down to the river to wash my body and brush my teeth. There is a small bar of soap left in my pack. As I touch the cold river water, my visions of a total body bath are quickly reduced to a whore bath. I brush my teeth and head back to camp. Maybe tomorrow I will bathe in the cold, icy Inn River.

"The Germans give us the first food in two days late today. It consists of watery barley soup and a loaf of bread for 18 men. Thank God for the Red Cross parcels. We would have died long ago if we had to survive only on food from the Germans.

"Today, for the first time in 16 months, I see the discipline of the guards starting to break down. They are only half-hearted in performing

their duties when an officer is present and very little when none are around. During the day we are allowed to have fires. The guards try to share them with us. This would never have happened, even a week ago. We reject their attempts. It appears they have given up and are more concerned about their personal rather than their military future. In contrast, we Americans are getting organized and are beginning to act more like a military unit. On a daily basis, I feel authority slipping from our captors to us. We all realize that the end of the war is near, but it is not over yet and all, both friend and foe, must survive until then.

"Friday, April 29th begins cold and hungry. It is around 0800 hours and a loud commotion is heard from the Russian sector of our temporary camp. I learn that groups of starving Russians are rioting for a few potatoes on a truck. The German solution to the riot, even at this late stage of the war, is to march them into the woods and shoot them. Based on a later rumor, about twelve Russians were shot to death. Extreme hatred still exists between these two foes. The Germans hope, with all their hearts, that the Americans and not the Russian Army will capture them. They know the Reds will shoot them.

"After the shooting of the Russians, the Germans line us up for a roll count but fail to count our entire group, which is more evidence of German lack of discipline. The guards are running out of food and have no shelter. They try to be friendly; we reject them.

"Today is spent in beefing up our shelter and adding more roof to the open space. We are almost free here. I went down to the river and brushed my teeth, but I have no courage for a bath yet. Then I wandered in the woods just to pass time. Late this afternoon, we receive raw barley from the Germans. The sun is out, it is warm, my clothes are dry, and my spirits begin to soar. Things are looking up for a change, which immediately makes me leery.

"Saturday, April 28th and Sunday, April 29th, rain, rain, and more rain. Things are looking down, as usual. Rations are few, only a hard biscuit. Our pine shelter has collapsed from the heavy rains. I am cold, wet, and very hungry.

"Monday, April 30th, the last day of April and my 16th month as a POW. It seems like 16 years. I am shocked when I observe how my fellow POWs have aged in just a year and a half. Almost all have lost a great deal of weight, most are malnourished, and all are weak from the lack of a proper diet. (Sam, during his 16 months as a POW, lost a total of 80 pounds. His weight at this time is about 105 pounds.)

"The weather remains cold, damp, and always threatens to rain. We try to stay warm. Our food is almost gone. Today only a spoonful of dry beans and one of barley is provided.

"A welcome sound, in the distance around Braunau, is the sound of heavy gunfire and explosions drawing closer to our temporary POW camp. It rains all night.

"Early Tuesday morning, May 1st, I am awakened by the sound of tanks firing in the distance. I spring out of our makeshift pine hut and see German tanks hightailing it to the west in full retreat. A loud cheer thunders from the camp. The American Army is kicking butt. Our tanks are now shelling Braunau from across the river. We hear that Braunau is surrounded by our troops. Hitler's birthplace will soon be in American control. It is ironic that the Butcher of Berlin was born here and we hope to have a rebirth of freedom here, also. Today, I shaved but did not bathe in the frigid Inn River, maybe tomorrow

"A world of white greets me as I awake this Wednesday, May 2nd and crawl out of our pine shelter. It snowed last night and the area is completely covered. It is cold and almost impossible to get the wet wood to ignite to start a fire. I am soaked to the skin and chilled to the bone. Early in the afternoon the sun is trying to make an appearance, but fails.

"The camp is consumed with rumors. We are like schoolboys, we believe any and all. We hear that Braunau has fallen to our troops. Good rumor. We hear that Hitler is dead. Better rumor. Not a rumor, but a fact, is that there is no food left for POWs or Germans.

"Late this morning American Army engineers complete a pontoon bridge across the Inn River and our tanks are coming across. Braunau puts up a little resistance but is quickly occupied by the U.S. Army. White sheets flutter from all houses, businesses, and even church steeples.

"At approximately 1800 hours three jeeps with an American Army reconnaissance captain[3] in charge pulls into our camp. Then with the words we had longed to hear he announces, 'You are no longer prisoners of war. You are now United States soldiers.'

"Sixteen months of fear, boredom, hunger, coldness, and isolation converts into streams of tears flowing from my eyes as I hear these words. And so this unholy life that began on January 4, 1944 will end this May 2, 1945. Thank God for his mercy.

"The next day, Thursday, May 3rd, in the late morning, a full company of American infantry arrive in the camp. We are ordered by the same Army captain to stay in the camp until trucks come to pick us up *but we have been fenced in too long and our stomachs are too empty to obey this order. We spread out like wildfire in all directions looking for farmhouses to sleep in and food to eat.*

"Late Friday afternoon, May 4th the Army sends out units to advise us that we will be leaving the Rossbach area the next day. Anyone not there will be left. We only have to be told once!

"Saturday, May 5th, we anxiously await the trucks to carry us from this place. The day passes slowly but about 1800 hours the trucks appear. We load up and depart the Rossbach area only to be moved a few miles south to a temporary American Rest and Rehabilitation (R&R) area. We are housed in a factory building in the village of Ranshofen.

"The stay here is short, three days, and we are moved across the Inn River and north about 45 miles to an abandoned airfield near the Bavarian City of Pocking, Germany. The American Red Cross is here and has set up a club with coffee and doughnuts. I make a special effort to thank them for my life saving food parcels over the last 16 months. Without them many of us surely would have died of starvation."

On Thursday, May 10, 1945 T/Sgt. Honeycutt along with Sgts. Gilrane, Craden, Peifer, Parker, and Polley are evacuated from the airfield at Pocking, Germany. C-47 transport planes fly them to LeHavre, France and Army trucks complete the journey to the infamous Camp Lucky Strike.[4] Shorty, who has a way of getting to the point, while gazing out over the camp declares, "We are damn lucky to have survived this war and to make it to Camp Lucky!"

Epilogue

The lucky crew of the *What's Cookin, Doc?* endured 16½ combat missions, a crash landing, 16 months as prisoners of war and still came home to their beloved America, safe and sound. There were no parades or welcome home ceremonies. They did not expect or desire any such recognition. What they wanted was to get on with their lives and to put the nightmare of war behind them. They did just that.

William (Bill) Kaczaraba

Bill was released early from the Army Air Corps in November, 1945 (Official Discharge date January 15, 1946) to attend Princeton University. While a student at Princeton, he met Helny Ingeborg Wahlberg, a student cadet nurse. They met in April 1947 at a banquet for graduating senior nurses of St. Peters School of Nursing in New Brunswick, New Jersey.

Bill and Helny became engaged on October 31, 1947 for Helny's 21st birthday. They were married on June 19, 1948 in the Princeton University Chapel.

Their greatest happiness was their children: Patricia Mary Rodriquez, an architect (born 1948); Linda Doris, a public relations person and also a writer (born 1950); and William Steven, a cable executive news director (born 1958). The Kaczaraba family is still growing with two granddaughters, Danika and Francesca Rodriquez.

At Princeton University, Bill was awarded his degree on October 1, 1948 because he completed his course work in three years instead of four. He received a Bachelors Degree Cum Laude in Economics and was considered a member of Princeton's Class of 1949. Bill also earned a law degree and was awarded the Degree of Juris Doctor on June 10, 1953 from the University of Miami. He practiced law in the Miami area from October 1953 until his death.

He died on July 10, 1969 in Miami from a massive pulmonary thromboembolism complicated by diabetes and arteriosclerosis. He is buried in Barrancas National Cemetery, Naval Air Station in Pensacola, Florida.

Bill was the first *Doc* crew member to leave us, however, in all brave men's hearts, he will always be *The Bold Leader*.

Myron (Mike) Clinton Morgan, Sr.

Mike landed at Newport News, Virginia on August 15, 1945. The next two weeks were spent in quarantine and processing paper work prior to returning home to Morgantown, West Virginia in September, 1945, with 30 days leave.

During his leave he wed the love of his life, Madelyn, but all too soon had to leave her again. His orders were to report, at the end of his leave, to San Antonio, Texas.

In Texas he was to be trained in flying B-29s, however, this was circumvented when the atomic bomb abruptly ended the war. He was discharged in November, 1945, to begin a new civilian life.

Mike and Madelyn were graced with two children, Michele (born in 1948) in Eric, Pennsylvania and Myron C. Morgan, Jr. (born in 1952) in Schnectady, New York. In addition, Mike and Madelyn have five grandchildren (Matthew and Meghan Morgan; Jacelyn, Jennifer, and Colin McCoal.)

The majority of Mike's career was with Mohawk Container Company. He was an engineer and designer of their offices and products.

He died unexpectedly in New Hartford, New York in 1982 at the age of 62 of a massive heart attack. Mike is buried in Smithfield, Pennsylvania. We are minus a hero for he was *As Brave As They Come*.

Theodore (Ted) Matthew Wirth

Ted was discharged from the Army Air Corps in October, 1945 and returned to his family farm partnership in Nebraska City, Nebraska. He is alive today and still farms with two of his sons, James and Gerald. Ted has two other sons: Donald, a family practice Doctor in Grand Island, Nebraska, and John, an attorney in Denver, Colorado. His only daughter, Mary Lou, is a high school teacher in Omaha, Nebraska. He has been additionally blessed with ten grandchildren. Ted told me that, "all in all, I have been very fortunate." We are blessed that brave men like Ted are still with us and hope to have him around for many more farming seasons. He is still *The Quiet Warrior.*

Marvin Lewis Horsky

Marvin was discharged from the Army Air Corps in October, 1945. He enrolled at the University of Minnesota on the GI bill and graduated with a Bachelor of Science degree in Accounting in 1949. Hughes Aircraft Company employed him in Los Angeles, California for a number of years. He then moved to Austin, Texas where he was employed as a Certified Public Accountant until his retirement in 1985. Death occurred in 1992 at the age of 72. One thing is sure, heaven has an abundance of humor with the presence of *The Joker.*

Peter (Pete) Parker

Pete was discharged from the Army Air Corps in early September, 1945. He went to work for General Motors in the Cleveland area as a stockman. He died of bleeding ulcers during the late '80s, which would put him in his 60s at the time of death. Rest in peace, *Old War Horse.*

George Gibson (Gibby) Polley, Jr.

Gibby was discharged from the Army Air Corps in October, 1945. After the war, he started a local cab company in Marblehead, Massachusetts called Gibby's Taxi. In 1949 he enrolled at Boston University on the GI Bill, graduating in 1953 with a Bachelor of Science degree in Motion Pictures. He married Vernelle Ball in 1946 and they were blessed with two children: a son, George Gibson, III, in January of 1947, and a daughter, Virginia Ann, in March, 1951.

After working in television advertising and later the Martin Aircraft Co. missile program, he and his family moved back to Marblehead,

Massachusetts, where he became a prominent real estate broker. He died in a boating accident on September 4, 1974 at the age of 52. Heaven's pearly gates are well protected by Gibby, the crew's outstanding combat ace. A loving husband and father in peace, in war *A Crack Shot*.

Harry Alexander (Gilly) Gilrane

Harry was discharged from the Army Air Corps in September, 1945, and returned to his home in Brooklyn, New York. Harry married Dorothy, the girl he left behind, on June 25, 1947. Enrolling at the City College of New York under the GI Bill, he earned a Bachelor of Science Degree in Systems Engineering and later earned his Professional Engineering Certification.

After graduation he had a job with Funk Eddie, a shipping firm, as an agent for the SCAN American Inc. Then a stint as a life insurance broker with MONY. Finally, he joined a small manufacturing company that fabricated abrasive castings. Through hard work and dedication he became Chief Executive Officer of the company. The fightin' Irishman was then challenged to make it profitable. This he did as the company became the leading fabricator of abrasive castings in the country with designs and shipments all over the world. Many years later he sold the company to a foundry and retired to Pinehurst, North Carolina in 1990.

He is now a volunteer with the U. S. Army Special Forces Survival, Escape, Resistance, and Evasion (SERE) Program at Fort Bragg and Camp McCall, North Carolina, addressing the graduation classes in rotation with other former POWs. The Army believes his POW experience will benefit the Special Forces troops, if captured.

Harry and his wife have three children: Michael Patrick, a graduate of the State University of New York at Cortland; Timothy Brant, a medical doctor and graduate of Albright College, Reading, Pennsylvania; and Deborah Lynn, a graduate of Syracuse University, Syracuse, New York.

I have visited Harry on several occasions during the preparation of this book and consider him a close friend. May his little guy keep this *Fightin' Irishman* with us for many more Saint Patrick's Days to come.

Solomon (Sol) Craden

Sol was discharged from the Army Air Corps on October 13, 1945, and returned to his hometown of Milwaukee, Wisconsin. Friends introduced him to a local Milwaukee girl, Virginia Ann Ellingson. After a courtship of several months, Sol and Virginia were married on December 12, 1948.

Sol and Virginia have four children: two sons, Steven and Paul, and two daughters, Jane Pollpeter and LeAnn Kurey. Their greatest gifts are their four beautiful grandchildren: Nicholas and Abbey Pollpeter; Ben and Luke Kurey.

Sol established his own automatic screw machine shop business in 1948 (Craden Manufacturing, Inc.), and this was his primary occupation until his retirement in 1990. Sol and his wife presently live in Menomonee Falls, Wisconsin. May this *Gallant Fighter* remain with us many more years.

Wilbur Allen Peifer

Wilbur was discharged from the Army Air Corps in September, 1945. He returned to his home in Pontiac, Michigan. No other information is known of his civilian life. It is not known if he is still alive today. He was *German by Birth, American by Choice* and he served his adopted country with honor.

John Samuel (Sam) Honeycutt

After reporting to Washington, DC for MIS-X debriefing and the signing of papers pledging never to reveal his code user activities, Sam arrived home to his wife, Pauline, on June 12, 1945. She was then living with her parents in Virgilina, Virginia, a town of about 300 souls. The word got around town that Sam was home. The town's population converged on the home to greet him and stayed well past midnight.

After a 30-day leave, he was ordered to report to Lackland AFB in San Antonio, Texas for B-29 engineer training in preparation for the war against Japan. While at Lackland, the war ended and he was discharged on October 12, 1945.

Sam and Pauline have three children. Their eldest son, Darwin, was born in 1950 and is employed in the investment business. A second son, Roger, was born in 1952 and is employed in the instrument manufacturing business. Finally in 1954, they had a daughter, Valarie, who is employed with a major computer company. Their family grew with the addition of five grandchildren: Ginger, Dale, Sean, and Samantha Honeycutt and Nicholas Sottile.

The majority of Sam's career was with Monarch Elevator Company located in Greensboro, North Carolina as a shop foreman. In 1989, he was diagnosed with Parkinson's Disease. Parkinson's is a disease affecting the basal ganglia of the brain for which no cause has been found, and therefore, no cure. This disease is a disorder of middle-aged and elderly people characterized by tremor, rigidity, and a poverty of spontaneous movement. Sam's first and most prominent symptom was tremors, which affected his right hand, then spread first to the leg on the same side and then to his other limbs, interfering with such actions as holding a fork or spoon. Next his face became expressionless causing an unmodulated voice. Later, he had an increasing tendency to stoop. A shuffling run was required to maintain his balance.

During a weekend in March, 1992, my wife and I were visiting Sam and my sister, Pauline. The purpose of the visit was to spend time with him before his second heart operation.

About 2 A.M. Saturday night I was awakened by my sister's excited voice calling, "Honey, what are you doing?" Sam was standing in the corner of their bedroom and he replied, "I'm peeing in the corner of my hut, it's okay, everybody does it. If I go outside at night the Germans will shoot me." His mind was reliving his POW nightmares. It seems Sam couldn't live with his memories and he couldn't live without them.

My sister called to me for assistance to help him into the bathroom. I cradled this man, my lifelong hero, in my arms as I assisted him. His legs had now stiffened to where he could not bend them at all. He was embarrassed, but helpless to refuse my aid. As I placed this man that I loved back into bed, I knew I held a treasure; one of the last of a dying breed.

On March 23, 1992, Sam traded in his old tarnished Air Force wings for a brand new shiny pair from his Lord. The memorial poem below was read at his funeral, however, I believe it also applies equally to his *What's Cookin, Doc?* crewmates of so many years ago.

John Honeycutt

A man of faith, strength and vision
was what he was to me.
His life was lived in true distinction
filled with integrity.

He touched my life in many ways
hard to explain though I wish I could.
A finer Christian I'm sure you'll never find
just in case you thought you ever would.

You knew once that you met him
of his great capacity to care.
And also of his love for his Maker
he so humbly expressed in his prayer.

A gentle giant, a man of faith
are words to describe this gentleman.
We all would do well to follow the
example of his life,
if we can.[1]

He loved his God, his family, and his country. I believe he had his values in the proper order. His crew can honestly state that during combat he *Led by Example* and I can faithfully testify that is exactly how he lived his life.

★★★★★

During the '80s there was a song by the Statler Brothers entitled, *Whatever Happened to Randolph Scott?* It was a plea for a return to heroes that America once produced. Such as the young men like the crew of *What's Cookin' Doc?* who rose to the challenges of World War II and fought the bloody air battles over Europe.

Above all, the most important thing to each crew member of *Doc* was his sense of values. Prior to combat each had doubts as to how, when presented with a challenge, he would rise to it. How would he react? Would he have the courage and endurance to ignore the flak and fighters and still possess the ability to stay the course even though death would be his constant companion?

In the years after the war these fine men can look back and think upon those challenges that confronted each of them at the time. Each can look straight into any man's eye and know that their values were straight and true, and when presented with the challenges of combat, they met them head on and conquered them admirably.

Each deserves imperishable praise for the service and sacrifices rendered to our country in its darkest hour. By these faithful acts they have assuredly earned a hallowed niche in this nation's hall of glory with or without official recognition or reward. Men may never raise monuments to honor these brave men but their's is a timeless memorial that no chisel can trace; their bravery and honor are graven, not in stone, but in the living hearts of all who cherish freedom.

In writing this book, these men have given me a tremendous opportunity to commemorate their heroism, and to honor their sacrifices. They surrendered their youth to achieve a great and lasting victory. It is a tribute to them that such valor and steadfastness remain strong in our memories today. The least I can say to each of them is that I, and the United States of America, salute them and all that they stood for.

Let us remember and celebrate their sacrifices. We owe them more than we can ever repay for they are truly the last of *A Dying Breed*.

Combat Missions

Mission	Day/Date	Duration (Hours & Minutes)	Target
01	Saturday/10/2/43	7:00	Emden, Germany
02	Friday/10/8/43	6:45	Bremen, Germany
03	Saturday/10/9/43	9:00	Anklam, Germany
04	Sunday/10/10/43	7:00	Munster, Germany
05	Wednesday/10/20/43	5:45	Duren, Germany
06	Wednesday/11/3/43	6:30	Wilhelmshaven, Germany
07	Friday/11/5/43	7:00	Gelsenkirchen, Germany
08	Tuesday/11/16/43	8:45	Knaben, Norway
09	Friday/11/26/43	6:20	Bremen, Germany #2
10	Monday/11/29/43	6:40	Bremen, Germany #3
11	Saturday/12/11/43	6:45	Emden, Germany #2
12	Monday/12/13/43	6:15	Bremen, Germany #4
13	Wednesday/12/22/43	5:40	Osnabruck, Germany
14	Friday/12/24/43	4:15	Croisette, France
15	Thursday/12/30/43	8:00	Ludwigshafen, Germany
16	Friday/12/31/43	9:30	Southwestern France
*17	Tuesday/1/4/44	(MIA)	Kiel, Germany

*The *What's Cookin,' Doc?* was scheduled for repairs and maintenance on 1/4/44, therefore, A/C #2-5838, *Mad Money II* was assigned to Lt. William Kaczaraba and his crew. Fighter aircraft and ground fire hit *Mad Money II* over Kiel, Germany. In an attempt to fly to neutral Sweden, the crew crash-landed 5 km. SW of Kalundborg, Denmark.

Three days later on 1/7/44, the *What's Cookin,' Doc?* flown by 2nd Lt. Walter E. Garner was hit by fighter aircraft over Ludwigshafen, Germany and crash-landed near Amiens, France. Enemy fighters killed the navigator and left waist gunner.

APPENDIX

Image Credits

Image#	Credit
1.1	Mrs. Hilny Kaczaraba (wife of 1st Lt. Bill Kaczaraba)
1.2, 3.4, 28.4	Mrs. Madelyn Morgan (wife of 2nd Lt. Mike Morgan)
1.3, 25.6, 25.9, 26.1, 27.1, 29.5, 29.6 29.7, 29.6	Mr. Theodore (Ted) Wirth
1.4, 8.2, 28.1,28.2	Mrs. Pauline Honeycutt (wife of T/Sgt. John Honeycutt)
1.5, 30.3	Mr. Harry Gilrane
3.5	National Air & Space Museum, Washington, DC.
2.1, 2.2, 2.3, 2.4, 2.5,2.6, 2.7, 2.8, 2.9, 2.10, 2.11, 2.12, 2.13, 2.14, 2.15, 2.16, 2.17, 2.18, 2.19, 2.20, 2.21	Mr. Dan Patterson
3.1, 3.2, 3.3, 5.1, 24.1	*As Briefed*, published by Edward Stern & Company, Inc.
8.1	*B-17s Over Berlin*, published by Brasseys, Washington and London
25.1, 28.5, 28.6, 28.7, 28.8, 28.9, 29.1, 29.2, 33.1	Mighty Eighth Air Force Heritage Museum, Savannah, Georgia.
28.3, 29.3, 29.4, 29.8	Sketches by Col. Charles Ross Greening (sketched during his internment in Stalag Luft I)
29.5, 29.6	Mr. Sol Craden
30.1	National Archives, Washington, DC

Image#	**Credit**
28.10, 30.2, 34.1	Sketch and picture contained in T/Sgt. Ben H. Phelper's *Kriegie Memories* book
25.2, 25.7, 25.8	Department of the Air Force, Air Force Historical Research Agency Maxwell Air Force Base, Alabama.
26.1	Special appreciation to Vera Farmer Welk of Martinez, Georgia for English translation of local Danish newspaper article.

Endnotes

Book I: A Gathering of Eagles

Chapter 1: Eaglets

1. In addition to the specialized training required for each crew member's primary duties, each is also required to understand the basics of all other crew member's duties.

2. Information from Mike Morgan's memoirs, *Fly for Your Life*.

3. Letter from Ted Wirth to the author, dated January 1997.

4. Information from the *Milwaukee Journal*, dated January 21, 1944.

5. Statements from Harry Gilrane during interviews in December 1996.

6. Information provided by George Gibson Polley, III (son of S/Sgt. George Gibson Polley, Jr.).

Chapter 2: Crew Duties and Training

1. Flak is the Eighth Air Force airmen short term for the German word, *Fliegerabwehrkanone*, which means antiaircraft gunfire.

2. Accurate bombing is a function of many variables as follows:

   A. Altitude, controlled by Lt. Kaczaraba, determines the length of time the bombs are in flight and affected by atmospheric conditions. The forward travel of the bombs (range) and deflection (distance the bombs drift in a crosswind with respect to the aircraft's ground track) are a function of time from release to impact. The altimeter must be calibrated correctly and Lt. Kaczaraba must maintain the assigned altitude as accurately as possible. For every additional 100 feet above the assumed bombing altitude of 20,000 feet, bombing error increases by 30 feet.

   B. True airspeed, controlled by Lt. Kaczaraba, is the measure of the B-17's speed through the air. The true airspeed of the bomber determines the trail of the bomb — the horizontal distance the bomb lags behind the bomber at the moment of impact. Once the bomber airspeed and altitude are entered into the bombsight they must be maintained. For erroneous airspeed, bombing error increases approximately 170 feet for a 10 MPH change.

C. Bomb ballistics tables for each type of bomb describes their intended trajectory from bomber to target.

D. Trail, mentioned earlier, is available from bombing tables and set in the bombsight by Lt. Wirth. Trail is affected by altitude, airspeed, bomb ballistics and air density — the first two factors are controlled by Lt. Kaczaraba.

E. Actual time of fall is affected by altitude, type of bomb, and air density.

F. Ground speed, the speed of the B-17 in relation to the earth's surface, affects the range of the bomb and varies with airspeed, which is controlled by Lt. Kaczaraba.

G. Drift, determined by the direction and velocity of the wind, is the distance the bomb travels downwind from the aircraft on its journey to the target. Lt. Wirth sets drift on the bombsight.

3. To obtain this information, the author measured the internal dimensions of a B-17G restored as *Nine-O-Nine* (S/N 44-83575, 91st Bomb Group, 323rd Squadron, stationed at Bassingbourn, England during World War II).

4. Today, 56 years later, the U.S. Government's Department of Energy, Hanford Nuclear Site occupies the desert area where this crew made many practice bomb runs. The author visited this area in 1993 and was surprised to learn that the road to the bomb practice area is still called "Bomb Run Road."

5. Letter from Ted Wirth to the author dated January 1997.

6. This was a term used by the U.S. troops stationed in England during World War II. It came about because of the continuous touring of this area by movie and theater stars entertaining the troops. The entertainers referred to their visits as the "European Theater" and the generals added "Operations." Thus, all Eighth Air Force operations were labeled the European Theater of Operations or ETO.

Book II: War Eagles
Chapter 3: Life at Grafton-Underwood

1. Roger A. Freeman, *The Mighty Eighth* (Motorbooks International), pages 253–254. The following provides information to assist the reader in relating to the 384th Bomb Groups History and composition.

Group Designations: Bombardment Groups are popularly termed Bomb Groups and a group usually consists of 48 aircraft at full strength.

Assignment Eighth Air Force: Assignment usually dates from the arrival of group personnel on the British soil. In the case of bomber groups, where ground and air echelons traveled separately, assignment is dated from either the arrival of the Commanding Officer (who would fly in) or the arrival of the Group Headquarters party (by sea) dependent on which is first.

Component Squadrons: There are usually four squadrons within a Bomb Group. Squadrons activated with a group usually remain as components of that group throughout hostilities.

Stations: These are the official British Air Ministry names. In most instances the name is that of the parish in which the airfield is located, but it often happens that the station overlaps into parts of two or three villages and in such cases the name of the station is usually that of the village. This is the case of the 384th Bomb Group located at Grafton-Underwood, England.

Operational Statistics: The 384th Bomb Group is a component of the 1st Air Division. The totals for missions, bomb tonnage, sorties, and enemy aircraft claims are derived from the final statistical summaries of the 1st Air Division.

History

Activated December 1, 1942, Gowen Field, Idaho. Formed and began training January 2, 1943 to April 1, 1943. Moved to Sioux City AAB, Iowa for final training.

Departed for European Theater of Operations (ETO) from Camp Kilmer, New Jersey on May 9, 1943. Began operations May 25, 1943 from Grafton-Underwood, England (Station 106).

Flew 316 combat missions, June 22, 1943 to April 25, 1945.

Dropped 22,415.4 tons of bombs. Completed 9,348 sorties.

Lost 159 B-17s in combat.

Claimed 165 enemy aircraft destroyed, 34 probable, 116 damaged.

*Lost 485 men killed in action (KIA). Lost 771 men as POWs, 23 evaded or escaped.

Total casualties: 1,379

Note: Twelve A/C MIAs with no crew status, assumed crews (120) KIA.

Squadrons

544th, 545th, 546th, 547th.

Major Awards

Received two Presidential Distinguished Unit Citations — January 11, 1944 (all 1st BD Group), Oberpfafenhofen and on April 24, 1944. Dropped last Eighth Air Force bombs of war on April 25, 1945.

Subsequent History

The group was used for occupational air forces and moved to Istres, France in June 1945 to participate in Green Project moving U.S. troops to staging areas. Absorbed aircraft and personnel into the 306th BG in late 1945.

Inactivated at Istres, France on February 28, 1946.

Total of four years and three months as an operational group during WWII.

Commanding Officers

Col. Budd J. Peaslee: December 18, 1942–September 6, 1943.

Col. Julius K. Lacey: September 6, 1943–November 23, 1943.

Col. Dale O. Smith: November 23, 1943–October 24, 1944.

Lt. Col. Theodore R. Milton: October 24, 1944–June 16, 1945.

Lt. Col. Robert W. Fish: June 17, 1945–October 18, 1945.

2. In less than a month, on October 14, 1943 on a mission known as "Black Thursday" to Schweinfurt, Germany this crew will be shot down. All ten crew members will be killed, wounded, or missing in action.

3. The "tail-end Charlie" is the flight formation position assigned to new crews.

It is in the extreme rear location of a formation and is most likely to receive most of the enemy fighter's attacks. The practice of assigning new crews to this position is based on the belief that they will be shot down and killed or become prisoners of war quickly. New crews will be missed less than old hands.

4. Pounders is a term used for a bomb weight (i.e., 1,000 pounds).

5. Flight Records of T/Sgt. John S. Honeycutt from May 1943 through September 1943.

Chapter 4: Pitiful Pioneers

1. Condensed from Clinton H. Orean's *Facts & Happenings* document.

Chapter 5: Welcome to Air Combat

1. The military clock is used throughout this book. For the readers not familiar with military time — if it is 1430 hours subtract 1200 from it, and it is 2:30 P.M. Civilian time. Before noon is just as it reads — 0400 hours is 4:00 A.M.

2. After the war Travis Air Force Base, located at Fairfield, California was named in honor of General Travis.

3. The PFF method is where all the aircraft in a formation release their bombs when the lead aircraft, which has PFF equipment installed, releases.

Chapter 6: Heroes Reprimand

1. Information from Mike Morgan's memoirs, *Fly for Your Life*.

2. Positions of enemy aircraft are given in relation to the hour hands on the crew's watches. If a fighter is at 12 o'clock then he is attacking directly from the front of the aircraft. If at 6 o'clock then it is attacking directly from the rear and so on.

3. Authors Note: The following are reasons why this crew should have been presented the Silver Star or the Distinguished Flying Cross for their uncommon valor above and beyond the call of duty for this mission on October 8, 1943 to Bremen, Germany.

   This crew flew its mission, as briefed, destroying nine enemy aircraft and probably destroying one other. The nine confirmed kills by this crew, on a single mission, was not equaled by any other Eighth Air Force aircraft (bomber or fighter) during World War II. The five kills by the tail gunner were not equaled by any other individual on a single mission during World War II.

   Their unselfish actions and love for their comrades not only allowed them to return safely to England, but also saved the two crippled aircraft and the lives of 20 airmen.

Chapter 7: Anguish after Anklam

1. "Happy Valley" is the Eighth Air Force Crew's nickname for Germany's industrial Ruhr Valley. It is well protected by enemy fighters and flak, thus the name happy.

Chapter 8: Holly Terror

1. "Wash" is a term used by aircrews for an aircraft propeller's air exhaust.

Chapter 10: Double Duren

1. Recall is the command given by headquarters or the lead aircraft commander for the formation to abort (terminate) the mission and return to base. The recall is usually due to poor weather conditions.

2. Brass is the military term given officers, usually above the rank of Colonel. When this rank is achieved, the officer has accumulated many medals that are made of brass.

Chapter 11: Brown Bomber

1. Stand down is the term for all aircraft to stay on the ground, usually due to bad weather.

2. SOS is the military abbreviation for shit on shingle. SOS is finely chopped meat and gravy on toast.

3. Bad news curtain refers to a curtain that covers a large map of Europe with the designated targets for that day's mission.

4. Pathfinder method of bombing is where all aircraft in a formation drop their bombs at the same time in concert with the lead ship or the Pathfinder ship. This ship has special equipment used in bad weather when visibility is poor.

Chapter 12: Happy Valley

1. USAAF: United States Army Air Force

2. RAF: Royal Air Force.

3. An 8/10 cloud cover means that ground visibility is 80 percent obscured. A 10/10 cloud cover means that ground visibility is 100 percent obscured, and so forth.

4. Chow hall is a building where meals are served to military personnel.

Chapter 13: Needle in a Haystack

1. A balloon barrage is a line of anchored balloons holding up nets and cables used for antiaircraft defense.

2. Triangle P is the 384th Bomb Group designation and is painted on the tail vertical section of each B-17.

Chapter 15: The Hitchhiker

1. Time hack is when crew members synchronize their watches during briefing.

2. *Fuehrer* means Father and refers to Hitler.

3. Salvo is when all aircraft drop bombs together on a signal from the lead aircraft.

Chapter 16: Frozen Flyboys

1. On May 8, 1944, Lt. Allison, on a mission to Sottevost, France crash-landed his A/C No. 43-31211 due to extensive flak damage. Five of this crew would be killed, three taken prisoners, and two would evade. Two of the five killed were S/Sgt. Vernon Kaufmann and T/Sgt. William Clements.

Chapter 19: Bremen Is Blazing

1. V speed is the speed on takeoff when the aircraft cannot abort. Its speed is such that if full brakes were applied it would overshoot the end of the runway.

2. WT is a message meaning wait or slow down to allow other formations to catch up. Usually speeds are reduced or an S pattern is implemented to use up time.

3. Let down is the Air Force term for the formation to start descending in preparation for landing.

Chapter 20: Code Users

1. The Air Medal (one enemy plane shot down) and the Air Medal with Oak Leaf Cluster (for each additional plane shot down) presented to the *Doc* crew did not include enemy planes destroyed on the first Bremen mission. (See Chapter 6, Heroes Reprimand.) Bremen mission kills were later allowed, enemy plane totals are then:

Crew Member	Kills
S/Sgt. George G. Polley	7
T/Sgt. John S. Honeycutt	3
S/Sgt. Harry A. Gilrane	2
S/Sgt. Peter F. Parker	2
S/Sgt. Wilber A. Peifer	2

2. By war's end, the system had become so efficient that MIS-X was able to maintain constant communication with American POWs in virtually every German POW camp. So well selected were these code users that not one ever broke security. Not until 1986, at a Stalag Luft III reunion in Seattle, Washington, was the identity of a single World War II CU ever revealed — 41 years after the war had ended!

Chapter 21: Targets of Opportunity

1. Dead reckoning is a navigational method of determining the aircraft's position relative to the earth. It calculates distance, speed, and other factors between two fixed points on earth.

Chapter 25: KO over Kiel

1. In performing his duty, T/Sgt. John Samuel (Sam) Honeycutt was well aware of the risk to his life. While attempting to ignite the gasoline he knew the B-17 would very likely explode. He knew this but was willing to risk his life to carry out his duty. For this heroic action, T/Sgt. Honeycutt, on May 29, 1945 would receive the Air Force high award of the Distinguished Flying Cross. He also had the satisfaction of knowing that the Germans did not salvage a single section from his plane except a small piece of the tail section.

2. Based on a 1992 letter to Mr. Ted Wirth from a local man, Mr. Ole Rasmussen, this pro-German Danish fisherman from the local town of

Havnemark quickly phoned the Germans to report an American bomber crash landing. A couple of weeks later, in protest, a blacksmith in the near-by town of Melby made a swastika of iron and sent it anonymously to the fisherman.

3. This medieval castle is actually a palace known as Lerchenborg Palace. It is located five miles south-southwest of the city of Kalundborg, Denmark on the Peninsula of Asnaer. The palace was built in the Baroque style in 1745 for General Lerchen, a rich Danish landowner. The three-winged edifice, the lower ancillary buildings, offices, stables, riding arena and park are grouped around a central axis. Two memorial rooms in one wing of the palace are dedicated to Hans Christian Andersen who was often a guest there. The park laid out partly in the French style and partly in English, today has a beautiful rose garden.

Chapter 26: Destination: Dulag Luft

1. The train station that the crew was taken to is in the city of Kalundborg. The train trip from Kalundborg to Copenhagen, Denmark was about 60 miles.

2. An identification metal plate about one inch by two inches with name, serial number, blood type, and religion stamped on it. It is worn around the neck on a chain.

3. See Image 28.1 for listing and locations of permanent camps.

Chapter 29: Stalag Luft I: No Country Club

1. This chapter contains information obtained from Mike Morgan's memoirs entitled, *Fly for Your Life* and information from Ted Wirth. It also contains material gathered from official German Stalag Luft I record and American Red Cross Prisoners of War Bulletins published during 1944–45. The dates provided are not exact so I have rounded them off to beginning, middle, or end of a month. This chapter tells of the circumstances under which Lts. Kaczaraba, Morgan, Wirth, and Horsky lived and the common enemies they faced. Enemies like hunger, boredom, constant cold, and the uncertainty of the length of their confinement. It also tells of the activities in which these Kriegies participated in during their 15 months of confinement at Stalag Luft I.

2. The American Red Cross *Prisoners of War Bulletin* in February 1944 provided the following information on Stalag Luft I.

The camp for British and American officer-airmen at Barth, in north Germany, known as Stalag Luft I, also carries the designation "Friegsgefanenelager No. 1 der Luftwaffe" (Prisoners of War Camp No. 1 of the Air Force). The American strength at this camp at the end of January 1944 is about 2000 and substantially in excess of the British strength. Col. J. R. Byerly is the American senior officer and Maj. M. S. Dillingham, his assistant. (Formally the 384th BG, 547th SQ Commander.)

The camp is run entirely as an Oflag (officers' camp) and is composed of a "Vorlager" (receiving area) and two compounds. The American and British prisoners are not separated, and the camp is run by a joint British-American staff. The men can move from one compound to another during the daytime.

In all the barracks the men sleep in triple-tier wooden bunks. The building of new barracks has not kept pace with the rapid influx of prisoners, with the result that practically all the camp's facilities are seriously inadequate.

Considering the lack of facilities for cooking, laundry, and bathing, the state of health at the camp is considered good. This is perhaps partly due to the camp's healthy location near the seashore.

Chapter 30: Stalag 17B: More Than Just a Hollywood Movie

1. This chapter contains information obtained from T/Sgt. Honeycutt, S/Sgts. Polley, Gilrane, and Craden. In addition, it contains information from official German Stalag 17B Records and American Red Cross *Prisoners of War Bulletins* published during 1944–45. The dates provided are not exact so I have rounded them off to beginning, middle, and end of a month. This chapter tells of the circumstances under which the NCOs lived. It also tells of the activities these Kriegies participated in during 15 months of confinement at Stalag 17B.

2. Protecting power refers to the country responsible for enforcing the Geneva Convention articles of war. In the case of Stalag 17B, the United States is the protecting power.

3. Man of Confidence is the literal translation of *Homme de Confiance* used in the French text of the Geneva Prisoners of War Convention. The *Homme de Confiance* is the elected representative by the prisoners in a camp containing enlisted men, or the senior officer in an officers' camp. The Germans refer to him as the camp leader; the Americans call him the camp spokesman; and the British often call him the camp captain. Regardless of his military rank, the camp spokesman in a German Stalag (even if it contains officer-prisoners) represents all the prisoners of his nationality in relations with German authorities, the Warring Power, and welfare.

4. During a phone conversation with Ralph Lavoie in May 1999 he related how he came to be a POW and the actual story of his now famous escape attempt.

   How he came to be a POW began on the morning of June 25, 1943:

   His Flying Fortress named *Yankee Powerhouse* took off with the 384th Bomb Group from its base in England and headed for Hamburg, Germany. Ralph was in the ball turret. Flak and fighter opposition was very heavy, and three of the group's bombers were shot down, including the *Yankee Powerhouse*.

During a fighter attack a shell exploded in the cockpit, killing the copilot. The pilot was also hit and was left with only one hand to try to keep control of the plane. He dived out of the formation to avoid collision with other B-17s.

One of a fighter's shells had exploded in the power unit of the ball turret. Although Ralph could unlock the double latches of his escape door, he could not roll the turret to bring that door up inside the fuselage. Meanwhile, the mortally wounded pilot pulled out of the dive and ordered "bail-out."

As the plane leveled, the weight of the ammunition in Ralph's turret shifted and, without power, rolled into position so that the door swung open inside the fuselage and not out into open space. Ralph climbed out, clamped on his chute, helped two of his crewmates out, and then dived through the waist hatch himself. Worried that he was still well above 10,000 feet and without oxygen, he delayed opening his chute as long as he dared, falling several thousand feet before pulling the ripcord.

As he floated down, a German fighter circled him, perhaps to point out the jumper's location to people on the ground so they could be waiting to take him prisoner. When he hit the ground, it was a farmer with a pitchfork who made the capture. After being interrogated at Frankfort, he was then transported by rail to Stalag 17B in Krems, Austria.

The Escape Attempt Began on December 2, 1943:

Jim Proakis had already tried an escape once; climbing on the undercarriage of a garbage wagon that was leaving the camp. The guards spotted him. He and Ralph learned of a plan being organized, involving one of the guards whom had agreed to a bribe of a big sum of money after the end of the war.

The guard's part was to make a cut in the outer fence while a group of POWs cut their way through the inner fence and the coils between. Jim and Ralph decided they would follow the group through the fences and to freedom. The bribe offer, however, was reported to the German staff and the organizers were warned not to proceed.

Word of that did not get to Jim and Ralph. They crawled out to the proposed location of the fence-cut as scheduled. It was cold and snowy and they thought that the guards would be less alert. They crossed the single-strand warning wire back of Barracks #36 and crawled toward the high inner fence on their stomachs. They were almost immediately caught in the beam of the corner guard tower's spotlight.

As they quickly turned to crawl back, the tower guard began shooting and Ralph heard the bullets whizzing overhead. Over Ralph's protest, Jim leaped up to run toward a nearby air raid trench. He was immediately cut down by machine gun fire. Ralph kept crawling until a bullet hit his left leg. The force of it knocked him over onto his back.

The shooting continued — later it was estimated by some POWs to have been more than a hundred shots. Ralph's only injury up to now, however, was the leg wound.

As Ralph lay there on his back the firing stopped and he saw against the tower lights, the silhouettes of two men approaching. One was a guard with a rifle; the other was an officer with his pistol drawn.

Ralph was not unduly concerned that they had their weapons ready. After all, it was wartime and he was a prisoner who had tried to escape. But what came next was totally unexpected. The officer, seeing that Ralph was still alive, aimed his pistol directly at him and fired. He was standing right over Ralph and trying to murder him. "No, no, don't shoot!" Ralph pleaded with him, but he took a step back and got ready to fire again.

Using his good leg Ralph tried to roll back and forth so as not to be such an easy target. He fired and missed. Telling the guard to hold Ralph down with the butt of his rifle against his chest, he began firing again.

One bullet went through Ralph's right shoulder, others through his neck, left side, off his ribs and one actually went through his cheek and out his mouth, which was open wide as he yelled at the shooter. He fired about five shots, which emptied his pistol. Ralph suddenly went very weak and thought the end had come.

The same officer had used one shot to fire into the head of Jim Proakis as he lay there, perhaps already dead, Ralph was later told.

The six months following the shooting were difficult ones for Ralph in the Lazarette. Although he says that the staff people went far out of their way to help him, their facilities and medications were limited and recovery from all of the effects of the shooting meant many days and nights of pain and suffering.

He remembers regaining consciousness at one point and finding a tube stuck in his arm, the other end in someone else's arm. It was one of the POW staff, giving a transfusion of his own blood, since there was no other source of Ralph's type immediately available.

It was in August 1944 when Ralph was brought before the Medical Repatriation Board. After the doctors' examinations he was declared totally unfit and disabled. With several others, including amputees, blind, and severely crippled or sick prisoners, he was carried down to the Krems railroad station.

At Stockholm they were put on board the Swedish hospital ship *Gripsholm*, which steamed to Liverpool, England, for their first stop and then to the United States.

Was the tragic escape attempt a total failure for Ralph? Well, he did get back to the United States nine months before the rest of the POWs in Stalag 17B, and that has to be taken into consideration.

Chapter 34: Eagles Can Walk Too

1. This and other pictures were taken in secret with possible death as punishment by T/Sgt. Ben H. Phelper. After the war he published a collection of these pictures in a book entitled *Kriegie Memories*.

2. Mauthausen was originally built by Germany as a concentration camp to imprison Austrian political undesirables. The Nazis set up the camp north of the Danube River near the village of Mauthausen, 19 kilometers southeast of Linz. It became the killing camp for European Jews. Any Jew sent to Mauthausen was automatically stamped with a death sentence.

3. This reconnaissance unit is from the 67th Company, 13th Armored Division, Patton's 3rd Army.

4. Camp Lucky Strike is a sprawling tent city set up by the U.S. government to temporarily house returning POWs. The camp's population, by this time, is about 50,000.

Chapter 35: Epilogue

1. Memorial poem written by Deacon Eric Kyles of the Hope Valley Baptist Church in Durham, North Carolina.

Secret Letter Codes

This simulated POW letter from T/Sgt. Sam Honeycutt to his brother, Kenneth, reveals how a message can be hidden within a seemingly innocuous letter. The decoded solution and grid reveal the message. For purposes of illustration, the key words are underlined in the letter.

3-3-44

Hello Ken and family,

It's cold and snowing here today.

The snow on the <u>Danube</u> River is beautiful. Coming out <u>of</u> the east and the <u>north</u>, it covers the entire camp <u>and</u> the area. Inside the <u>camp</u> we are given shovels made <u>of</u> wood to clear roads <u>east</u> of camp. We shoveled two <u>miles</u> on this day. Tomorrow <u>four</u> of us must muster the <u>concentration</u> to clear the remaining <u>German</u> roads of the ice and <u>heavy</u> snow. It's a miracle we have strength to do any work given the meager amounts of food we get.

Could you send me some fishing and hunting books to read. I would be most grateful. My health is OK, just nothing to do but pass time until this war is over.

Your little brother,

Runt

To Decode Letter

In the letter, a date written out such as "March 3, 1944" would inform the MIS-X decoder that there is no code in the letter. A date line using all numerals, such as "3-3-44" indicates a code is included in the letter.

In order to determine the number of coded words in the message, multiply the number of letters in the first two words of the first line. For example, in Sam's letter, "Its cold" is 3 times 4 letters, for a total of 12 words.

A grid block is drawn with three squares across (horizontal) and four squares down (vertical). The code words are entered into the grid block beginning at the top left square, proceeding to the right until all squares are filled in.

The code word frequency in Sam's letter is 5/6, meaning that beginning with the second line, first the fifth word DANUBE, and then the sixth word, OF, are entered into the grid. Continuing, the fifth word, NORTH, and the sixth word, AND, are entered into the grid. The words are counted and entered until all of the blocks in the grid are filled. The letter is signed "RUNT," which is the code name the MIS-X assigned to Sam as a code user.

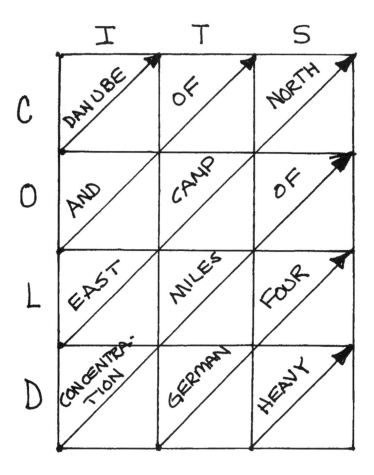

The grid is read in the direction of the arrows, beginning with the bottom right box. The code message reads:

Heavy German Concentration Four Miles East of Camp and North of Danube

WELCOME TO
HELLGATE PRESS

THE UNEXPECTED STORM

The Gulf War Legacy
by Steven Manchester

ISBN: 1-55571-542-7
260 pages, Hardcover: $21.95

After rigorous physical exams, soldiers were trained to fight, infused with rage, and sent to strike—only to watch biology and technology do their jobs for them. Operation Desert Storm was a war like no other. What our troops brought home with them as a result of experimental vaccines, radioactive depleted uranium, and so much pent-up rage, is just beginning to surface. This is one soldier's story.

LIFE IN THE FRENCH FOREIGN LEGION

How to Join and What to Expect When You Get There
by Evan McGorman

ISBN: 1-55571-532-X
250 pages, Hardcover: $22.95

Five years is a long time to commit to anything—especially when your life could be at stake. Consider, prepare, and plan before you enlist. *Life in the French Foreign Legion* is based on this insider's account of what life is really like in one the most mysterious military organizations in the world.

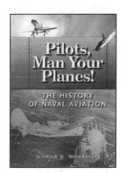

PILOTS, MAN YOUR PLANES!

A History of Naval Aviation
by Wilbur H. Morrison

ISBN: 1-55571-466-8
474 pages, Hardcover: $33.95

An account of naval aviation from Kitty Hawk to the Gulf War, *Pilots, Man Your Planes!* tells the story of naval air growth from a time when planes were launched from battleships to the major strategic element of naval warfare it is today. This book is filled with rare photographs, detailed maps, and accurate accounts that can be found nowhere else. Ideal for anyone interested in aviation.

1-800-228-2275

**VISIT YOUR FAVORITE BOOKSTORE
OR ORDER DIRECT**
Hellgate Press, P.O. Box 3727, Central Point, OR 97502

ARMY MUSEUMS
West of the Mississippi
by Fred L. Bell, SFC, Retired

ISBN: 1-55571-395-5
318 pages, Paperback: $17.95

A guide book for travelers through 23 museums of the west. *Army Museums* contains detailed information about the contents of each museum and the famous soldiers stationed at the forts and military reservations where the museums are located. It is a colorful look at our heritage and the settling of the American West.

FROM HIROSHIMA WITH LOVE
by Raymond A. Higgins

ISBN: 1-55571-404-8
320 pages, Paperback: $18.95

Written from detailed notes and diary entries, *From Hiroshima With Love* is the remarkable story of Lieutenant Commander Wallace Higgins and his experiences in Hiroshima. As Military Governor, Higgins was responsible for helping rebuild a ravaged nation. In doing so, he developed an unforeseen respect for the Japanese, their culture, and one special woman.

WALKING AWAY FROM THE THIRD REICH
The Experiences of a Teenager in Hitler's Army
by Claus W. Sellier

ISBN: 1-55571-513-3
308 pages, Paperback: $15.95

Seventeen-year-old boys are the same everywhere. This is a gripping story of a well-to-do German boy who is eager to serve, but learns the hard way that war is not a game. From the shelter of his private boys' school, to the devastating battle fields of Germany, he learns what is truly important to him.

THIS WOMAN'S ARMY
The Dynamics of Sex and Violence in the Military
by Marie deYoung

ISBN: 1-55571-507-9
392 pages, Paperback: $16.95

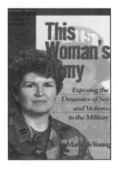

A powerful, personal account of one officer's exposure to the social problems and gender conflicts that are endemic throughout the Army. It defends women's rights to serve in any role where they can "hold their own," at the same time placing responsibility for much sexual misconduct squarely on their shoulders. It deals with the eroded standards for physical, mental, and emotional fitness at the root of the Army's problems.

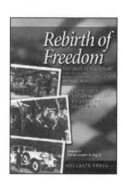

REBIRTH OF FREEDOM

From Nazis and Communists to a New Life in America   ISBN: 1-55571-492-7
by Michael Sumichrast   **324 pages, Paperback: $16.95**

"…a fascinating account of how the skill, ingenuity and work ethics of an individual, when freed from the yoke of tyranny and oppression, can make a lasting contribution to Western society. Michael Sumichrast's autobiography tells of his first loss of freedom to the Nazis, only to have his native country subjected to the tyranny of the Communists. He shares his experiences of life in a manner that makes us Americans, and others, thankful to live in a country where individual freedom is protected."

– General Alexander M. Haig, Secretary of State

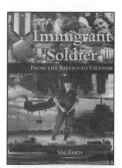

IMMIGRANT SOLDIER

From the Baltics to Vietnam   **ISBN: 1-55571-512-5**
by Vic Pakis   **240 pages, Paperback: $15.95**

The story of a family whose fortunes changed dramatically due to the rise of Communism and Nazism and a flight for freedom to the United States. A son describes his family's experiences as they flee Latvia, and how he joins the U.S. Army to fight against Communism and oppression in Southeast Asia.

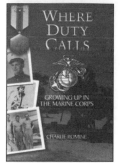

WHERE DUTY CALLS

Growing Up in the Marine Corps   ISBN: 1-55571-499-4
by Charlie Romine   **114 pages, Paperback: $12.95**

An eighteen-year-old, out to experience the world for the first time, joins the Marine Corp in 1942 and serves during World War II and Korea. He had never been away from home, but when the Japanese bombed Pearl Harbor, he rushed to join. This is his personal coming-of-age story.

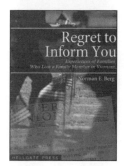

REGRET TO INFORM YOU

Experiences of Families Who Lost A Family Member in Vietnam   ISBN: 1-55571-509-5
by Norman Berg   **168 pages, Paperback: $16.95**

How do you cope with the knowledge that a loved one is missing in action, remains not recovered? Thirty years later, real people still wait for the war in Vietnam to end—to know what happened to their loved ones. *Regret to Inform You* is a moving glimpse at the human strength and persistence it takes to survive the maze of government bureaucracy, miscommunication, and inconclusive evidence. Eight families relate their stories as only they ca

THE WAR THAT WOULD NOT END
U.S. Marines in Vietnam, 1971-1973
by Major Charles D. Melson, USMC (Retired)

ISBN: 1-55571-420-X
388 pages, Paperback: $19.95

When South Vietnamese troops proved unable to take over the war from their American counterparts, the Marines had to resume responsibility. Covering the period 1971-1973, Major Charles D. Melson describes the battle strategies of the units that broke a huge 1972 enemy offensive. The book contains a detailed look at this often ignored period of America's longest war. Featured as an alternate selection in the DoubleDay Book Club.

PROJECT OMEGA
Eye of the Beast
by James E. Acre

ISBN: 1-55571-511-7
228 pages, Paperback: $13.95

"CNN tried its level best to dishonor the reputation of the brave men of Special Operations Group. ... Acre's beautifully written and accurate portrayal of some of the actions of that noble unit will allow the reader to see how these daring young men made accomplishing the impossible routine and to also set the record straight."
— David Hackworth, Author of *About Face and Hazardous Duty*

GULF WAR DEBRIEFING BOOK
An After Action Report
by Andrew Leyden

ISBN: 1-55571-396-3
318 pages, Paperback: $18.95

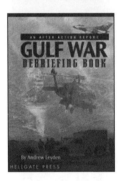

Available in the George Bush Presidential Library Museum Store. Now you can draw your own conclusion as to what happened during the seven-month period between late 1990 and early 1991. The *Gulf War Debriefing Book: An After Action Report* provides you with a meticulous review of the events. It includes documentation of all military units deployed, the primary weapons used during the war, and a look at the people, places, and politics behind the military maneuvering.

HOW IT WAS
A Vietnam Story
by John Patrick O'Hara

ISBN: 1-55571-516-8
125 pages, Paperback: $12.95

How it Was is not a blow-by-blow record, but a shoebox of memories presented as they flashed inside the mind of a Vet trying to come to terms with what he had seen and done during his tour. It is a non-traditional, thought-provoking journey into a war-torn mind.

ORDER OF BATTLE
Allied Ground Forces of Operation Desert Storm
by Thomas D. Dinackus

ISBN: 1-55571-493-5
407 pages, Paperback: $17.95
Contains photographs of medals, ribbons, and unit patches

Based on extensive research—containing information not previously available to the public—*Order of Battle: Allied Ground Forces of Operation Desert Storm* is a detailed study of the Allied ground combat units that served in the conflict in the Persian Gulf. In addition to showing unit assignments, it includes the type of insignia and equipment used by the various units in one of the largest military operations since the end of WWII.

GREEN HELL
The Battle for Guadalcanal
by William J. Owens

ISBN: 1-55571-498-6
284 pages, Paperback: $18.95

This is the story of thousands of Melanesian, Australian, New Zealanders, Japanese, and American men who fought for a poor insignificant island in a faraway corner of the South Pacific Ocean. For the men who participated, the real battle was of man against jungle. This is the account of land, sea, and air units covering the entire six-month battle. Stories of ordinary privates and seamen, admirals and generals who survived to claim the victory that was the turning point of the Pacific War.

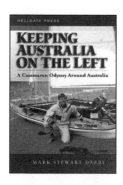

KEEPING AUSTRALIA ON THE LEFT
A Catamaran Odyssey Around Australia
by Mark Stewart Darby

ISBN: 1-55571-508-7
232 pages, Paperback: $13.95

A wonderful tale of an Australian man, his American girlfriend, and a small open catamaran called *Tom Thumb*. It is a precarious adventure that unfolds among the desolate seaports and motley characters of the Australian coastline. Sharks, crocodiles, deadly jellyfish, storms, wild seas, and limestone cliffs are only part of this unique two-year journey.

OH, WHAT A LOVELY WAR

by Stanley Swift, transcribed and edited by Evelyn Luscher   ISBN: 1-55571-502-8

96 pages, Paperback: $10.95

This book tells you what history books do not. It is war with a human face. It is the unforgettable memoir of British soldier Gunner Stanley Swift through five years of war. Intensely personal and moving, it documents the innermost thoughts and feelings of a young man as he moves from civilian to battle-hardened warrior under the duress of fire.

THROUGH MY EYES

91st Infantry Division, Italian Campaign, 1942-1945
by Leon Weckstein   ISBN: 1-55571-497-8

208 pages, Paperback: $14.95

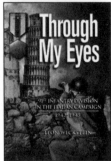

Through My Eyes is the true account of an Average Joe's infantry days before, during, and shortly after the furiously fought battle for Italy. The author's front row seat allows him to report the shocking account of casualties and the rest-time shenanigans during the six weeks of the occupation of the city of Trieste. He also recounts in detail his personal roll in saving the historic Leaning Tower of Pisa.

WORDS OF WAR

From Antiquity to Modern Times   ISBN: 1-55571-491-9
by Gerald Weland   176 pages, Paperback: $13.95

Words of War is a delightful romp through military history. Lively writing leads the reader to an understanding of a number of soldierly quotes. The result of years of haunting dusty libraries, searching obscure journals, and reviewing microfilm files, this unique approach promises to inspire many casual readers to delve further into the circumstances surrounding the birth of many quoted phrases.

MIGHTY MIDGETS AT WAR

The Saga of the LCS(L) Ships from Iwo Jima to Vietnam   ISBN: 1-55571-522-2
by Robin L. Rielly   270 pages, Paperback: $18.95

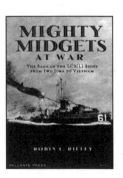

Extensively researched, *Mighty Midgets at War* accurately chronicles the history of the Mighty Midgets—Landing Craft Support vessels—and the terror-filled duty into which sailors aboard them were thrust. Based exclusively on original sources such as ship's logs, action reports, and correspondence and interviews with actual wartime participants, it includes over 100 photos and illustrations, and follows the careers of these great ships from WWII to Vietnam. In several cases, it follows these ships to their eventual retirement or sale to other countries.

WIDOW-MAKERS & RHODODENDRONS
Loggers: The Unsung Heroes of WWII
by Doris Winter Hubbard

ISBN 1-55571-525-7
172 pages, Paperback: $19.95

A vivid account of life in a logging community during WWII, when men risked their lives to fill the sky-rocketing demand for wood for the contonments, packaging, dunnage for ships, explosives, and paper vital for our victory. It is a compassionate look at the families who worried whether their men would make it home from the muddy slopes.

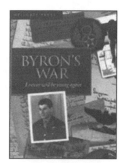

BYRON'S WAR
I never will be young again...
by Byron Lane

ISBN: 1-55571-402-1
298 pages, Hardcover: $21.95

Offered by The Aviators' Guild Book Club, *Byron's War* is based on letters and a personal journal that tells the story of WWII through the eyes of a young air crew officer. It is a tribute to the changes he experiences as he goes through cadet training, flies the North Atlantic as a crew member, and faces awesome responsibility during those critical times.

COAST GUARD ACTION IN VIETNAM
Stories of Those Who Served
By Paul Scotti

ISBN: 1-55571-528-1
250 pages, Paperback: $17.95

Written by the author of *Seaports: Ships, Piers, and People* and *Police Divers,* this well-crafted lively and engaging history will rejuvenate one's pride in the American miliary with its little-known details of the Coast Guard's involvement in Vietnam. The fact that they were in Vietnam at all is a surprise to many. What they were doing there will be an even bigger surprise!

THE PARROT'S BEAK
U.S. Operations in Cambodia
by Paul B. Morgan

ISBN: 1-55571-543-5
200 pages, Paperback: $14.95

By the author of *K-9 Soldiers: Vietnam and After,* Morgan's latest book divulges secret insertion techniques and information about Nixon's secret war that the government still refuses to acknowledge.

Order Direct FROM HELLGATE PRESS

Titl	Price	Quantity	Cost
Army Museums	$17.95		
Byron's War (hardcover)	$21.95		
Coast Guard Action in Vietnam	$17.95		
A Dying Breed	$15.95		
From Hiroshima With Love	$18.95		
Gulf War Debriefing Book:	$18.95		
Keeping Australia on the Left	$13.95		
Legacy of Leadership (hardcover)	$17.95		
Life in the French Foreign Legion (hardcover)	$22.95		
Mighty Midgets at War	$18.95		
Night Landing	$13.95		
Order of Battle	$17.95		
Parrot's Beak	$14.95		
Patriot Dreams (hardcover)	$21.95		
Pilots, Man Your Planes! (hardcover)	$33.95		
Rebirth of Freedom	$16.95		
Regret to Inform You	$16.95		
Right Foot in the Pacific, Left Foot in the Atlantic	$17.95		
The War That Would Not End	$19.95		
This Woman's Army	$16.95		
Widow-Makers & Rhododendrons	$19.95		
Words of War	$13.95		
Memories Series			
After The Storm	$14.95		
Green Hell	$18.95		
Honor & Sacrifice (hardcover)	$21.95		
How it Was	$12.95		
Immigrant Soldier	$15.95		
K-9 Soldiers	$13.95		
Oh, What A Lovely War!	$10.95		
Project Omega	$13.95		
Survival	$14.95		
Through My Eyes	$14.95		
The Unexpected Storm (hardcover)	$21.95		
Walking Away From the Third Reich	$15.95		
Where Duty Calls	$12.95		
	Subtotal		$
	Shipping		$
	Grand Total		$

Ordering Information

Name:

Address:

City: State: Zip:

Daytime Phone: Email:

Ship To

If different than above:

Name:

Address:

City: State: Zip:

Daytime Phone: ☐ Check if this is a gift

Payment Information

☐ **Check** (Make payable to PSI Research)   Charge: ☐ VISA ☐ MasterCard ☐ AMEX ☐ Discover

Card Number: Expires:

Signature: Name on Card:

To order, simply complete the order and payment information and mail to:

Hellgate Press

P.O. Box 3727

Central Point, OR 97502-0032

Phone Orders   1-800-245-6502

Phone orders accepted Monday through Friday, 6:30 A.M. to 5:00 P.M. (Pacific). Please have your credit card and order information available.

Fax Orders   1-541-245-6505

You may fax orders 24 hours-a-day. If a transmission problem occurs, please mark your second fax as a duplicate.

International Orders 1-541-245-6502

We are happy to take international orders; however, all shipments outside of the U.S. must have the proper international delivery charge included on an international money order. Please call for additional information and pricing.

Shipping

We ship regular UPS Ground; however, rush service is available. Please call for additional information and pricing.

Return Policy

If you're not completely satisfied, please return any item within 15 days of purchase for a prompt refund (less shipping and handling). Please explain your reason for returning the item and enclose your packing slip to ensure proper processing.

Shipping Chart:

If your purchase is:	U.S.A. Shipping:
$0-25	$5.00
$25.01 – $50	$6.00
$50.01 – $100	$7.00
$100.01 – $175	$9.00
$175.01 – $250	$13.00
$250.01 – $500	$18.00
$500.01 +	4% of total

Visit us online at:
http://www.psi-research.com/hellgate.htm

If you have questions or need assistance, email us at:
info@psi-research.com